DOMESDAY BOOK

Berkshire

History from the Sources

DOMESDAY BOOK

A Survey of the Counties of England

LIBER DE WINTONIA

Compiled by direction of

KING WILLIAM I

Winchester
1086

DOMESDAY BOOK

General editor

JOHN MORRIS

5

Berkshire

edited by
Philip Morgan

from a draft translation prepared by
Alison Hawkins

PHILLIMORE
Chichester
1979

1979

Published by

PHILLIMORE & CO. LTD.,
London and Chichester

Head Office: Shopwyke Hall,
Chichester, Sussex, England

ISBN 0 85033 171 4 (case)
ISBN 0 85033 172 2 (limp)

Printed in Great Britain by
Titus Wilson & Son Ltd.,
Kendal

BERKSHIRE

Introduction

The Domesday Survey of Berkshire

Notes
Index of Persons
Systems of Reference
Index of Places
Map
Technical Terms

History from the Sources
General Editor: John Morris

The series aims to publish history
written directly from the sources
for all interested readers, both
specialists and others. The first
priority is to publish important
texts which should be widely
available, but are not.

DOMESDAY BOOK

The contents, with the folio on which each county begins, are:

1	Kent	I	1	20	Bedfordshire	209
2	Sussex		16	21	Northamptonshire	219
3	Surrey		30	22	Leicestershire	230
4	Hampshire		37	23	Warwickshire	238
5	Berkshire		56	24	Staffordshire	246
6	Wiltshire		64	25	Shropshire	252
7	Dorset		75	26	Cheshire	262
8	Somerset		86	27	Derbyshire	272
9	Devon		100	28	Nottinghamshire	280
10	Cornwall		120	29	Rutland	293
11	Middlesex		126	30	Yorkshire	298
12	Hertfordshire		132	31	Lincolnshire	336
13	Buckinghamshire		143		Claims, Yorkshire	373
14	Oxfordshire		154		Lincolnshire	375
15	Gloucestershire		162		Yorkshire, summary	379
16	Worcestershire		172			
17	Herefordshire		179	32	Essex	II	1
18	Cambridgeshire		189	33	Norfolk	109
19	Huntingdonshire		203	34	Suffolk	281

Domesday Book is termed *Liber de Wintonia* (The Book of Winchester) in column 332c

INTRODUCTION

The Domesday Survey

In 1066 Duke William of Normandy conquered England. He was crowned King, and most of the lands of the English nobility were soon granted to his followers. Domesday Book was compiled 20 years later. The Saxon Chronicle records that in 1085

> at Gloucester at midwinter ... the King had deep speech with his counsellors ... and sent men all over England to each shire ... to find out ... what or how much each landholder held ... in land and livestock, and what it was worth ... The returns were brought to him.[1]

William was thorough. One of his Counsellors reports that he also sent a second set of Commissioners 'to shires they did not know, where they were themselves unknown, to check their predecessors' survey, and report culprits to the King.'[2]

The information was collected at Winchester, corrected, abridged, chiefly by omission of livestock and the 1066 population, and fair-copied by one writer into a single volume. Norfolk, Suffolk and Essex were copied, by several writers, into a second volume, unabridged, which states that 'the Survey was made in 1086'. The surveys of Durham and Northumberland, and of several towns, including London, were not transcribed, and most of Cumberland and Westmorland, not yet in England, was not surveyed. The whole undertaking was completed at speed, in less than 12 months, though the fair-copying of the main volume may have taken a little longer. Both volumes are now preserved at the Public Record Office. Some versions of regional returns also survive. One of them, from Ely Abbey,[3] copies out the Commissioners' brief. They were to ask

> The name of the place. Who held it, before 1066, and now?
> How many *hides*?[4] How many ploughs, both those in lordship and the men's?
> How many villagers, cottagers and slaves, how many free men and Freemen?[5]
> How much woodland, meadow and pasture? How many mills and fishponds?
> How much has been added or taken away? What the total value was and is?
> How much each free man or Freeman had or has? All threefold, before 1066,
>   when King William gave it, and now; and if more can be had than at present?

The Ely volume also describes the procedure. The Commissioners took evidence on oath 'from the Sheriff; from all the barons and their Frenchmen; and from the whole Hundred, the priests, the reeves and six villagers from each village'. It also names four Frenchmen and four Englishmen from each Hundred, who were sworn to verify the detail.

The King wanted to know what he had, and who held it. The Commissioners therefore listed lands in dispute, for Domesday Book was not only a tax-assessment. To the King's grandson, Bishop Henry of Winchester, its purpose was that every 'man should know his right and not usurp another's'; and because it was the final authoritative register of rightful possession 'the natives called it Domesday Book, by analogy

---

[1] Before he left England for the last time, late in 1086.   [2] Robert Losinga, Bishop of Hereford 1079-1095 (see *E.H.R.* 22, 1907, 74).   [3] *Inquisitio Eliensis*, first paragraph.   [4] A land unit, reckoned as 120 acres.   [5] *Quot Sochemani.*

from the Day of Judgement'; that was why it was carefully arranged by Counties, and by landholders within Counties, 'numbered consecutively ... for easy reference'.[6]

Domesday Book describes Old English society under new management, in minute statistical detail. Foreign lords had taken over, but little else had yet changed. The chief landholders and those who held from them are named, and the rest of the population was counted. Most of them lived in villages, whose houses might be clustered together, or dispersed among their fields. Villages were grouped in administrative districts called Hundreds, which formed regions within Shires, or Counties, which survive today with minor boundary changes; the recent deformation of some ancient county identities is here disregarded, as are various short-lived modern changes. The local assemblies, though overshadowed by lords great and small, gave men a voice, which the Commissioners heeded. Very many holdings were described by the Norman term *manerium* (manor), greatly varied in size and structure, from tiny farmsteads to vast holdings; and many lords exercised their own jurisdiction and other rights, termed *soca*, whose meaning still eludes exact definition.

The Survey was unmatched in Europe for many centuries, the product of a sophisticated and experienced English administration, fully exploited by the Conqueror's commanding energy. But its unique assemblage of facts and figures has been hard to study, because the text has not been easily available, and abounds in technicalities. Investigation has therefore been chiefly confined to specialists; many questions cannot be tackled adequately without a cheap text and uniform translation available to a wider range of students, including local historians.

Previous Editions

The text has been printed once, in 1783, in an edition by Abraham Farley, probably of 1250 copies, at Government expense, said to have been £38,000; its preparation took 16 years. It was set in a specially designed type, here reproduced photographically, which was destroyed by fire in 1808. In 1811 and 1816 the Records Commissioners added an introduction, indices, and associated texts, edited by Sir Henry Ellis; and in 1861-1863 the Ordnance Survey issued zincograph facsimiles of the whole. Texts of individual counties have appeared since 1673, separate translations in the Victoria County Histories and elsewhere.

This Edition

Farley's text is used, because of its excellence, and because any worthy alternative would prove astronomically expensive. His text has been checked against the facsimile, and discrepancies observed have been verified against the manuscript, by the kindness of Miss Daphne Gifford of the Public Record Office. Farley's few errors are indicated in the notes.

---

[6] *Dialogus de Scaccario* 1,16.

The editor is responsible for the translation and lay-out. It aims at what the compiler would have written if his language had been modern English; though no translation can be exact, for even a simple word like 'free' nowadays means freedom from different restrictions. Bishop Henry emphasized that his grandfather preferred 'ordinary words'; the nearest ordinary modern English is therefore chosen whenever possible. Words that are now obsolete, or have changed their meaning, are avoided, but measurements have to be transliterated, since their extent is often unknown or arguable, and varied regionally. The terse inventory form of the original has been retained, as have the ambiguities of the Latin.

Modern English commands two main devices unknown to 11th century Latin, standardised punctuation and paragraphs; in the Latin, *ibi* ('there are') often does duty for a modern full stop, *et* ('and') for a comma or semi-colon. The entries normally answer the Commissioners' questions, arranged in five main groups, (i) the place and its holder, its hides, ploughs and lordship; (ii) people; (iii) resources; (iv) value; and (v) additional notes. The groups are usually given as separate paragraphs.

King William numbered chapters 'for easy reference', and sections within chapters are commonly marked, usually by initial capitals, often edged in red. They are here numbered. Maps, indices and an explanation of technical terms are also given. Later, it is hoped to publish analytical and explanatory volumes, and associated texts.

The editor is deeply indebted to the advice of many scholars, too numerous to name, and especially to the Public Record Office, and to the publisher's patience. The draft translations are the work of a team; they have been co-ordinated and corrected by the editor, and each has been checked by several people. It is therefore hoped that mistakes may be fewer than in versions published by single fallible individuals. But it would be Utopian to hope that the translation is altogether free from error; the editor would like to be informed of mistakes observed.

The maps are the work of Jim Hardy and Alison Hawkins.

The preparation of this volume has been greatly assisted by a generous grant from the Leverhulme Trust Fund.

This support, originally given to the late Dr. J. R. Morris, has been kindly extended to his successors. At the time of Dr. Morris's death in June 1977, he had completed volumes 2, 3, 11, 12, 19, 23, 24. He had more or less finished the preparation of volumes 13, 14, 20, 28. These and subsequent volumes in the series were brought out under the supervision of John Dodgson and Alison Hawkins, who have endeavoured to follow, as far as possible, the editorial principles established by John Morris.

Conventions

*	refers to a note to the Latin text
[ ]	enclose words omitted in the MS.

( )   enclose editorial explanations.

HIC ANNOTANTVR TENENTES TRAS IN BERROCHESSCIRE.

.I.REX WILLELMVS.

.II.Eps Wintonienſis.

.III.Eps Sariſbcrienſis.

.IIII Eps Dunelmenſis.

.V.Eps Execeſtrenſis.

.VI.Eps Conſtantienſis.

.VII.Abbatia Abandoniens.

.VIII Abbatia Glaſtingebeꝝ.

.IX.Abbatia Weſtmonaſt.

.X.Abbatia Wintoniens.

.XI.Abbatia Certeſyg.

.XII Abbatia S Albani

.XIII Abbatia S PETRI Surdiue.

.XIͬ.Abbatia de Labatailge.

.XV Abbatiſſa de Winceſtre.

.XVI Abbatiſſa de Ambreſberie.

.XVꟾ Comes Ebroicenſis.

.XVꟾ Comes Hugo.

.XIX Comes Moritonienſis.

.XX.Walterius gifard.

.XXI.Henricus de Ferieres.

.XXII.Wills filius Anſculf.

.XXIͬ.Wills de ouu.

XXIͬ.Wills peurel.

.XXV.Wills de braioſe.

.XXVI.Wills Loueth.

.XXVII.Wills filius corbucion.

XXVꟾ Wills filius Ricardi.

.XXIX Wills de Calgi.

.XXX.Walterius filius ponz.

.XXXI.Walterius filius Other.

.XXXII.Eudo filius Huƀti.

.XXXIII.Milo criſpin.

XXXIͬ.Ghilo fr Anſculfi.

.XXXV.Haſcoit muſard.

.XXXVI Giſleƀtus de Breteuile.

.XXXVII Giſlebertus de gand.

.XXXVꟾ Goiffrid de manneuile.

.XXXIX.Oſbernus Gifard.

.XL.Robertus filius Girold.

.XLI.Robertus de Olgi.

.XLII.Roƀtus de Stadford.

.XLIII.Ricardus puingiand.

.XLIIII Rogerius de Juri.

.XLV.Rogerius de Laci.

.XLVI.Radulf de Mortemer.

.XLVII.Radulfus de Todeni.

.XLVIII.Radulfus filius comitis.

.XLIX.Radulfus filius Seifrid.

.L.Ernulfus de Heſding.

.LI.Hugo filius baldri.

.LII.Hugo de Porth.

.LIII.Hunfrid camerarius.

.LIͬ.Hunfrid uiſdeleuu.

.LV.Turſtin filius Rolf.

.LVI.Albertus

.LVII.Aiulfus uicecomes.

.LVꟾ.Hugolin Stirman

.LIX.Maci de Moretania.

.LX.Bernard Accipitrarius.

.LXI.Reinbaldus pƀr

.LXII.Grinbald

.LXIII.Teodricus Aurifaƀ Odo 7 alij plures taini.

BERKSHIRE
LIST OF LANDHOLDERS IN BERKSHIRE

1	King William	32	Eudo son of Hubert
2	The Bishop of Winchester	33	Miles Crispin
3	The Bishop of Salisbury	34	Giles brother of Ansculf
4	The Bishop of Durham	35	Hascoit Musard
5	The Bishop of Exeter	36	Gilbert of Bretteville
6	The Bishop of Coutances	37	Gilbert of Ghent
7	Abingdon Abbey	38	Geoffrey de Mandeville
8	Glastonbury Abbey	39	Osbern Giffard
9	Westminster Abbey	40	Robert son of Gerald
10	Winchester Abbey	41	Robert d'Oilly
11	Chertsey Abbey	42	Robert of Stafford
12	St. Albans Abbey	43	Richard Poynant
13	St. Pierre-sur-Dives Abbey	44	Roger of Ivry
14	Battle Abbey	45	Roger of Lacy
15	The Abbess of Winchester	46	Ralph of Mortimer
16	The Abbess of Amesbury	47	Ralph of Tosny
17	The Count of Evreux	48	Ralph the Earl's son
18	Earl Hugh	49	Ralph son of Siegfried
19	The Count of Mortain	50	Arnulf of Hesdin
20	Walter Giffard	51	Hugh son of Baldric
21	Henry of Ferrers	52	Hugh of Port
22	William son of Ansculf	53	Humphrey the Chamberlain
23	William of Eu	54	Humphrey Visdeloup
24	William Peverel	55	Thurstan son of Rolf
25	William of Braose	56	Albert
26	William Lovett	57	Aiulf the Sheriff
27	William son of Corbucion	58	Hugolin the Steersman
28	William son of Richard	59	Matthew of Mortagne
29	William of Cailly	60	Bernard the Falconer
30	Walter son of Poyntz	61	Reinbald the Priest
31	Walter son of Othere	62	Grimbald
		63	Theodoric the Goldsmith
		[64	Stephen son of Erhard]
		[65]	Odo and several other thanes

IN BVRGO DE WALINGEFORD HABVIT REX EDWARD

.VIII . virgatas træ.7 in his erant . CC.LXX VI . hagæ.

reddentes . XI . lib de gablo.7 qui ibi manebant

faciebant feruitiũ regis cũ equis uel p aquã ufq

ad Blidberiã . Reddinges . Sudtone . Befentone.

7 hoc facientibus dabat ppofit mercedẽ non de .

cenfu regis . fed de fuo.

Modo funt in ipfo burgo cfuetudines oms ut ante fuer.

Sed de Hagis funt . XIII . min . p caftello funt . VIII.

deftruftæ.7 monetarius ht unã quietã quãdiu facit

monetã . Saulf de oxeneford ht unã . Filius Alfi

de Ferendone unã . quã rex ei dedit ut dicit.

Hunfrid uifdeLeuu ht unã . de quã reclamat regẽ

Nigell unã de Henrico p hæreditatẽ Soarding . fed

burgenfes teftificant fe nunq habuiffe.

De iftis . XIII . non ht rex confuetudinem.7 adhuc

Wilts de Warene ht unã hagã . de quã rex ñ ht cfuetud.

De fup plus funt . XXII . mafuræ francigeñ . reddtes

VI . folid 7 v . denar.

Rex . E . habuit . XV . acras . in quibʒ maneb hufcarles.

Milo tenet eas . nefciunt quom . Vna ex his jacet in

Witeham ᴍ Walterij gifard.

Walchelin eps ht . XXVII . hagas . de . XXV . folid.7 funt

appciatæ in Bricfteuuelle ᴍ ejus.

Abb de abbendone hab . II . acras . in qbʒ funt . VII.

mafuræ de . IIII . folid.7 ptin ad oxeneford.

B In the Borough of WALLINGFORD
1 King Edward had 8 virgates of land, and in them were 276 sites,
   which paid £11 in tribute. Those who lived there did service for
   the King with horses, or by water, as far as Blewbury, Reading,
   Sutton (Courtenay) and Benson. The reeve gave wages or allowances
   to those who did so, not from the King's tribute, but from his own.

   All customary dues in this Borough are now as they were before.

   But there are 13 fewer sites. 8 were destroyed for the castle;
   a moneyer has 1, exempt so long as he coins money; Saewulf of Oxford
   has 1; Alfsi of Faringdon's son 1, which the King gave him,
   as he states; Humphrey Visdeloup has 1, for which he calls the King
   to warrant; Nigel 1 from Henry, through Swarting's inheritance,
   but the burgesses testify that they never had it.

   The King does not have the customary dues of these 13, and, further,
   William of Warenne has 1 site from which the King does not have
   customary dues. In addition there are 22 Frenchmen's dwellings which
   pay 6s 5d. King Edward had 15 acres in which his Guards lived;
   Miles Crispin holds them; the (burgesses) do not know how; one of them
   lies in (the lands of) (Long) Wittenham, Walter Giffard's manor.

2 Bishop Walkelin has 27 sites at 25s; they are assessed in his manor
   of Brightwell. The Abbot of Abingdon has 2 acres, in which
   are 7 dwellings at 4s; they belong to Oxford.

ℾMilo . xx . maſuras de . xɪɪ . ſoł 7 x . denar̅.7 jaceɴ̄

in Neuuehā.7 iterū unā acrā in qua ſunt . vɪ . hagæ de

xvɪɪɪ . denar̅. In Haſelie . vɪ . maſuras redd . xʟɪɪɪɪ . deñ.

In Eſtoche unā maſurā de . xɪɪ . deñ. In Celgraue . ɪ . ma

ſurā de . ɪɪɪɪ . denar̅.7 In Suttone una acra in qua ſunt

vɪ . maſuras de . xɪɪ . denar̅.7 In Braio una acra.7 ibi

ℾeſt tam̄ in Walengeford.
xɪ . maſuras de , ɪɪɪ . ſolid . Tota ħ terra p̧tinᵇad oxenefordſcire.

ℾRainald ħt unā acrā in qua ſunt . xɪ . maſuræ de . xxvɪ .

denar̅.7 p̧tiñ in Eldeberie quæ . e̅ in Oxeneford.

gifard
ℾArchiep̄s . vɪ . maſuras de . xxvɪ . denar̅.ℾWalterius ħt

unā acrā 7 x . maſuras de . vɪ . ſolid 7 ɪɪɪ . oboł.ℾRoƀt

de olgi . ɪɪɪɪ . maſuras de . xx . deñ.ℾGiſleƀt de gand

magn'
unā mas . de . ɪɪ . deñ 7 obolo.ℾHugo . ɪ . maſurā de . ɪɪɪɪ .

denar̅.ℾR . fili Seifridi . ɪɪ . hagas de . xɪɪ . deñ . ℾHugo

peurel
de Molebec . ɪ . haga de . ɪɪɪɪ.deñ.ℾRannulf una de . ɪɪɪɪ . deñ.

f. other
Louet
Walter . vɪ . hagas de . ɪɪɪɪ . deñ 7 oboł miñ.ℾWiłłs unū

fruſtū træ de . ɪɪɪɪ . deñ. In Eldeſlei . ɪɪɪ . maſuræ . de . ɪɪɪ .

deñ . v . maſuras in bercheſire ħt aƀƀ de Labatailge

de . xx . deñ.ɪ . haga quæ fuit ep̄i petri de . ɪɪɪɪ . denar̅.

ℾRex.ɪɪɪ.hagas de . vɪ . deñ.ℾHenric̜ de ferrarijs . vɪ . hagas

quæ . T.R.E.7 etiā T.R.W.deder̅ . ʟxɪɪ . denar̅ con

ſuetudinalit̅ in firma regis . m̄ nichil dant.

Ep̄s Remigi̅ . ɪ . haga de . ɪɪɪɪ . deñ.ℾHugo . ɪ . haga de . xvɪ . deñ.

56 c
Godric .ɪ.haga de . ɪɪ . deñ . Doda .ɪ . ħaga de . ɪɪ . deñ.

Algar . ɪ . de . ɪɪ . deñ . Fabri . v . hagas de . x . denar̅.

Miles, 20 dwellings at 12s 10d; they lie in (the lands of)
Newnham (Murren); moreover, 1 acre, in which are 6 sites at 18d;
in Haseley, 6 dwellings which pay 44d; in (North) Stoke 1 dwelling at 12d;
in Chalgrove 1 dwelling at 4d; in Sutton (Courtenay) 1 acre, in which
are 6 dwellings at 12d; in Bray 1 acre, and 11 dwellings there at 3s.

All this land belongs to Oxfordshire; however it is in Wallingford (lands).

3 Reginald has 1 acre, in which are 11 dwellings at 26d; they belong
to Albury, which is in Oxford[shire].
The Archbishop, 6 dwellings at 26d.
Walter Giffard has 1 acre and 10 dwellings at 6s and 3 halfpence.
Robert d'Oilly, 4 dwellings at 20d.
Gilbert of Ghent, 1 dwelling at 2½d.
Hugh Grant, 1 dwelling at 4d.
Ralph son of Siegfried, 2 sites at 12d.
Hugh of Bolbec, 1 site at 4d.
Ranulf Peverel, 1 at 4d.
Walter son of Othere, 6 sites at 4d less ½d.
William Lovett, a piece of land at 4d.

4 In (East) Ilsley, 3 dwellings at 3d.
The Abbot of Battle has 5 dwellings in Berkshire at 20d.
1 site, which was Bishop Peter's, at 4d.
The King, 3 sites at 6d.
Henry of Ferrers, 6 sites which customarily gave 62d, before 1066
and also after, in the King's revenue; but now they give nothing.
Bishop Remigius, 1 site at 4d.
Earl Hugh, 1 site at 16d.
Godric, 1 site at 2d.   56 c
Doda, 1 site at 2d.
Algar, 1 at 2d.
The smiths, 5 sites at 10d.

Ƭ Rex in Ældremaneſtone . ii . hagas de . v . denaꝛ.

Comes ebroicens . ii . hagas de . ii .7 oboł . Hugo . i . haga
de . ii . den . Rogꝛ. i . hagā de . xii . den . Roƀt . i . hagā

Ƭ Rex . i . haga de . vi . den . Eꝑs Oſmund . vii . ∧ de . vi . den.
hagas de . xxviii . den . Roƀt de Oilgi . ii . hag de . x . den.

Rog de Laci . v . hag de . xxi . den . Radulf pcehaie . vii.
ƀag de . l . den . Rainbald . i . hag de . iiii . den . Scs Albaꞑ
.i . hag ſinga 7 c̄ in calūnia . Briſtiſt . i . hag de . ii . den.

Leueua . i . hag de . ii . den . Goduiꞑ . i . hag de . ii . den.
Aluuiꞑ . i . hag de . ii . den . Ælmer pƀr 7 ali Elmer
7 Bruman 7 Eduui 7 Edmund 7 Wilłs fili Oſmundi 7 Lefłot
7 Lanƀt pƀr . Aluuold 7 Godric hn̄t gaƀlū de domiƀꝥ
ſuis . 7 ſanguinē ſi-ibi effundit. ſi recept fuerit homo
int antequā calūnict á ꝓpoſito regis . excepto ſaƀƀo
ꝓpt mercatū ꝗa tc̄ rex hꝛ foriſſaƈturā . 7 de adulte
rio 7 Latrocinio hn̄t ipſi emendā in ſuis domiƀꝥ . alie
ū foriſſaƈturæ ſunt regis.

T.R.E. uałƀ . xxx . liƀ . 7 poſt. xl . liƀ . Modo. lx . liƀ.
7 tam̄ redd de firma . ꝗt xx . liƀ ad numeꝛ.

Qd ptiꞵ ad adbrei. vii . ſoł . 7 tꞃa milonis . xxiiii.
Qd aƀƀ de abendone hꝛ. viii . ſoł . Qd Rogꝛ. vii . ſoł.
Qd Rainald. iiii . ſoł.

Hi ſubſcripti taini de Oxenefordscire . habueꝛ
tꞃā in Walingeford.

Lanfranc Archieꝑs . iiii . domos In Niwetvne redd
vi . ſoł . Remigi eꝑs unā dom̄ ptiꞵ ad Dorkeceſtre
redd . xii . denaꞃ . Aƀƀ de S Albano unā domū de . iiii.
ſolid . R . aƀƀ unā dom̄ in Auuilma . redd . iii . ſolid.

5 The King, in Aldermaston, 2 sites at 5d.
The Count of Evreux, 2 sites at 2½d.
Hugh (of) Bolbec, 1 site at 2d.
Roger of Lacy, 1 site at 12d.
Robert d'Oilly, 1 site at 6d.

6 The King, 1 site at 6d.
Bishop Osmund, 7 sites at 28d.
Robert d'Oilly, 2 sites at 10d.
Roger of Lacy, 5 sites at 21d.
Ralph Piercehedge, 7 sites at 50d.
Reinbald the priest, 1 site at 4d.
St. Albans, 1 site, contested (?); it is in dispute.
Brictric, 1 site at 2d.
Leofeva, 1 site at 2d.
Godwin, 1 site at 2d.
Alwin, 1 site at 2d.

7 Aelmer the priest, another Aelmer the priest, Bruman, Edwy, Edmund,
William son of Osmund, Leofled, Lambert the priest, Alfwold and
Godric have the tribute from their houses, and the (fines for)
blood shed there, if any. If a man should be taken therein before
he was charged by the King's reeve... except on Saturdays,
because of the market, for then the King has the fine.
They have the fines for adultery and for robbery, in their own houses.
But other fines are the King's.

8 Value before 1066 £30; later £40; now £60; however, it pays £80
at face value in revenue; what belongs to *Adbrei*, 7s; Miles Molay's
land, 24[s]; what the Abbot of Abingdon has, 8s; what Roger of Lacy
(has), 7s; what Reginald (has), 4s.

9 The undermentioned Oxfordshire thanes had land in Wallingford:
Archbishop Lanfranc, 4 houses which belong in Newington, paying 6s.
Bishop Remigius, 1 house which belongs to Dorchester, paying 12d.
The Abbot of St. Albans, 1 house at 4s.
Abbot R....... 1 house, in Ewelme, paying 3s.

ꝼ Comes Hugo . ɪ . doṁ in Piritune . redꝺ . ɪɪɪ . folid.

ꝼ Walter⁹ gifard . ɪɪɪ . domos in Çauereſhã . redꝺ . ɪɪ . folid.

ꝼ Roƀt de Olgi . ɪɪ . domos in Watelintune . redꝺ . ɪɪ . folid

7 in Perie . ɪ . domũ de . ɪɪ . folid.   ꝼ folid.

Ilƀt⁹ de Laci 7 Roger⁹ . F . Seifridi 7 Orgaɼ . ɪɪɪ . domos de . ɪɪ

ꝼ Hugo de bolebec . ɪɪɪ . domos in Crem . redꝺ . ɪɪɪ . folid.

ꝼ Hugo grando de ſcoca . ɪ . domũ de . xɪɪ . denaɼ.

ꝼ Drogo in Sireburne . 7 in Weſtune . tres domos . de . ɪɪɪɪ . fot.

ꝼ Roƀt armenteres in Auuilme . ɪ . domũ de . xɪɪ . den.

ꝼ Wazo unã domũ in Auuilme . redꝺ . ɪɪɪ . folid.

Quando gelꝺ dabat T . R . E . cõmunit ꝑ totã Berchefcirã
dabat hida . ɪɪɪ . denaɼ 7 obolũ ante natale dñi . 7 tantꝺ
ad Pentecoſt . ꝼ Si rex mitteƀ alicubi exercitũ . de . v .
hiꝺ tant uñ miles ibat . 7 ad ej⁹ uiƈtũ ł ſtipendiũ de una
quaq̧ hida dabant ei . ɪɪɪɪ . folidi . ad . ɪɪ . menſes.
Hos ũ denaɼ regi ñ mittebant ſed militiƀ dabant.
Siꝗs in expeditionẽ fũmonit ñ ibat . totã trã fuã erga
regẽ foriffaciebat Qꝺ fiꝗs remanendi hñs aliũ ꝓ ſe mit
tere ꝓmitteret . 7 tañ ꝗ mittendus erat remaneret . ꝑ . ʟ . fot
ꝺetus erat dñs ej⁹ . ꝼ Taiñ uel miles regis dñic⁹ moriens . ꝓ re
leuaṁto dimitteƀ regi oṁia arma fua . 7 equũ . ɪ . cũ ſella.
aliũ fine ſella . Qꝺ fi . ẻent ei canes ł accipitres . ꝓfentabant
regi ut fi uellet accipet . ꝼ Siꝗs occiꝺet hominẽ pace regis
habentẽ . 7 corꝑ fuũ 7 oṁem fubſtantiã foriffacieƀ erga regẽ.
ꝼ Q̇ ꝑ noƈtẽ effringeƀ ciuitatẽ . c . fot emꝺaƀ regi ñ uicecomiti.
ꝼ ꝗ monit aꝺ ſtabilitionẽ uenationis ñ ibat . ʟ . fot regi emꝺabat.

Earl Hugh, 1 house, in Pyrton, paying 3s.
Walter Giffard, 3 houses, in Caversham, paying 2s.
Robert d'Oilly, 2 houses, in Watlington, paying 2s; and, in
(Water)perry, 1 house at 2s.
Ilbert of Lacy, Roger son of Siegfried, and Ordgar, 3 houses at 4s.
Hugh of Bolbec, 3 houses, in Crowmarsh (Gifford), paying 3s.
Hugh Grant of *Scoca*, 1 house at 12d.
Drogo, 3 houses, in Shirburn and in (South) Weston, at 4s.
Robert of Armentières, 1 house, in Ewelme, at 12d.
Wace, 1 house, in Ewelme, paying 3s.

10 When tax was given before 1066, commonly throughout Berkshire
the hide gave 3½d before Christmas and as much at Whitsun.

If the King sent an army anywhere, one man-at-arms only
went from 5 hides and for his supplies or pay 4s were given to him
for 2 months from each hide; they did not send this money to
the King, but gave it to the men-at-arms.

If anyone was summoned for an expedition, but did not go,
he forfeited the whole of his land to the King.
But if anyone who had (the reason to) stay behind promised to
send another man in his place, but the man who was to be sent
stayed behind, his lord was cleared for 50s.

At his death, a thane or a King's household man-at-arms sent to
the King as death-duty all his arms and horse, one with a saddle,
another without a saddle; but if he had dogs or hawks, they were
presented to the King, to accept if he wished.

11 If anyone killed a man who had the King's peace, his body and all
his substance were forfeit to the King.

Whoever broke into the City at night paid 100s fine to the King,
not to the Sheriff.

A man who, summoned for game-beating for a hunt, did not go
paid the King 50s fine.

TERRA REGIS.

Rex Wills ten *Windesores* in dnĩo . Rex . E . tenuit.

Ibi . xx . hidæ . Tra . ē. In dnĩo . ē una car . 7 xxii . uilti

7 ii . borđ cũ . x . car . Ibi uñ feruus . 7 pifcaria de . vi . folid 7 viii.

denar . 7 xl . ãc p̃ti . Silua . de . l . porc de pafnag . 7 alia filua

miffa . ē in defenfa . 7 adhuc funt in uilla . c . hagæ . v . miñ . Ex his

funt . xxvi . q̇etæ de gablo . 7 de alijs exeunt . xxx . folidi.

De tra huj M) ten Albt unā hid 7 dimiđ . 7 tciā parte uni denæ.

Walt fili Other unā hid 7 dim 7 unā v 7 tant filuæ unde

exeuꝛ . v . porci de pafnag . Giflebt maminot . iii . uirg . Wilts

unā hid . Aluric . i . hid . 7 alt Aluric dimiđ hid . 7 p̃br uillæ

unā hid 7 dim . 7 ii . feruientes curiæ regis dimiđ hid . Eudo dapif

T . R . E . ualb xv . lib . 7 poft . vii . lib . Modo . xv . lib.   f̃ ii . hiđ.

Rex ten *Taceha* in dnĩo . Rex . E . tenuit . *In Taceha Hvnđ*.

Tc fe defđ ꝓ . ii . hiđ . 7 nunq̃ geld . Tra . ē . xxv . car . Ibi funt

xxxv . uilti 7 xii . borđ cũ . xxv . car . 7 ibi xii . hagæ redđtes

de firma . lv . fot . 7 ii . molini de xxii . fot 7 vi . deñ . 7 cxlvii.

ãc p̃ti . Silua . de . lx . porc.

Æcctam huj M) ten . ii . clerici cũ . iii . hiđ . quæ ꝑtiñ ibi 7 geld

cũ comitatu . 7 uat . iii . lib.

T . R . E . ualb xx . lib . modo . xxx . lib 7 tam̃ redđ xxxiiii . lib.

Rex ten *Coceha* in dnĩo . Rex . E . tenuit . *In Benes Hvnđ*.

Tc . xx . hide . fed nunq̃ geld . Tra . ē . xxv . car . Ibi . xxxii . uilti

7 xxi . cot cũ . xx . car ı 7 ibi . iiii . ferui . 7 ii . moliñi . de . xxii . fot

7 vi . deñ . 7 ii . pifcar de xiii . folid 7 iiii . deñ . 7 l . ãc p̃ti.

Silua . de . c . porc . 7 alia medietas ē in forefta de Windefores.

De nouo mercato qđ ibi . ē modo . xx . fot.

Tot T . R . E . ualb . l . lib . 7 poft . l . fot . Modo . xxx.vi . lib . 7 tam̃

redđ . xlv . lib.

[In RIPPLESMERE Hundred]

1 King William holds WINDSOR in lordship. King Edward held it. 20 hides.
Land for.... In lordship 1 plough;
22 villagers and 2 smallholders with 10 ploughs.
1 slave; a fishery at 6s 8d; meadow, 40 acres; woodland at 50 pigs
from pasturage; another woodland has been put in (the King's)
Enclosure; further, there are 100 sites less 5 in the town; 26 of
them are exempt from tribute, and 30s comes from the others.
Albert the Clerk has 1½ hides of the land of this manor, and the
third part of a pig pasture; Walter son of Othere, 1½ hides and 1
virgate and as much woodland as 5 pigs come from in pasturage;
Gilbert Maminot 3 virgates; William Bellett 1 hide; Aelfric 1 hide;
a second Aelfric ½ hide; the village priest 1½ hides; 2 Servants of
the King's Court ½ hide; Eudo the Steward 2 hides.
Value before 1066 £15; later £7; now £15.

The King holds in lordship

in THATCHAM Hundred

2 THATCHAM. King Edward held it. Then it answered for 2 hides;
it never paid tax. Land for 25 ploughs.
35 villagers and 12 smallholders with 25 ploughs.
12 sites which pay 55s in revenue; 2 mills at 22s 6d;
meadow, 147 acres; woodland at 60 pigs.
Two clerics hold the church of this manor, with 3 hides
which belong there and pay tax with the County; value £3.
Value before 1066 £20; now £30; however, it pays £34.

in BEYNHURST Hundred

3 COOKHAM. King Edward held it. Then 20 hides, but it never paid tax.
Land for 25 ploughs.
32 villagers and 21 cottagers with 20 ploughs.
4 slaves; 2 mills at 22s 6d; 2 fisheries at 13s 4d; meadow, 50 acres;
woodland at 100 pigs; the other half is in Windsor Forest;
from the new market which is now there 20s.
Value of the whole before 1066 £50; later [£?] 50s; now £36;
however, it pays £45.

De his . xx . hiđ . hŧ Reinbald de rege . i . hiđ 7 dim̃ in elemoſina.

7 æcclam ipſi ꝏ . cū . viii . cot 7 una car̃ . 7 xv . acs p̃ti . Val l . ſol.

Duo alij clerici hñt inde dim̃ hiđ . 7 ii . cot cū . ii . car̃ . 7 viii . acs p̃ti.

Rex ten in dñio WALTHA . Eddid regina tenuit ⌐ Val . v . ſol.

Tc̃ ꝑ . viii . hiđ . modo ꝑ nichilo . Tra . e̅ . xvi . car̃ . In dñio ſunt . ii.

7 xxxii . uiłłi 7 iiii . cot cū . xv . car̃ . Ibi . iiii . ſerui . Silua . de . c . l.

porc . T . R . E . 7 poſt . ualb̃ xii . lib̃ . Modo ⸴ x . lib̃ . tam̃ redđ . xv . lib̃ . ad

Rex ten in dñio BLITBERIE . Rex . E . IN BLITBERIE HĎ . ⌐ penſa.

tenuit . Tc̃ 7 m̃ . iii . hiđ . Tra . e̅ . xx . car̃ . In dñio ſunt . iiii . car̃.

7 xxiiii . uiłłi 7 lviii . cot cū . xv . car̃ . 7 ibi . iii . molini de xxxvii.

ſoliđ 7 vi . deñ . 7 xvi . ac p̃ti . T . R . E . 7 poſt ⸴ ual . l . lib̃ . Modo ⸴ lx . lib̃.

De iſto ꝏ ten Wiłłs æcclam cū . v . uirg̃ træ . Aluric tenuit

de rege . E . Ibi . iii . cot 7 x . ac p̃ti . Val 7 ualuit . c . ſol.

Rex ten in dñio ESTONE . Vxor Lanc tenuit de rege . E . Tc̃

ꝑ xv . hiđ . m̃ ꝑ . v . hiđ . Tra . e̅ . vii . car̃ . In dñio . e̅ una . 7 xiiii.

uiłłi cū . vii . car̃ . 7 ibi . iii . ſerui 7 lx . ac p̃ti.

T . R . E . ualb̃ xv . lib̃ . 7 poſt . xii . lib̃ . Modo ⸴ ix . lib̃ . IN HESLITESFORD HĎ.

Rex ten in dñio CELSEA . Rex . E . tenuit . Tc̃ ibi . xxiii . hidæ.

ſed ꝑ . xxii . ſe defđb̃ . Tra . e̅ . xxvii . car̃ . De tota hac tra hŧ rex

xi . hiđ quæ ñ gelđ . 7 ibi in dñio . iiii . car̃ . 7 xvii . uiłłi 7 lxxi . cot.

cū . xvi . car̃ . Ibi . vi . ſerui . 7 iii . molini de . lxii . ſol . 7 c . ac p̃ti.

In hoc ꝏ fuer̃ . x . libi hões . T . R . E . 7 teneb̃ xii . hiđ 7 dimiđ

de tra ejđ ꝏ . ſed inde recede ñ poterant.

Modo de hac tra ten Ricarđ puingiant . viii . hiđ . quæ ꝑ . iii.

hiđ ſe defđt m̃ . De Ricardo ten Wiłłs . iii . hiđ . 7 Hugo . i . hidã.

57 a

Ibi . iii . car̃ in dñio . 7 iiii . uiłłi 7 xi . cot 7 xxvi . ac p̃ti . 7 vii . ſerui.

⌐ De tra ejđ ten Giſleb̃t de rege . v . uirg̃ . 7 ꝑ una v ſe defđ.

Of these 20 hides, Reinbald the priest has 1½ hides from the King
in alms, and the church of this manor, with
   8 cottagers and 1 plough; meadow, 15 acres; value 50s.   r
Two other clerics have ½ hide of it and
   2 cottagers with 2 ploughs; meadow, 8 acres; value 5s.

4 WALTHAM. Queen Edith held it. Then for 8 hides; now for nothing.
Land for 16 ploughs. In lordship 2.
   32 villagers and 4 cottagers with 15 ploughs.
   4 slaves; woodland at 150 pigs.
Value before 1066 and later £12; now £10;
however, it pays £15 by weight.

in BLEWBURY Hundred
5 BLEWBURY. King Edward held it. Then and now 3 hides.
Land for 20 ploughs. In lordship 4 ploughs;
   24 villagers and 58 cottagers with 15 ploughs.
   3 mills at 37s 6d; meadow, 16 acres.
Value before 1066 and later £50; now £60.
   William Beaufour holds the church of this manor, with 5 virgates
of land. Aelfric held it from King Edward.
   3 cottagers; meadow, 10 acres. The value is and was 100s.

6 ASTON (Tirrold). Lank's wife held it from King Edward. Then
for 15 hides, now for 5 hides. Land for 7 ploughs. In lordship 1;
   14 villagers with 7 ploughs.
   3 slaves; meadow, 60 acres.
Value before 1066 £15; later £12; now £9.

in SLOTISFORD Hundred
7 CHOLSEY. King Edward held it. 23 hides there then, but it answered
for 22. Land for 27 ploughs. Of all this land the King has 11 hides
which do not pay tax. In lordship 4 ploughs;
   17 villagers and 71 cottagers with 16 ploughs.
   6 slaves; 3 mills at 62s; meadow, 100 acres.
In this manor there were 10 free men before 1066, who held
12½ hides of the land of this manor, but could not withdraw from it.
Now Richard Poynant holds 8 hides of this land, which now answer
for 3 hides. From Richard William holds 3 hides and Hugh 1 hide.
In lordship 3 ploughs;   57 a
   4 villagers and 11 cottagers.
   Meadow, 26 acres; 7 slaves.
Gilbert holds from the King 5 virgates of land of this manor.
It answers for 1 virgate.

7 Herueus ten de rege . III . hid 7 unā v̇ quæ n̄ geld . In dn̄io fuṅ

II . car̔.7 un uitts 7 XIIII . cot cū , I . car̔ 7 dim̄.7 II . ferui.7 III . ãc

p̄ti . Totū T . R . E .7 poſt uatḃ . LXIIII . liḃ . Modo . dn̄iū regis .

XLVII . liḃ ad numer̄ . Pars Ricardi 7 alioɀ.́ XVII . liḃ.7 XV . folid .

ꝼ De hoc c̄ō ten̄ abbatia de monte ̄S Michaelis de rege unā

æcctam cū . I . hida.7 ibi.ē.I.car̔ cū . IIII . cot.7 VII . ãc p̄ti.Vat.III.liḃ .

ꝼ Duo etiā p̄bri in ead uilla ten̄ de rege in decima 7 æccta qd̄

uat.IIII . liḃ .

Rex ten̄ in dn̄io *BASTEDENE* de feuo Rogerij comit' . Aileua liḃa

femina tenuit T . R . E . Tc̄ ꝑ xx . hid . modo ꝑ . VI . hid . Tra . ē . XX .

car̔ . In dn̄io . V . car̔ funt.7 XXVIII . uitti 7 XV . cot cū XIIII . car̔ .

7 molin̄ de xv . fot.7 XIII . ferui.7 In Walingeford . III . hag̔æ

de . IX . den̄.7 XXX . ãc p̄ti . Silua . de . cxx . porc̄ .

T . R . E .7 m̄ uat.xxv . liḃ . Cū recep̄.́ xx . liḃ .

De iſto c̄ō hn̄t . II . p̄bri . II . æcctas cū una hida.7 idē ipſi tenuer̄

T . R . E . Ibi hn̄t . II . car̔ .   Vat 7 ualuit XL . fot .

Rex ten̄ in dn̄io *WANETINZ* . Rex . E . tenuit . IN *WANETINZ HD̆* .

Tc̄ | IIII . hidæ . Nunꝗ geld . Tra . ē . xxi . car̔ . In dn̄io funt . v . car̔ .
  ⁷ modo

7 xxx uitti cū . XL . cot hn̄t XVII . car̔ . Ibi . v . ferui . Vat.LXI.liḃ .
                                        olī.́Lv.liḃ.

ꝼ In hoc c̄ō tenuit Petrus . II . partes æcctæ cū . IIII . hid . ibi ꝓtinent .
         cp̄s   or

Nunꝗ geld . Modo funt in manu regis q̇a n̄ eraṅ de epiſcopatu .

Ibi . ē una car̔.7 III . uitti 7 VII . cot cū. I . car̔.7 molin̄ de . c . den̄ .

7 XII . ãc p̄ti . Tra . ē . II . car̔ . Valuit . III . liḃ . Modo.́IIII . liḃ .

ꝼ Tertiā parte̅ p̄dictæ æcctæ ten̄ Witts diacon de rege . cū . I . hida .

quæ n̄ geld . Ibi funt.IIII.uitti cū.I.car̔.Valuit.xxv.fot.m̄.́xxx.fot .

Rex ten̄ in dn̄io *SPERSOLT* . Tres liḃi hōes tenuer̄ . T . R . E .
                                                  uicecom̄ 9

ꝑ . III.c̄ō.Froger poſt habuit 7 fecit un̄ c̄ō.Tc̄ fe defd̄ ꝑ XVI .

hid . modo ꝑ nichilo . Tra . ē . x.car̔ . In dn̄io funt . II . car̔.7 XXVIII .

uitti 7 XVII . cot cū . v . car̔.Ibi . III . ferui.7 LXXXIIII . ãc p̄ti .
                                              octogi'

Hervey holds from the King 3 hides and 1 virgate which do not
pay tax. In lordship 2 ploughs;
1 villager and 14 cottagers with 1½ ploughs.
2 slaves; meadow, 3 acres.
Value of the whole before 1066 and later £64; now, the King's
lordship, £47 at face value; Richard's part, and the others', £17 15s.
Of this manor the Abbey of Mont St. Michel holds from the
King one church, with 1 hide. 1 plough there, with
4 cottagers; meadow 7 acres. Value £3.
Also, two priests in the same village hold from the King,
in the tithes and the church, the value of £4.

8 BASILDON, from Earl Roger's holding. Aelfeva, a free woman,
held it before 1066. Then for 20 hides; now for 6 hides.
Land for 20 ploughs. In lordship 5 ploughs;
28 villagers and 15 cottagers with 14 ploughs.
A mill at 15s; 13 slaves.
In Wallingford, 3 sites at 9d; meadow, 30 acres;
woodland at 120 pigs.
Value before 1066 and now £25; when acquired £20.
Two priests have the two churches of this manor, with 1 hide;
they also held them before 1066, they have 2 ploughs there.
The value is and was 40s.

in WANTAGE Hundred
9 WANTAGE. King Edward held it. Then and now 4 hides. It
never paid tax. Land for 21 ploughs. In lordship 5 ploughs.
30 villagers with 40 cottagers have 17 ploughs. 5 slaves.
Value £61; formerly £55.
In this manor Bishop Peter held two parts of the church
with 4 hides which belong there; they never paid tax; they are
now in the King's hand, because they were not the Bishopric's,
1 plough there.
3 villagers and 7 cottagers with 1 plough.
A mill at 100d; meadow, 12 acres. Land for 2 ploughs.
The value was £3; now £4.
William the Deacon holds from the King the third part of the
said church, with 1 hide which does not pay tax.
4 villagers with 1 plough. The value was 25s; now 30s.

10 SPARSHOLT. Three free men held it before 1066 as three manors.
Froger the Sheriff had it later and made it one manor.
Then it answered for 16 hides; now for nothing.
Land for 10 ploughs. In lordship 2 ploughs;
28 villagers and 17 cottagers with 5 ploughs.
3 slaves; meadow, 84 acres.

Tot̃ T.R.E.ualb̃ .ix.lib̃.7 poſt.́xv.lib̃.Modo.xix.lib̃.7 v.ſolid.
7 tam̃ redd̃ xxiii.lib̃.

Huj̃ m̃ æcclam cũ.i.hida ten̄ Edred.7 ipſe.T.R.E.tenuit.
Ibi hr̃.i.car̃.7 i.cot̃ 7 iiii.ac̃s p̃ti.H̃ hida n̄ geld.Val̃.xx.ſol̃.

R̃ex ten̄ in dñio CERLETONE.Elmer un̄ lib̃ hõ tenuit.T.R.E.
Tc̃ ,p.viii.hid̃.modo ,p.vii.hid̃.Tra.̃e.iiii.car̃.Petrus ep̃s
tenuit poſtea.Ibi.i.car̃ in dñio.7 un̄ uill̃s 7 vii.cot̃ cũ.i.car̃.
Ibi.iii.ſerui.7 xxiiii.ac̃ p̃ti.7 molin̄ de vii.ſol̃ 7 vi'.den̄.qũe
Walt̃ gifard ten̄ injuſte ut Hund̃ dicit.

T.R.E.ualb̃.viii.lib̃.7 poſt.iiii.lib̃.Modo.́viii.lib̃.

R̃ex ten̄ in dñio BEDRETONE.Vluric un̄ lib̃ hõ tenuit.T.R.E.
Tc̃ ,p.x.hid̃.modo ,p.ii.hid̃ una v̄ min.Tra.̃e.iiii.car̃.In dñio
̃e una car̃ 7 dim̃.7 iiii.uilli 7 v.cot̃ cũ.ii.car̃.

T.R.E.ualb̃.vi.lib̃.7 poſt.́iii.lib̃.Modo.́c.ſolid.

Ibi hr̃ rex dim̃ v̄ quã Vlflet tenuit T.R.E.7 potuit ire quo uoluit.
Tc̃ ,p dim̃ v̄.m̃ ,p nichilo.Robt̃ ten̄ in firma de Wanetinz.ſed
nunꝗ ibi p̃tinuit.Val̃.xvi.den̄ 7 ualuit

In Sudtone ten̄ Rex dim̃ v̄.quã Leflet tenuit T.R.E.7 potuit
ire quo uoluit.Tc̃ ,p dim̃ v̄.m̃ ,p nichilo.Robt̃ ten̄ in firma de Sudton.
ſ; ꝋi n̄ p̃tin̄.Val̃ 7 ualuit.xvi.den̄.

57 b

R̃ex ten̄ in dñio WARWELT.Eddid IN RIPLESMIERE H̃D.
regina tenuit.Tc̃ 7 m̃ ſe defd̃ ,p.x.hid̃.T̃ra.̃e   Ibi
xiii.uilli cũ.viii.car̃.Silua de.c.porc̃.

T.R.E.7 poſt.ualb̃.xii.lib̃.Modo.́vi.lib̃.

ꝼ Prbr Goiſfridi de magne uile hr̃ inde.i.hid̃.quæ ſep fuir
de iſto m̃.ſed iſte miſit in m̃ dñi ſui. IN CERLEDONE H̃D.

R̃ex hr̃ in dñio WEREGRATE.Eddid regina tenuit.
Tc̃ ,p xxxiii.hid̃.modo ,p nichilo T̃ra.̃e xxix.car̃.In
dñio ſunt.ii.car̃.7 xli.uill̃s 7 xiiii.bord̃ cũ.xxv.car̃.

Value of the whole before 1066 £9; later £15; now £19 5s;
however, it pays £23.
Edred the priest holds the church of this manor with 1 hide.
He held it himself before 1066; he has 1 plough and
1 cottager; meadow, 4 acres. This hide does not pay tax.
Value 20s.

11 CHARLTON. Aelmer, a free man, held it before 1066. Then for
8 hides; now for 7 hides. Land for 4 ploughs. Bishop Peter
held it later. 1 plough in lordship;
1 villager and 7 cottagers with 1 plough.
3 slaves; meadow, 24 acres; a mill at 7s 6d which
Walter Giffard holds wrongfully, as the Hundred states.
Value before 1066 £8; later £4; now £8.

12 BETTERTON. Wulfric, a free man, held it before 1066.
Then for 10 hides; now for 2 hides less 1 virgate.
Land for 4 ploughs. In lordship 1½ ploughs;
4 villagers and 5 cottagers with 2 ploughs.
Value before 1066 £6; later £3; now 100s.
The King has ½ virgate there which Wulfled held before 1066;
she could go where she would. Then for ½ virgate, now for
nothing. Robert holds it in the Wantage revenue, but it never
belonged there. The value is and was 16d.

13 In 'SUTTON' the King holds ½ virgate which Leofled held before 1066;
she could go where she would. Then for ½ virgate; now for nothing.
Robert holds it in the Sutton revenue, but it does not belong there.
The value is and was 16d.

In RIPPLESMERE Hundred   57b
14 The King holds in lordship WARFIELD. Queen Edith held it.
Then and now it answered for 10 hides. Land for....
13 villagers with 8 ploughs.
Woodland at 100 pigs.
Value before 1066 and later £12; now £6.
A priest of Geoffrey de Mandeville's has 1 hide from it
which always was this manor's, but he put it in his lord's manor.

In CHARLTON Hundred
15 The King has in lordship WARGRAVE. Queen Edith held it.
Then for 33 hides; now for nothing. Land for 29 ploughs.
In lordship 2 ploughs;
41 villagers and 14 smallholders with 25 ploughs.

Ibi . vi . ſerui . 7 moliñ de . ix . ſoliđ 7 ii . deñ . 7 iii . piſcarie
de . iii . Mił anguił . 7 xvi . ãc p̃ti . Silua de . c . porc̃.

T . R . E . ualb̃ . xxxi . lib̃ . 7 poſt | xxvii . lib̃ . 7 vi . ſoł 7 viii . deñ.

Rex ten in dñio *RAMEHA* . Eddid regina tenuit . Tc̃
⫟p xii . hiđ . modo ⫟p . iiii . hiđ . Tra . ē   In dñio
ſunt . ii . car̃ . 7 xx . uiłłi 7 iiii . borđ cũ ꝟi . car̃ . Ibi . iiii.
ſerui . 7 moliñ de . xx . ſoł . 7 mił anguił . 7 lii . ãc p̃ti.
Silua ad clauſurā . T . R . E . ualb̃ . xv . lib̃ . 7 poſt 7 m̃ : x . lib̃.

Rex ten in dñio *SOANESFELT* . Sexi tenuit de rege . E.
in alođ.   Tra . ē . vii . car̃ . In
dñio ſunt . ii . car̃ . 7 viii . uiłłi 7 viii . borđ . cũ . v . car̃.
Ibi . ii . ſerui . 7 moliñ de . l . deñ . 7 piſcariæ . v . de xl . deñ.
7 xii . ãc p̃ti . Silua de . xx . porc̃.

T . R . E . 7 poſt : ualb̃ . vii . lib̃ . Modo : viii . lib̃ 7 vi . deñ.

Rex ten in dñio *SELINGEFELLE* . Sexi tenuit in alođ
de rege . E . Tc̃ ⫟p . v . hiđ . m̃ ⫟p nichilo . Tra . ē . vi . car̃ . In
dñio . ē una . 7 viii . uiłłi 7 v . borđ cũ . vii . car̃ . Ibi . ii.
ſerui . 7 moliñ de . v . ſoł 7 cl . anguił . 7 v . piſcariæ
de qñgent 7 l . anguił . 7 xvi . ãc p̃ti . Silua de q̃t xx.
7 x . porc̃ . Valuit . vii . lib̃ . Modo : viii . lib̃.

Rex ten in dñio *FINCHAMESTEDE* . Herald com̃ 9 tenuit.
Tc̃ ⫟p . v . hiđ . m̃ ñ gełd ſed redđ firmā in Radinges.
Tra . ē . xv . car̃ . In dñio . ē una . 7 xvi . uiłłi 7 viii . borđ
cũ . xiiii . car̃ . Ibi . vi . ſerui . 7 moliñ de . vii . ſoł 7 vi . deñ.
7 iiii . ãc p̃ti . Silua de . cc . porc̃ . Valet . viii . lib̃ 7 ualuit.

Rex ten in dñio *BERCHEHA* . Ælmer tenuit de rege . E.
Tc̃ 7 m̃ ⫟p . iii . hiđ . Tra . ē . iii . car̃ . In dñio . ē una . 7 vi.
uiłłi 7 iiii . borđ cũ . iii . car̃ . Ibi . v . ãc p̃ti . Silua de . xl . porc̃.
Valuit . iiii . lib̃ . T . R . E . 7 poſt 7 m̃ : iii . lib̃.

57 b

6 slaves; a mill at 9s 2d; 3 fisheries at 3,000 eels;
meadow, 16 acres; woodland at 100 pigs.
Value before 1066 £31; later and now £27 6s 8d.

The King holds in lordship
16 REMENHAM. Queen Edith held it. Then for 12 hides; now for 4 hides.
Land for.... In lordship 2 ploughs;
20 villagers and 4 smallholders with 6 ploughs.
4 slaves; a mill at 20s and 1,000 eels; meadow, 52 acres;
woodland for fencing.
Value before 1066 £15; later and now £10.

17 SWALLOWFIELD. Saxi held it from King Edward in freehold.
Land for 7 ploughs. In lordship 2 ploughs;
8 villagers and 8 smallholders with 5 ploughs.
2 slaves; a mill at 50d; 5 fisheries at 40d; meadow, 12 acres;
woodland at 20 pigs.
Value before 1066 and later £7; now £8 6d.

18 SHINFIELD. Saxi held it in freehold from King Edward.
Then for 5 hides, now for nothing. Land for 6 ploughs.
In lordship 1;
8 villagers and 5 smallholders with 7 ploughs.
2 slaves; a mill at 5s and 150 eels; 5 fisheries
at 550 eels; meadow, 16 acres; woodland at 90 pigs.
The value was £7; now £8.

19 FINCHAMPSTEAD. Earl Harold held it. Then for 5 hides; now
it does not pay tax but it pays revenue in Reading.
Land for 15 ploughs. In lordship 1;
16 villagers and 8 smallholders with 14 ploughs.
6 slaves; a mill at 7s 6d; meadow, 4 acres;
woodland at 200 pigs.
The value is and was £7.

20 BARKHAM. Aelmer held it from King Edward. Then and now
for 3 hides. Land for 3 ploughs. In lordship 1;
6 villagers and 4 smallholders with 3 ploughs.
Meadow, 5 acres; woodland at 40 pigs.
Value before 1066 £4; later and now £3.

Rex ten in dnio *HERLEI* . Almar tenuit in alođ
de rege.E. Tc p.v.hiđ.modo p.IIII.hiđ.Tra.e.vi.car.
In dnio.e una car.7 vi.uiłłi 7 un borđ cu.III.car.
Ibi.II.ſerui.7 una haga in Radinges.7 II.piſcarie
de.vii.ſoł 7 vi.den.7 xx.ac p̃ti.Silua de.lxx.porc.
T.R.E.uałb.c.ſoł.7 poſt 7 m̃:´L.ſoł. *IN BRAI HĐ.*
Rex ten in dnio *BRAI*.Rex.E.tenuit.Ibi.xviii.
hidæ.7 n̄ geldauer.Tra.e   In dnio ſunt
.III.car.7 lvi.uiłłi 7 vii.borđ.cu xxv.car.Ibi.IIII.
ſerui.7 æccła.7 III.milites.7 l.ac p̃ti.Silua de.lx.porc.
Rainbald ten.I.hidā quæ ptin æcclæ.7 ibi hr.I.car.
Tot T.R.E.uałb.xxv.lib.7 poſt.xviii.lib.Modo:´xvii.lib.
Rex ten in dnio *BORCHEDEBERIE*. *IN BORCHEDEBERIE HĐ.*
Rex.E.tenuit.Ibi.II.hidæ.ſed n̄ geld.Tra.e   In dnio
e una car.7 xviii.uiłłi 7 xvi.borđ.cu.xx.car.Ibi.I.ſeru.
7 æccła ad q ptin dim hida.7 uał xv.ſoł.Ibi.xi.ac p̃ti.
Silua de.c.porc.Valet 7 ualuit xi.lib.7 tam redđ.xvi.lib.

57 c   £ 7 x.ſolid.
Rex ten in dnio *NACHEDEDORNE*. *IN NACHEDEDORN HĐ.*
Edric tenuit in alođ de rege.E. Tc p xx.hiđ.m̃ p
ix.hiđ una v min.Tra.e.xii.car.In dnio ſunt.ii.car.
7 viii.uiłłi 7 iiii.borđ cu.ii.car.
De iſto m̃ ten Radulf æcclam cu.i.hida 7 dim v.
7 Rainald.ii.hiđ 7 dimiđ v.Ibi.i.car 7 un uiłłs.
Tot T.R.E.uałb xv.lib.7 poſt:´xii.lib.Modo.x.lib.
qđ rex hr.Qđ Radulf:´xl.ſoł.Qđ Rainald:´xxx.ſoł.
Rex ten *CONTONE* in dnio.Rex.E.tenuit.Ibi.iii.hidæ
una v min.Tra.e.viii.car.In dnio ſunt.ii.car.7 vi.
uiłłi 7 xii.borđ.cu.vi.car.Ibi.iii.ſerui.7 iiii.ac p̃ti.
Silua de.iii.porc.Hanc ſiluā ten Henric de ferreres.
T.R.E.7 poſt:´ualuit.vi.lib.Modo:´viii.lib.

21 EARLEY. Aelmer held it in freehold from King Edward.
Then for 5 hides; now for 4 hides. Land for 6 ploughs.
In lordship 1 plough;
  6 villagers and 1 smallholder with 3 ploughs.
  2 slaves; 1 site in Reading; 2 fisheries at 7s 6d;
    meadow, 20 acres; woodland at 70 pigs.
Value before 1066, 100s; later and now 50s.

in BRAY Hundred
22 BRAY. King Edward held it. 18 hides; they did not pay tax.
Land for.... In lordship 3 ploughs;
  56 villagers and 7 smallholders with 25 ploughs.
  4 slaves; a church; 3 men-at-arms; meadow, 50 acres;
    woodland at 60 pigs.
  Reinbald holds 1 hide which belongs to the church;
    he has 1 plough there.
Value of the whole before 1066 £25; later £18; now £17.

in BUCKLEBURY Hundred
23 BUCKLEBURY. King Edward held it. 2 hides, but they do not
pay tax. Land for .... In lordship 1 plough;
  18 villagers and 16 smallholders with 20 ploughs.
  1 slave; a church to which belongs ½ hide, value 15s;
    meadow, 11 acres; woodland at 100 pigs.
The value is and was £11, however it pays £16 10s.

in COMPTON Hundred   57c
24 'BARETHORN'. Edric held it in freehold from King Edward.
Then for 20 hides; now for 9 hides less 1 virgate.
Land for 12 ploughs. In lordship 2 ploughs;
  8 villagers and 4 smallholders with 2 ploughs.
Ralph the priest holds the church of this manor with 1 hide
  and ½ virgate; Reginald, 2 hides and ½ virgate. 1 plough and
  1 villager.
Value of the whole before 1066 £15; later £12; now, what the
King has, £10; what Ralph (has),40s; what Reginald (has), 30s.

25 COMPTON. King Edward held it. 3 hides less 1 virgate.
Land for 8 ploughs. In lordship 2 ploughs;
  6 villagers and 12 smallholders with 6 ploughs.
  3 slaves; meadow, 4 acres; woodland at 3 pigs.
    Henry of Ferrers holds this woodland.
Value before 1066 and later £6; now £8.

Rex ten̄ in dn̄io *CHENETEBERIE*. *IN CHENETEBERIE HD̆*.

Rex.E.tenuit.Ibi.ii͏ͤ.hidæ.Tra.ē.x.car̄.In dn̄io

funt.ii.car̄.7 xv.uilłi 7 xvi.borđ.cū.viii.car̄.Ibi

ii.ſerui.7 ii.molini de xxxii.ſoł 7 vi.den̄.7 xl.ãc

p̄ti.Silua.de.iii.porc̄.T.R.E.7 poſt.7 m̄.ʼuał.x.lib̄.

Henric̄ de fereres ten̄ de hoc m̄.xliii.ac̄s træ.que

fuer̄ in firma regis.T.R.E.ſic̄ ſcira dicit.Dicunt aut̄

qđ Godric uicecom̄ fecit ibi paſcua equis ſuis.ſed

neſciunt quomodo.

Rex ten̄ in dn̄io *ESELDEBORNE*.Rex.ē.tenuit.

Ibi.vi.hide 7 dimiđ.Tra.ē.x.car̄.In dn̄io ſunt

.iii.car̄.7 xiiii.uilłi 7 xiii.borđ.cū.vi.car̄.Ibi.iii.

ferui.7 molin̄ de.x.ſoł.7 viii.ãc p̄ti.Silua ad clau

ſurā.T.R.E.7 poſt.uałb̄.xii.lib̄.Modo.ʼxx.lib̄.

De iſto m̄ ſunt.ii.hide 7 dim̄ in m̄ Henrici miſſæ.

una hida fuit de Reue Land.alia de uillanis.

7 dim̄ ᵈhida fuit de firma regis.ſed tp̄r Godrici uicecom̄

fuit foris miſſa.Hoc atteſtat̄ tota ſcira.

Rex ten̄ *EDDEVETONE* in dn̄io.Azor tenuit in

alođ de rege.E.Tc̄ ₚ.x.hiđ.modo ₚ.ii.dim̄ v

min̄.Tra.ē.vi.car̄.In dn̄io.ē una car̄.7 vi.uilłi

7 ii.borđ cū.ii.car̄.Ibi.i.feru.7 molin̄ de.xv.ſoł.

7 xxxiiii.ãc p̄ti.Silua de.x.porc̄.

T.R.E.uałb̄.vi.lib̄,7 poſt.ʼc.ſoł.Modo.ʼlxx.ſoł.

Rex ten̄ in dn̄io *LAMBORNE*. *IN LĀBORNE HD̆*.

Rex.E.tenuit.Ibi.xx.hidæ.Tra.ē xlii.car̄.

In dn̄io ſunt.iiii.car̄.7 xliiii.uilłi 7 lx.borđ cū

xx.v.car̄.Ibi.vi.ferui.7 æccła cū.i.hida ei p̄tin̄.

7 ii.molini de.xx.ſoliđ.Silua de.x.porc̄.

T.R.E.uałb̄.xlix.lib̄.7 poſt.ʼxxxiiii.lib̄.Modo.ʼxlii�‖.lib̄.

1

26 KINTBURY. King Edward held it. 2 hides. Land for 10 ploughs.
In lordship 2 ploughs;
 15 villagers and 16 smallholders with 8 ploughs.
 2 slaves; 2 mills at 32s 6d; meadow, 40 acres;
  woodland at 3 pigs.
Value before 1066, later and now £10.
 Henry of Ferrers holds 43 acres of land of this manor
which were in the King's revenue before 1066, as the Shire
states; moreover, they state that Godric the Sheriff made a
pasture there for his horses, but they do not know how.

27 SHALBOURNE. King Edward held it. 6½ hides. Land for 10 ploughs.
In lordship 3 ploughs;
 14 villagers and 13 smallholders with 6 ploughs.
 3 slaves; a mill at 10s; meadow, 8 acres; woodland for fencing.
Value before 1066 and later £12; now £20.
 Of this manor 2½ hides were put in Henry's manor;
one hide was Reeve's land, the other was the villagers';
the half-hide was of the King's revenue, but in the time of
Godric the Sheriff it was put outside. This the whole Shire confirms.

28 EDDINGTON. Azor held it in freehold from King Edward.
Then for 10 hides; now for 2 less ½ virgate.
Land for 6 ploughs. In lordship 1 plough;
 6 villagers and 2 smallholders with 2 ploughs.
 1 slave; a mill at 15s; meadow, 34 acres; woodland at 10 pigs.
Value before 1066 £6; later 100s; now 70s.

in LAMBOURN Hundred
29 LAMBOURN. King Edward held it. 20 hides. Land for 42 ploughs.
In lordship 4 ploughs;
 44 villagers and 60 smallholders with 25 ploughs.
 6 slaves; a church, with 1 hide which belongs to it;
 2 mills at 20s; woodland at 10 pigs.
Value before 1066 £49; later £34; now £44.

In *FALESLEI* ten̂ Rex . i . hiđ . Rex . E . tenuit . *IN EGLEI HĎ.*

T̂ra . ē . iii . car̂ . In dn̄io funt . ii . car̄ . cū . vi . borđ . 7 iii .

ac̄ p̊ti . Val 7 ualuit . xl . fol.

Rex ten̂ in dn̄io *LEDENCV̄BE* . Rex . E . tenuit . Ibi . iii .

hidæ . T̂ra . ē . xvi . car̂ . In dn̄io funt . iii . car̄ . 7 un̊ uilłs

7 xxx . borđ . 7 xviii . burs . 7 ii . ferui . cū xiii . car̂ .

Ibi . v . molini de . iiii . lib̄ . 7 cc . 7 xxv . ac̄ p̊ti .

Æcctam huj̊ Ṁ ten̂ abbatia de Ambref̄bie . cū una v̂ .

Tot̄ T . R . E . 7 poft̄ . 7 m̂ ual . lv . lib̄ . tam̄ redđ . lx . lib̄ .

Rex ten̂ in dn̄io *SPERSOLT.* *IN HILLESLAV HĎ.*

Rex . E . tenuit . Ibi . x . hidæ . T̂ra . ē . xiii . car̂ .

In dn̄io funt . iii . car̄ . 7 xxv . uilłi 7 iii . borđ cū . x . car̂ .

57 d

Ibi . iii . ferui . 7 cc . ac̄ p̊ti . Ƒ xxvi . lib̄ .

T . R . E . ualb̄ . xv . lib̄ . 7 poft̄ ; xviii . lib̄ . Modo ; xx . lib̄ . Tam̄ redđ

De ifto Ṁ ten̂ Henric̊ de Fereres unā v̂ tre 7 xii . ac̄s p̊ti . 7 unā

uacariā de . vi . penfis cafeoₜ . quæ fic̄ fcira teftat̄ remanfer̄

in firma regis qdo Godric̊ uicecomitatū pđiđit .

Rex ten̂ in dn̄io *SERIVEHA* . Rex . E . tenuit . *IN SERIVEHA HĎ.*

Ibi . xlvi . hidæ . T̂ra . ē . xxxiii . car̂ . In dn̄io funt . iiii . car̄ .

7 qt̂ xx . uilłi 7 xvii . borđ . cū . xxx . car̂ . Ibi eccła cū . v . hiđ

de eađ tra . 7 ibi . i . car̄ 7 iiii . uilłi 7 v . borđ cū . ii . car̄ .

In Ṁ funt . ii . molini de . xx . fol . 7 ccxl . ac̄ p̊ti . Silua de . xx .

porc̄ . T . R . E . ualb̄ . xxx . v . lib̄ . 7 poft̄ ; xx . lib̄ . Modo ; xlv . lib̄ .

Qđ pb̄r ht̄ ; iiii . lib̄ . *IN WIFOL HĎ.*

Rex ten̂ in dn̄io *FERENDONE* . Herald̊ tenuit . Tc̄ fe defđ

ꝑ xxx . hiđ . modo n̄ gelđ . T̂ra . ē . xv . car̂ . In dn̄io funt . iii . car̂ .

7 xvii . uilłi 7 x . borđ cū . x . car̄ . Ibi . x . ferui . 7 molin̄ cū

pifcaria de . xxxv . fol . 7 ix . hagæ in eađ uilla de . xl . foliđ .

7 cxxx . ac̄ p̊ti . Silua ad claufurā .

In EAGLE Hundred

30 In (Little) FAWLEY the King holds 1 hide. King Edward held it.
Land for 3 ploughs. In lordship 2 ploughs, with
6 smallholders.
Meadow, 3 acres.
The value is and was 40s.

The King holds in lordship
31 LETCOMBE (Regis). King Edward held it. 3 hides.
Land for 16 ploughs. In lordship 3 ploughs;
1 villager, 30 smallholders, 18 boors and 2 slaves
with 13 ploughs.
5 mills at £4; meadow, 225 acres.
Amesbury Abbey holds the church of this manor, with 1 virgate.
Value of the whole before 1066, later and now £55;
however, it pays £60.

in HILLSLOW Hundred
32 KINGSTON LISLE. King Edward held it. 10 hides. Land for 13
ploughs. In lordship 3 ploughs;
25 villagers and 3 smallholders with 10 ploughs.
3 slaves; meadow, 200 acres.   57d
Value before 1066 £15; later £18; now £20; however, it pays £26.
Of this manor Henry of Ferrers holds 1 virgate of land;
12 acres of meadow; a dairy, at 6 weys of cheese, which
remained in the King's revenue when Godric lost the Sheriffdom,
as the Shire testifies.

in SHRIVENHAM Hundred
33 SHRIVENHAM. King Edward held it. 46 hides. Land for 33 ploughs.
In lordship 4 ploughs;
80 villagers and 17 smallholders with 30 ploughs.
A church with 5 hides of this land; 1 plough there and
4 villagers and 5 smallholders with 2 ploughs.
In the manor 2 mills at 20s; meadow, 240 acres;
woodland at 20 pigs.
Value before 1066 £35; later £20; now £45;
what the priest has, £4.

in WYFOLD Hundred
34 (Great) FARINGDON. Harold held it. Then it answered for 30 hides; now it
does not pay tax. Land for 15 ploughs. In lordship 3 ploughs;
17 villagers and 10 smallholders with 10 ploughs.
10 slaves; a mill with a fishery at 35s; 9 sites in this
village at 40s; meadow, 130 acres; woodland for fencing.

De ifto ⳩ hℾ Ofmund eꝑs . ɪ . hidã cũ æccɫa.

7 Alfi hℾ . ɪɪɪɪ . hiđ.7 in dñio.ɪɪ.caℾ.7 ɪɪ.borđ.7 vɪ.ſerui.

Toℾ T.R.E.uaℬ.xvɪ.liℬ.7 poſtʴxɪɪ.liℬ.Modoʴxxɪ.liℬ 7 vɪ.
ſoliđ 7 vɪɪɪ.deɴ.Qđ æccɫa ℓ ꝑℬrʴxʟ.ſoɫ.Qđ Alfiʴxxx.ſoliđ.

Rex teɴ in dñio *COCHESWELLE* . Herald tenuit . Tℭ ſe defđ
ꝑ xx . hiđ . m̊ ɴ gelđ . Tra.ē.vɪɪɪ.caℾ.In dñio funt.ɪɪ.caℾ.7 ɪx.
uiℓℓi 7 ɪɪɪɪ.borđ cũ.ɪɪɪ.caℾ.7 vɪɪ.ſerui.7 q̃ℓ xx.ãc p̊ti.ɪɪɪ.miɴ.
Æccɫa ibi.ē cũ dim̃ hida.

T.R.E.uaℬ.vɪɪɪ.liℬ.7 poſtʴvɪ.liℬ.Modoʴx.liℬ.

Rex teɴ in dñio aliã *COCHESWELLE*.Herald tenuit.Tℭ ꝑ.x.
hiđ.modo ɴ gelđ.Tra.ē.ɪx.caℾ.In dñio funt.ɪɪ.7 xɪ.uiℓℓi
7 vɪ.borđ cũ.vɪ.caℾ.7 cc.ãc p̊ti.Silua ad claufurã.

T.R.E.uaℬ.xvɪ.liℬ.7 poſtʴxɪɪ.liℬ.Modoʴxɪɪɪɪ.liℬ.

Rex teɴ *SVDTONE* in dñio.ꝑ.xxɪɪɪ.hiđ *IN SVDTONE HĐ.*
7 una v̆ ſe defđ T.R.E. modo ꝑ nichilo.Tra.ē.xx.caℾ.In dñio
funt.ɪɪɪ.caℾ.7 xʟvɪɪɪ.uiℓℓi 7 xxɪ.borđ.cũ.xvɪɪ.caℾ.Ibi.ɪɪ.ſerui.
7 ɪɪɪ.molini de.ʟ.ſoɫ.7 ccc.ãc p̊ti.Silua de xʟ.porℭ.
In Walingeford.ɪ.haga de.xvɪɪɪ.deɴ.ſ; waſta.ē.

T.R.E.uaℬ.xxx.liℬ.7 poſtʴxx.liℬ.Modoʴʟ.liℬ.Tam̃ redđ
ʟx.liℬ de firma ad numerũ.

Henriꞇ de Fereires teɴ in hoc ⳩ de dñica ℾra regis.cxx.aꞓs
ℾræ.7 ɪɪɪ.acras p̊ti.idõ ꝗa Godriꞇ anteceſſor ſuus cũ uicecom̃
eſſet.arauit eã ℾrã cũ ſuis caℾ.ſed ut diꞓ hunđ ad curiã regis
p̊tiɴ juſte.Godriꞇ enĩ occupauit injuſte.

Rex teɴ in dñio *HENRET*.Rex.E.tenuit.Tℭ ſe defđ ꝑ.ɪɪɪɪ.hiđ
7 dimiđ.m̊ ꝑ nichilo.Tra.ē.v.caℾ.In dñio funt.ɪɪ.caℾ.7 vɪɪɪ.
uiℓℓi 7 xɪɪɪ.borđ cũ.ɪɪ.caℾ.7 ɪɪ.ſerui ibi.7 moliɴ de.xʟɪɪ.ſoliđ.
7 ɪɪɪɪ.ãc p̊ti.T.R.E.uaℬ.x.liℬ.7 poſtʴvɪɪɪ.liℬ.Modoʴxv.liℬ.
7 tam̃ redđ.xx.liℬ.

Of this manor, Bishop Osmund has 1 hide, with the church.
Alfsi has 4 hides; in lordship 2 ploughs;
2 smallholders and 6 slaves.
Value of the whole before 1066 £16; later £12; now £21 6s 8d;
what the church or the priest (has) 40s; what Alfsi (has) 30s.

35 (Great) COXWELL. Harold held it. Then it answered for 20 hides;
now it does not pay tax. Land for 8 ploughs. In lordship 2 ploughs;
9 villagers and 4 smallholders with 3 ploughs; 7 slaves.
Meadow, 80 acres less 3; a church there, with ½ hide.
Value before 1066 £8; later £6; now £10.

36 (Little) COXWELL. Harold held it. Then for 10 hides; now it
does not pay tax. Land for 9 ploughs; in lordship 2;
11 villagers and 6 smallholders with 6 ploughs.
Meadow, 200 acres; woodland for fencing.
Value before 1066 £16; later £12; now £14.

in SUTTON Hundred
37 SUTTON (Courtenay). It answered for 23 hides and 1 virgate
before 1066; now for nothing. Land for 20 ploughs.
In lordship 3 ploughs;
48 villagers and 21 smallholders with 17 ploughs.
2 slaves; 3 mills at 50s; meadow, 300 acres;
woodland at 40 pigs.
In Wallingford 1 site at 18d; but it is waste.
Value before 1066 £30; later £20; now £50; however, it pays
£60 in revenue at face value.
Henry of Ferrers holds in this manor 120 acres of land
and 3 acres of meadow, of the King's household land, because
Godric, his predecessor, ploughed this land with his own ploughs
when he was Sheriff; but, as the Hundred states, it rightfully
belongs to the King's court for Godric appropriated it wrongfully.

38 (East) HENDRED. King Edward held it. Then it answered for 4½
hides; now for nothing. Land for 5 ploughs. In lordship 2;
8 villagers and 13 smallholders with 2 ploughs; 2 slaves.
A mill at 42s; meadow, 4 acres.
Value before 1066 £10; later £8; now £15; however, it
pays £20.

Henric̄ ten̄ ibi . i . hid̄ quæ fuerat in firma regis . Godric̄ tenuit.

Aluric̄ de Tacehā dicit ſe uidiſſe brevē regis qd̄ eā dederit

feminæ Godrici in dono . eo qd̄ nutriebat canes ſuos . Sed nemo.ē

in Hund̄ qui breuē uiderit p̄ter Aluricum.

Rex ten̄ in dn̄io STIVETVNE . Herald̄ tenuit . Tc̄ ſe defd̄ ⫽p . xx.

hid̄ . Modo ⫽p nichilo . Tra . ē . xx . car̄ . In dn̄io ſunt . iiii . car̄.

7 xxxviii . uiłłi 7 xxviii . bord̄ cū . x . car̄ . Ibi . ii . ſerui . 7 molini . iii.

de . xlv . ſolid̄ . 7 cclxviii . ac̄ p̄ti . Æccła . ē in m̄.   ⌐ xl . lib̄.

★ T . R . E . uałb̄ . xxv . lib̄ . 7 poſt.′xx . lib̄ . Modo.′xxii . lib̄ . Tam̄ redd̄

⌐ Ad hoc m̄ p̄tinuer̄ in Oxeneford . xiii . hagæ . redd̄tes . xii . ſolid̄

7 vi . den̄ . 7 uñ p̄tū de . xx . ſoł . Modo hōes de hund̄ dn̄t qd̄

★ Rob̄t de oilgi iſtud ten̄ut ſuſpicant̄.∣aliud ſciunt eo qd̄.ē

in alia ſcira.

Rex ten̄ in dn̄io ORDIA . Herald̄ tenuit T . R . E . IN GAMESFEL HD̄.

Tc̄ ſe defd̄ ⫽p xxxi . hida . modo ⫽p nichilo . Tra . ē . xvi . car̄ . In

dn̄io ſunt . iii . car̄ . 7 xxxii . uiłłi 7 xiii . bord̄ cū . xii . car̄ . Ibi

xiiii . ſerui . 7 moliñ de . xii . ſolid̄ 7 vi . den̄ . 7 piſcaria de . x.

ſolid̄ . 7 ccc . ac̄ p̄ti . xv . miñ.

De hac tra ten̄ Alſi . ii . hid̄ . quæ fuit uiłło⁊ . Ipſe tenuit T . R . E.

7 Aluiet . ii . hid̄ . 7 alt q̄dā Aluiet tenuit . In hac tra . i . car̄ in

dn̄io . cū . ii . bord̄ 7 uno ſeruo . 7 liiii . ac̄ p̄ti.

Tot̄ T . R . E . uałb̄ . xxx . lib̄ . 7 poſt.′xx . lib̄ . Modo . xxv . lib̄ 7 x . ſoł.

Rex ten̄ in dn̄io REDINGES . Rex . E . tenuit.′IN REDINGES HD̄.

Tc̄ 7 m̄ ſe defd̄ ⫽p . xliii . hid̄ . Tra . ē . xl . car̄ . In dn̄io . ē una.

7 lv . uiłłi 7 xxx . bord̄ cū . lv . car̄ . Ibi . iiii . molini de . xxxv.

ſolid̄ . 7 iii . piſcariæ de . xiiii . ſolid̄ 7 vi . den̄ . 7 cl . ac̄ p̄ti.

Silua . de . c . porc̄ . De paſtura.′xvi . ſolid̄ 7 vi . denar̄.

T . R . E . 7 poſt.′uałb̄ . xl . lib̄ . Modo.′xlviii . lib̄.

Henry holds 1 hide which was in the King's revenue.
Godric held it. Aelfric of Thatcham states that he has seen
the King's writ by which he had given it to Godric's wife
as a gift because she kenneled his dogs; but there is no one
in the 'Hundred who had seen the writ except Aelfric.

39 STEVENTON. Harold held it. Then it answered for 20 hides;
now for nothing. Land for 20 ploughs. In lordship 4 ploughs;
    38 villagers and 28 smallholders with 10 ploughs.
    2 slaves; 3 mills at 45s; meadow, 268 acres.
    There is a church in the manor.
Value before 1066 £25; later £20; now £32;
however, it pays £40.
    13 sites in Oxford belong to this manor, which pay 12s 6d,
and a meadow at 20s. Now the men of the Hundred state that,
as they suspect, Robert d'Oilly holds it; they know nothing else
because it is in another Shire.

in GANFIELD Hundred   58 a
40 LITTLEWORTH. Harold held it before 1066. Then it answered
for 31 hides; now for nothing. Land for 16 ploughs.
In lordship 3 ploughs;
    32 villagers and 13 smallholders with 12 ploughs.
    14 slaves; a mill at 12s 6d; a fishery at 10s;
        meadow, 300 acres less 15.
Alfsi holds 2 hides of this land, which was the villagers'.
He held it himself before 1066; Alfgeat (holds) 2 hides;
another Alfgeat held them. On this land 1 plough in lordship, with
    2 smallholders and 1 slave.
    Meadow, 54 acres.
Value of the whole before 1066 £30; later £20; now £25 10s.

in READING Hundred
41 READING. King Edward held it. Then and now it answered for
43 hides. Land for 40 ploughs. In lordship 1;
    55 villagers and 30 smallholders with 55 ploughs.
    4 mills at 55s; 3 fisheries at 14s 6d; meadow, 150 acres;
        woodland at 100 pigs; from the pasture 16s 6d.
Value before 1066 and later £40; now £48.

Rex hĩ in burgo de REDINGES . xxviii . hagas . reddtes

iiii . lib 7 iii . fot ᵽ omĩbᵹ c̃fuetudinib̃ . Tam̃ qui ten̊ redd̊

.c. folid̊ . ʄHenric̊ de Fereres hĩ ibi . i . hagã 7 dĩm v̊ træ.

in qua funt . iii . ãc p̃ti . Vat . vi . folid̊ . Godric̊ uicecom̃ tenuit hanc

trã ad hofpitiũ . id̊o Henricus ten̊.

ʄReinbald̊ fili̊ Petri ẽp̃i tenuit . i . hagã ibi . quã trahed ad ERLEI

ℂ̃O fuũ . Modo . ẽ in manu regis. 7 uat xvi . den̊.

PANDEBORNE jacuit in firma T.R.E. 7 poft tenuit Aluuold̊

camerari̊ . fed hund̊ nefcit quom̃ habuit. Frogeri̊ poftea

mifit in firma regis abfqᵹ placito 7 lege . Tc̃ fe defd̊ ᵽ . ii . hid̊.

modo ᵽ nichilo . Tra . ẽ . ii . car̃ . Ibi funt . iiii . uitti 7 v . bord̊.

7 molĩn de . xx . folid̊ . Vat 7 ualuit . xl . folid̊.

Rex ten̊ in dñio HELDREMANESTVNE . Herald̊ tenuit.

Tc̃ fe defd̊ ᵽ . xv . hid̊ . modo ᵽ nichilo . Tra . ẽ . xxx . car̃.

In dñio funt . ii . car̃. 7 xxxvi . uitti 7 xii . bord̊ cũ xviii . car̃.

Ibi . ii . ferui. 7 molĩn de . xx . folid̊. 7 ii ᵉ . pifcariæ de . v . folid̊.

Ibi æccta 7 cxxiiii . ãc p̃ti . Silua de . xxx . porc̃.

T.R.E. 7 poft 7 m̊ uat . xx . lib 7 x . folid̊ . Tam̃ de hac 7 de

Hocfelle quæ fubter eft redd̊ qui ten̊ . xxvi . lib̃.

In Eldremaneftune jacet HOCFELLE . Bricftuard̊ tenuit

de dono Heraldi . Tc̃ fe defd̊ ᵽ una hida 7 dimid̊ . modo pro

nichilo . Tra . ẽ . iii . car̃ . Ibi . iii . uitti 7 vi . bord̊ cũ . ii . car̃.

Ibi . ii . ferui. 7 vi . ãc p̃ti . Silua de . l . porc̃ . p̃ciũ ej̊ fupius.

In eod̊ HVND hĩ rex . i . hid̊. 7 jacet in Solafel quæ . ẽ in

Cerledone hd̊ . Sexi ten̊uit . T.R.E. Ibi. iiii or . uitti 7 ii . bord̊

cũ . iii . car̃ . Appciata . ẽ cũ Solafel qd̊ . ẽ cap̃ ℂ̃O.

Rex ten̊ WINTREBVRNE . De tra Eddid IN ROEBERG HD̃.

reginæ fuit . Lanc tenuit de ea . Teodric̊ ten̊ de rege ad firmã.

Tc̃ fe defd̊ ᵽ . v . hid̊ . modo ᵽ nichilo . Tra . ẽ . v . car̃ . In dñio eft

una car̃. 7 iiii. uitti 7 xi . bord̊ cũ . iiii . car̃. Ibi. ii. ãc p̃ti.

Silua de . iii . porc̃ . T.R.E. uatb . vi . lib̃. 7 poft:ʹl. fot. Modo:ʹiiii. lib̃.

58 a

42 In the Borough of READING the King has 28 sites which pay £4 3s
for all customary dues; however their holders pay 100s.
Henry of Ferrers has 1 site and ½ virgate of land, in which
are 3 acres of meadow. Value 6s. Godric, the Sheriff, held
this land for a lodging; therefore Henry holds it.
Reinbald, son of Bishop Peter, held 1 site there which he
transferred to his manor of Earley. Now it is in the King's hands;
value 16d.

43 PANGBOURNE lay in revenue before 1066. Later Alfwold the
Chamberlain held it, but the Hundred do not know how he had it.
Later, Froger put it in the King's revenue without plea and law.
Then it answered for 2 hides; now for nothing.
Land for 2 ploughs.
    4 villagers and 5 smallholders.
    A mill at 20s.
The value is and was 40s.

44 The King holds ALDERMASTON in lordship. Harold held it.
Then it answered for 15 hides; now for nothing.
Land for 30 ploughs. In lordship 2 ploughs;
    36 villagers and 12 smallholders with 18 ploughs.
    2 slaves; a mill at 20s; 2 fisheries at 5s.
    A church; meadow, 124 acres; woodland at 30 pigs.
Value before 1066, later and now £20 10s. However, from
this and from Wokefield, below, the holders pay £26.

45 In Aldermaston lies WOKEFIELD. Brictward held it by Harold's gift.
Then it answered for 1½ hides; now for nothing. Land for 3 ploughs.
    3 villagers and 6 smallholders with 2 ploughs.
    2 slaves; meadow, 6 acres; woodland at 50 pigs.
Its assessment, above.

46 In this Hundred the King has 1 hide. It lies in (the lands of)
Swallowfield, which is in Charlton Hundred. Saxi held it before 1066.
    4 villagers and 2 smallholders with 3 ploughs.
It is assessed with Swallowfield, which is the head of the manor.

In ROWBURY Hundred
47 The King holds WINTERBOURNE. It was of Queen Edith's land.
Lank held from her. Theodoric holds from the King at a revenue.
Then it answered for 5 hides; now for nothing.
Land for 5 ploughs. In lordship 1 plough;
    4 villagers and 11 smallholders with 4 ploughs.
    Meadow, 2 acres; woodland at 3 pigs.
Value before 1066 £6; later 50s; now £4.

TERRA WINTONIENS EPI. *IN HILLESLAV HD.*

★ .II. WALCHELIN eps Winton ht *OLVRICESTONE.*

de uictu monacho̫.T.R.E.fe defd ,p xx . hid.

Modo ,p x . hid . Tra.ē.xi.car.In dñio funt.ii.car 7 dim.

7 xii.uitti 7 xxiiii.bord cū.ii.car 7 dim.Ibi.x.ferui.

7 ii.molini de xii.fot.7 vi.den.7 cl.ac pti.

De ifto M̃ ten Rogeri.iii.hid 7 dim de epo.7 ibi ht.i.car.

T.R.E.uatb.xvi.lib.7 poft.xii.lib.Modo xviii.lib.

Tam̃ redd de firma.xx.ii.lib.Qd Rog ten.́iii.lib.

Ipfe eps ten *HARVVELLE. IN BLITBERIE HD.*

in dñio de epifcopatu fuo.Stigand eps tenuit T.R.E.

Tc ,p.xv.hid.modo ,p x.hid.Tra.ē.viii.car.

In dñio funt.ii.car.7 xviii.uitti 7 v.cot cū.vi.car.

Ibi.iiii.ferui.7 molin̄ de xxx.den.7 xlv.ac pti.

7 In Walengefort.iii.hagæ de.xv.denar.

T.R.E.7 poft.́uatb.xii.lib.Modo.́xvi.lib.

Ipfe eps ten *BRISTOWELLE IN ESLITEFORD HD.*

de epatu fuo.Stigand eps tenuit.T.R.E.Tc ,p xx.hid.

modo ,p.x.hid.Tra.ē.xvi.car.́In dñio funt.iiii.car.

7 xvii.uitti 7 xvi.cot.cū.ix.car.Ibi.xv.ferui.

7 molin̄ de.xx.folid.Ibi æccła.7 de placitis træ que in

Walingeford huic M̃ ptin̄.́xxv.fot.

T.R.E.7 poft.́uatb.xx.lib.Modo.́xxv.lib.

TERRA EPI SARISBERIENS. *IN CERLEDONE HD.*

.III. OSMVND eps Sarifberiæ ten *SONINGES.*

in dñio de epatu fuo.T.R.E.fe defd ,p.lx.hid.

Mod◌ ,p.xxiiii.hid.Tra.ē.xlvi.car.In dñio

funt.v.car.7 xl.vitti 7 xvi.bord.cū.xli.car.

Ibi.x.ferui.7 ii.molini de.xii.folid 7 vi.denar.

7 v.pifcariæ de.xxx.folid.7 xl.ac pti.Silua de.ccc.

porc.T.R.E.uatb.l.lib.7 poft.7 modo.́xl.lib.

In HILLSLOW Hundred
1 Walkelin, Bishop of Winchester, has WOOLSTONE for the supplies of
the monks. Before 1066 it answered for 20 hides; now for 10 hides.
Land for 11 ploughs. In lordship 2½ ploughs;
12 villagers and 24 smallholders with 2½ ploughs.
10 slaves; 2 mills at 12s 6d; meadow, 150 acres.
Roger of Ivry holds 3½ hides of this manor from the Bishop.
He has 1 plough there.
Value before 1066 £16; later £12; now £18; however it
pays £22 in revenue; what Roger holds, £3.

In BLEWBURY Hundred
2 The Bishop holds HARWELL himself, in lordship; of his bishopric.
Bishop Stigand held it before 1066. Then for 15 hides;
now for 10 hides. Land for 8 ploughs. In lordship 2 ploughs;
18 villagers and 5 cottagers with 6 ploughs.
4 slaves; a mill at 30d; meadow, 45 acres.
In Wallingford 3 sites at 15d.
Value before 1066 and later £12; now £16.

In SLOTISFORD Hundred
3 The Bishop holds BRIGHTWELL himself; of his bishopric.
Bishop Stigand held it before 1066. Then for 20 hides;
now for 10 hides. Land for 16 ploughs. In lordship 4 ploughs;
17 villagers and 16 cottagers with 9 ploughs.
15 slaves; a mill at 20s. A church; and from the pleas of the
land which belongs to this manor in Wallingford, 25s.
Value before 1066 and later £20; now £25.

3   LAND OF THE BISHOP OF SALISBURY

In CHARLTON Hundred
1 Osmund, Bishop of Salisbury, holds SONNING in lordship;
of his bishopric. Before 1066 it answered for 60 hides; now
for 24 hides. Land for 46 ploughs. In lordship 5 ploughs;
40 villagers and 16 smallholders with 41 ploughs.
10 slaves; 2 mills at 12s 6d; 5 fisheries at 30s;
meadow, 40 acres; woodland at 300 pigs.
Value before 1066 £50; later and now £40.

★ *ʃ*De appendicijs huj $\overset{9}{}$ $\overset{H}{\text{M}}$ tenuit de Albicus de Coci . xx . hiɗ.

in *HILDESLEI* . quæ juſte ꝑtiñ ſuꝑᵈdicᵗo $\overset{H}{\text{M}}$ epi.

ʃ Rogeȓ $\overset{9}{}$ pƀr teñ . 1 . æcclam in Walengeford . quæ

juſte ꝑtiñ huic $\overset{H}{\text{M}}$.   *IN WANETINZ HD.*

Iſdē eꝑs teñ de rege . 1 . hiɗ 7 dim̅.7 Tori de eo . Paȶ Tori

tenuit T.R.E.7 potuit ire quo uoluit . ſed ꝑ ſua defen

ſione ſe cōmiſit Hermanno eꝑo.7 Tori Oſ$\overset{eꝑo}{}$mundo ſimiliȶ.

Tc̄ 7 m̊ ꝑ una hidạ 7 dim̅ . Ṫra . ē . v . boƀ . In dñio tam̃

ē una caȓ . cū . 1 . coȶ.7 moliñ de . vi . ſoȴ 7 iii . deñ.

T.R.E. ualƀ . xv . ſoliɗ.7 poſtᷓxx . ſoȴ . Modoᷓxxx . ſoliɗ.

Iſɗ eꝑs teñ *WINTREBORNE*.7 $\overset{flāmart}{}$ Rannulf $\overset{9}{}$ *IN ROEBERG HD*

de eo . Herman $\overset{eꝑs}{}$ $\overset{9}{}$ tenuit . Tc̄ ſe defɗ ꝑ . 11 . hiɗ . modo ꝑ ni

chilo . Ṫra . ē . 1 . caȓ . In dñio dim̅ caȓ cū . iiii . borɗ . Vaȴ . xx . ſoȴ.

TERRA EꝐI DVNELMENSIS. *IN BENES HVND*.

.IIII. Eꝑs DVNELM̅SIS teñ de rege *WALTHA* in elemoſina.

V$\overset{canon'}{}$luuiñ $\overset{9}{}$ tenuit de Heraldo.7 æcclæ de Walthā $\overset{cō}{}$ ꝑtinuit.

Tc̄ 7 m̊ ꝑ . iii . hiɗ . Ṫra . ē . vi . caȓ . In dñio ſunȶ . ii.7 viii.

uiȴȴi 7 iii . coȶ cū . iiii . caȓ . Ibi . iii . ſerui.7 iii . ac̄ ꝑti.

Silua . de . vi . porc̄ . T.R.E. ualƀ . lx . ſoȴ.7 poſtᷓlxx . ſoȴ.

Modoᷓc . ſoliɗ.

58 c

TERRA EꝐI OSBERNI.

.V. OSBERN eꝑs teñ in dñio *BOCHELAND* . *IN GAMESFEL HD*.

de eꝑatu ſuo ut dicit . V$\overset{ch.np}{}$luric T.R.E. ibi manſit.

Vnde judiciū ñ dixeȓ . ſed ante rege ut judicet dimiſeȓ.

Tc̄ ſe defɗ ꝑ . xv . hiɗ 7 dim̅ . modo ꝑ . viii . hiɗ . Ṫra . ē

vi . caȓ . Ibi nil in dñio . ſed . ix . uiȴȴi 7 vii . coȶ . cū . iiii.

Aubrey of Coucy held 20 hides of the dependencies of this manor in (East) ILSLEY which rightfully belong to the said Bishop's manor.
Roger the priest holds 1 church in Wallingford which rightfully belongs to this manor.

In WANTAGE Hundred

2 The Bishop also holds 1½ hides from the King, and Thori from him. Thori's father held them before 1066; he could go where he would, but for his protection he committed himself to Bishop Herman, and Thori similarly to Bishop Osmund. Then and now for 1½ hides. Land for 5 oxen. In lordship however 1 plough, with
1 cottager.
A mill at 6s 3d.
Value before 1066, 15s; later 20s; now 30s.

In ROWBURY Hundred

3 The Bishop also holds WINTERBOURNE and Ranulf Flambard from him. Bishop Herman held it. Then it answered for 2 hides; now for nothing. Land for 1 plough. In lordship ½ plough, with
4 smallholders.
Value 20s.

4   LAND OF THE BISHOP OF DURHAM

In BEYNHURST Hundred

1 The Bishop of Durham holds (White) WALTHAM from the King in alms. Canon Wulfwin held it from Earl Harold. It belonged to the church of Waltham (Abbey). Then and now for 3 hides. Land for 6 ploughs. In lordship 2;
8 villagers and 3 cottagers with 4 ploughs.
3 slaves; meadow, 3 acres; woodland at 6 pigs.
Value before 1066, 60s; later 70s; now 100s.

5   LAND OF BISHOP OSBERN (OF EXETER)   58 c

In GANFIELD Hundred

1 Bishop Osbern holds BUCKLAND in lordship; of his bishopric, as he states. Wulfric Kemp lived there before 1066. Thereon (the men of the Hundred) did not give judgement, but referred it to the King to judge. Then it answered for 15½ hides; now for 8 hides. Land for 6 ploughs. Nothing in lordship, but
9 villagers and 7 cottagers with 4 ploughs.

car . Ibi æccla 7 vii . ferui . 7 molin de . xii . fol . 7 vi . den.

7 iiii . pifcariæ de . xx . folid 7 vi . den . 7 ccxx . ac p̄ti.

7 Wica de . x . penfis cafeo₇ . ualtes . xxxii . fol . 7 iiii.

den . T . R . E . ualb . xvi . lib . 7 poft: xii . lib . Modo: viii . lib.

TERRA EP̄I CONSTANTIENS. *IN NACHEDEDORNE HD.*

.VI. Eps Goisfridvs ten *CONTONE* . Oda tenuit de

rege . E . Tc fe defd ₚ . v . hid . modo ₚ . ii . hid 7 dimid.

Tra . e̅   In dn̄io funt . ii . car . 7 ix . uilti 7 iiii . bord.

cu . v . car . Ibi . v . ferui . Silua de . x . porc.

T . R . E . 7 poft . ualb . iiii . lib . modo: c . folid.

TERRA ÆCCLÆ ABENDONIENS *IN HORNIMERE HD.*

.VII. Abbatia De abbendone ten *COMENORE* . Sēp fuit

in abbatia . T . R . E . fe defd ₚ . l . hid . Modo ₚ . xxx.

hid . Tra . e̅ . l . car . In dn̄io funt . ix . car , 7 lx . uilti

7 lxix . bord cu . xxvi . car . Ibi . iiii . ferui . 7 ii . molini

de . l . folid . 7 de pifcarijs . xl . fol . 7 cc . ac p̄ti . Ibi æccla.

T . R . E . ualb xxx . lib . 7 poft 7 modo: l . lib.

De his . l . hid ten Anfchil . v . hid . Norman tenuit

T . R . E . ₚ uno M̄ . Seuacoorde . 7 n̄ potuit ire quó uoluit.

ₚ . v . hid geldau cu alijs fupioribȝ . Tra . e̅ . vii . car . In

dn̄io funt . ii . car . 7 xii . uilti 7 xv . bord cu . v . car.

T . R . E . ualb . c . fol . 7 poft . lxx . fol . Modo: viii . lib.

In Winteha ten Hubt de abbe . v . hid . de tra uilto₇.

fuer . iiii . 7 geldauer cu hid M̄ . Hida taini qeta fuit.

fed n̄ potuit ire quo uoluit . Tra . e̅ . ii . car . In dn̄io . e̅ . i . car

7 dim . 7 iiii . uilti 7 xi . bord . Ibi . lxiiii . ac p̄ti.

T . R . E . 7 poft: ualb . l . folid . Modo: iiii . lib.

Ex fup̄dictis hid ten Ofbn in Comenore . ii . hid 7 dim.

7 ₚ tanto geldauer cu alijs hid . Duo alodiarij tenuer

de abbe . Tra . e̅ . ii . car . In dn̄io . e̅ una car cu . i . uilto . 7 iii.

bord . ualuit . lx . fol . Modo: xl . folid.

A church; 7 slaves; a mill at 12s 6d; 4 fisheries at
20s 6d; meadow, 220 acres; a dairy, at 10 weys
of cheese, whose value is 32s 4d.
Value before 1066 £16; later £12; now £8.

6   LAND OF THE BISHOP OF COUTANCES

In COMPTON Hundred
1 Bishop Geoffrey holds COMPTON. Odda held from King Edward.
Then it answered for 5 hides; now for 2½ hides. Land for ....
In lordship 2 ploughs;
9 villagers and 4 smallholders with 5 ploughs.
5 slaves; woodland at 10 pigs.
Value before 1066 and later £4; now 100s.

7   LAND OF ABINGDON CHURCH

In HORMER Hundred
1 Abingdon Abbey holds CUMNOR. It was always in the Abbey (lands).
Before 1066 it answered for 50 hides; now for 30 hides.
Land for 50 ploughs. In lordship 9 ploughs;
60 villagers and 69 smallholders with 26 ploughs.
4 slaves; 2 mills at 50s; from the fisheries 40s;
meadow, 200 acres. A church.
Value before 1066 £30; later and now £50.

2 Of these 50 hides Askell holds 5 hides. Norman held them
before 1066 as one manor, called SEACOURT; he could not go
where he would. It paid tax for 5 hides with the others above.
Land for 7 ploughs. In lordship 2 ploughs;
12 villagers and 15 smallholders with 5 ploughs.
Value before 1066, 100s; later 70s; now £8.

3 In WYTHAM Hubert holds 5 hides of villagers' land from the Abbot.
There were 4, and they paid tax with the hides of the manor.
The thane's hide was exempt, but he could not go where he
would. Land for 2 ploughs. In lordship 1½ ploughs;
4 villagers and 11 smallholders.
Meadow, 64 acres.
Value before 1066 and later 50s; now £4.

4 From the said hides, Osbern holds 2½ hides in CUMNOR. They paid
tax for as much with the other hides. Two freeholders held them
from the Abbot. Land for 2 ploughs. In lordship 1 plough, with
1 villager and 3 smallholders.
The value was 60s; now 40s.

Rainald ten unā hiđ in Comenore.7 p una hiđ geldau

cū alijs . Tra . ē . I . car . Valuit . xx . fol. Modo . x . foliđ.

Ipſa abbatia ten BERTVNE in dnio . T.R.E. ſe defđ

p . LX . hiđ. Modo p . XL . hiđ . Tra . ē . XL . car. In dnio ſunt

III . car.7 LXIIII . uilli 7 XXXVI . borđ cū . XXXIIII . car.

7 x . mercatores ante portā æcclæ manentes redđ . XL . den.

.II.ſerui

7 In Bertune 7 XXIIII . colibti.7 II. molini de . XL . foliđ.

7 V . piſcariæ de XVIII . fol 7 IIII . den.7 cc . ac pti.7 xv.

foliđ de paſtura.7 II . molini in curia abbis ſine cenſu.

T.R.E . ualb xx . lib.7 poſt.7 modo: XL . lib.

De his . LX . hiđ ten Rainald de abbe in uadimonio

unū Ꝏ. SIPENE. Ednod Stalre tenuit T.R.E.7 n fuit tc

in abbatia . Hugo comes deđ abbi . Tc ſe defđ p . v. hiđ.

modo p una hida . Ibi in dnio ſunt . II . car.7 II. uilli 7 v.

borđ cū . I . car .7 IIII . ſerui.7 xx . ac pti.

Iſđ ten ibiđ de abbe . III . hiđ . Aluuard 7 Leuuin tenuer

de abbe . nec poterant recede . Tc 7 m ſe defđ p . III . hiđ.

In dnio ht . I . car. cū . I. borđ.7 XVIII . ac pti. piſcaria de. v.

den . Tra h eſt. IIII. car. T.R.E. ualb. VII. lib .7 poſt: c. fol.

Hugo coqus ten de abbe in Bertune   Modo: VI . lib.

.I. hiđ 7 dim.7 in Sanford. II. hiđ. Leuuin 7 Norman tenuer.

ſ; recede n potuer.

58 d

Ibi . I . car 7 dim. cū uno borđ.7 VI . ac pti. Tra. ē. II. car. Val. XL. foliđ.

Ex ſupdictis. LX. hiđ ten Anſchil 7 Giſlebt in BAIORDE. x. hiđ

de abbe. Vluric tenuit 7 recede n potuit . Hæ x. hidæ. p. VIII. ſe

defđt. Ibi ſunt. III. car.7 IX . uilli 7 VIII. borđ cū . IIII. car 7 dim.

Ibi. v. ſerui.7 LX. ac pti. Tra. ē. VIII. car. Valuit. x. lib. m. VIII. lib.

58 c, d

5 Reginald holds 1 hide in CUMNOR. It paid tax as 1 hide
   with the others. Land for 1 plough.
   The value was 20s; now 10s.

6 The Abbey holds BARTON itself, in lordship. Before 1066 it
   answered for 60 hides; now for 40 hides. Land for 40 ploughs.
   In lordship 3 ploughs;
       64 villagers and 36 smallholders with 34 ploughs.
       10 merchants dwelling in front of the church gate pay 40d.
   In Barton 2 slaves; 24 freedmen; 2 mills at 40s; 5 fisheries
       at 18s 4d; meadow, 200 acres; 15s from pasture;
       2 mills in the Abbot's court without dues.
   Value before 1066 £20; later and now £40.

7 Of these 60 hides Reginald holds one manor, SHIPPON, from
   the Abbot, in pledge. Ednoth the Constable held it before 1066,
   but it was not then in the Abbey (lands). Earl Hugh gave it to the
   Abbot. Then it answered for 5 hides; now for 1 hide.
   In lordship 2 ploughs;
       2 villagers and 5 smallholders with 1 plough; 4 slaves.
   Meadow, 20 acres.

8 He also holds 3 hides there from the Abbot. Alfward the priest
   and Leofwin the goldsmith held from the Abbot; they could
   not withdraw. Then and now it answered for 3 hides.
   In lordship he has 1 plough, with
       1 smallholder.
   Meadow, 18 acres; a fishery at 5d.
   This land is for 4 ploughs.
   Value before 1066 £7; later 100s; now £6.

9 Hugo Cook holds from the Abbot 1½ hides in BARTON and
   2 hides in (Dry) SANDFORD. Leofwin and Norman held them, but
   they could not withdraw. 1½ ploughs, with   58 d
       1 smallholder.
   Meadow, 6 acres. Land for 2 ploughs.
   Value 40s.

10 Of the said 60 hides, Askell and Gilbert hold 10 hides from the
   Abbot in BAYWORTH. Wulfric held them; he could not withdraw.
   These 10 hides answered for 8. 3 ploughs;
       9 villagers and 8 smallholders with 4½ ploughs.
       5 slaves; meadow, 60 acres. Land for 8 ploughs.
   The value was £10; now £8.

ʄ De eod ꝏ̄ 7 de ead t̄ra ten̄ Warin̄ in Sogoorde.IIII.hid.7 Ber
neri.v.hid in Soningeuuel 7 in Chenitun.7 Aluuin̄.I.hid
in Genetune.Sex Anglici tenuer̄.7 ab æccła recede n̄ potuer̄.

★ T̄ra.ē.VI.car̄.7 cū Alijs hid geldau.Ibi funt.III.car̄.7 VII.uiłłi
7 XVIII.bord cū.I.car̄.7 v.feruis.7 cx.aͨc p̊ti.Valuit.XII.lib.iꝰ

Ipfa abbatia ten̄ CIVELEI.Sēp   IN ROEBERG HVND.ʄ x.lib̄.

tenuit.T.R.E.fe defd ꝑ.XXVII.hid.modo ꝑ.VII.hid 7 dim̄.
T̄ra.ē.XX.car̄.In dn̄io funt.III.car̄.7 XXVIII.uiłłi 7 x.bord
cū XVIII.car̄.Ibi.III.ferui.7 IIII.aͨc p̊ti.Silua de.LX.porc̄.
De hac t̄ra ten̄ Wiłłs de abb̄e.v.hid.7 Godefrid.I.hid 7 dim̄.
7 ibi.una car̄.ē cū.III.uiłłis 7 II.bord hn̄tib̃.I.car̄.7 III.aͨs p̊ti.
Tot̄ T.R.E.7 poft:ͨ uałb̄.XII.lib̄.Modo:ͨx.lib̄ pars abb̄is.hoͤum:ͨL.folid.

Ipfa abbatia ten̄ WALIFORD.7 fēp tenuit.T.R.E.fe defd
ꝑ.L.hid.7 modo ꝑ.XXXVII.hid.T̄ra.ē.XXIIII.car̄.In dn̄io
funt.v.car̄.7 XXXIII.uiłłi 7 XXXIIII.bord cū XX.II.car̄.Ibi
IX.ferui.7 v.molini de.LX.foł.7 II.æcctæ.7 XL.aͨc p̊ti.Silua
de.XX.porc̄.T.R.E.7 poft 7 modo:ͨ uał.XXVII.lib̄.
De hac t̄ra huj ꝏ̄ ten̄ Reinbald LECANESTEDE.x.hid.
7 Wiłłs.IIII.hid.in WESTVN.7 Berneri.II.hid in BOʔSORE.
Has tenuer̄ Bricftuin̄ 7 Alfric̄ 7 ꝗda p̄pofit de abb̄e.nec potuer̄
recedere.T̄ra.ē.XI.car̄.Ibi funt.III.car̄.7 XII.uiłłi 7 XXIIII.
bord cū.VI.car̄.7 VI.feruis.7 II.aͨc p̊ti.7 Æccła.Vał 7 ualuit.x.lib̄.

Walteri de Riuere ten̄ de abb̄e BEDENE.Norman tenuit de
abb̄e.7 n̄ potuit ire quo uoluit.Tc̄ fe defd ꝑ x.hid.m̄ ꝑ VIII.
hid.Tam̄ fuit ꝑ.XV.hid.fed rex.E.c̄donauit ꝑ.XI.hid ut dn̄t.
T̄ra.ē.XI.car̄.In dn̄io funt.II.7 XI.uiłłi 7 x.bord cū.VI.car̄.
7 III.ferui ibi.De ipfa t̄ra ten̄ ꝗda miles.II.hidas.7 ibi ht̄.I.car̄
cū.III.bord.T.R.E.uałb̄.XI.lib̄.7 poft.VI.lib̄.modo:ͨVIII.lib̄.

11 Warin holds 4 hides of the same manor and the same land in
SUGWORTH; Berner, 5 hides in SUNNINGWELL and in KENNINGTON;
Alwin, 1 hide in KENNINGTON. Six Englishmen held them; they
could not withdraw from the church. Land for 6 ploughs and
they paid tax with the other hides. 3 ploughs;
   7 villagers and 18 smallholders with 1 plough; 5 slaves.
   Meadow, 110 acres.
The value was £12; now £10.

In ROWBURY Hundred
12 The Abbey holds CHIEVELEY itself and always held it. Before
1066 it answered for 27 hides; now for 7½ hides.
Land for 20 ploughs. In lordship 3 ploughs;
   28 villagers and 10 smallholders with 18 ploughs.
   3 slaves; meadow, 4 acres; woodland at 60 pigs.
William holds 5 hides of this land from the Abbot;
Godfrey 1½ hides. 1 plough there, with
   3 villagers and 2 smallholders who have 1 plough.
   Meadow, 3 acres.
Value of the whole before 1066 and later £12; now £10,
the Abbot's part; the men's, 50s.

13 The Abbey holds WELFORD itself. It always held it.
Before 1066 it answered for 50 hides; now for 37 hides.
Land for 24 ploughs. In lordship 5 ploughs;
   33 villagers and 34 smallholders with 22 ploughs.
   9 slaves; 5 mills at 60s; 2 churches; meadow, 40 acres;
     woodland at 20 pigs.
Value before 1066, later and now £27.

14 Of this land of this manor, Reinbald holds LECKHAMPSTEAD, 10 hides;
William, 4 hides in WESTON; Berner, 2 hides in BOXFORD.
Brictwin and Aelfric and a reeve held them from the Abbot;
they could not withdraw. Land for 11 ploughs. 3 ploughs there;
   12 villagers and 24 smallholders with 6 ploughs; 6 slaves.
   Meadow, 2 acres; a church.
The value is and was £10.

15 Walter of Rivers holds BEEDON from the Abbot. Norman held
from the Abbot; he could not go where he would. Then it
answered for 10 hides; now for 8 hides; however, it was
at 15 hides, but King Edward remitted it for 11 hides, as they state.
Land for 11 ploughs. In lordship 2;
   11 villagers and 10 smallholders with 6 ploughs; 3 slaves.
A man-at-arms holds 2 hides of this land; he has 1 plough, with
   3 smallholders.
Value before 1066 £11; later £6; now £8.

Ifd Walt ten in BENEHA. II. hid. Eddid tenuit. T.R.E.7 ꝑ tanto
fe defd tc 7 m̃. Ipfa Eddid poterat ire quo uellet. Tra.e.I.car.
Ibi funt.v bord.7 xx.ac p̃ti. nil aliud. Val 7 ualuit. xxx. fol.
H̃ tra ñ fuit in abbatia T.R.E. fed.e q̃eta regi.
Ipfa abbatia ten MERCEHA. Sep tenuit IN MERCEHA HD.
T.R.E.fe defd ꝑ.xx. hid. modo ꝑ x.hid. Tra.e.x.car. In
dñio funt. III. car.7 xviII. uilli 7 x.bord cũ.x.car. Ibi æccła
7 vi. ferui.7 molin de. xv. fol.7 c.ac p̃ti.
De hac tra ten Anfchil.I. hid. Aluuin tenuit de abbe.7 ibi
.e in dñio.I.car. Tot T.R.E.ualuit.xiI.lib 7 x.fol. Modo tntd.
Ipfa abbatia ten FRIELIFORD. Sep tenuit T.R.E. fe defd
ꝑ. x. hid.7 modo facit. In dñio funt. IIII. hidæ. Tra.e. IIII. car.
Ibi funt.viII.uilli cũ.II.car.7 xL. ac p̃ti. Val 7 ualuit. xL. fol.
De tra huj ꝏ ten Rainald. IIII. hid.7 Renbald. I. hid.
7 Saluui.I. hid. Quinq̨ teini tenuer de abbc. nec potuer
recedere. Tra. e. vi. car. Ibi funt. II. car 7 dim.7.vi.uilli 7 x.
bord cũ.II.car.7 II.feruis.7 Lx.ac p̃ti.
Tot T.R.E.ualb Lxx. folid.7 poft. fimilit. Modo vi. lib.
Rainbald ten de abbe.I. hid in TOBENIE. Norman 7 Aluric
tenuer T.R.E.7 m̃ fe defd ꝑ una hida. Tra.e. vi.car.In dñio
nichil. Ibi.II.|7 xvi.bord cũ.vi. car. Ibi. II. ferui.7 xv. ac p̃ti.
T.R.E.7 poft. ualuit. xL. fol. Modo. IIII. lib.
Willf ten de abbe LEIE.7 Norman tenuit T.R.E.de abbe.
Tc 7 m̃ fe defd ꝑ.I. hida. Tra. e. v. car. In dñio funt. II. car.
7 xII. bord cũ. III. car. Valuit. xL. folid. modo IIII. lib.
59 a
Ipfa abbatia ten WAREFORD.7 Sep tenuit. T.R.E. fe defd
ꝑ.x. hid.m̃ ꝑ.vi. hid. Abb he inde.viII. hid.7 Berneri. II. de co.

16 Walter also holds 2 hides in BENHAM. Edith held it before 1066. It answered for the same amount then and now. Edith herself could go where she would. Land for 1 plough.
    5 smallholders.
    Meadow, 20 acres; nothing else.
The value is and was 30s.
    This land was not in the Abbey (lands) before 1066 but it is exempt (from payment to) the King.

In MARCHAM Hundred
17 The Abbey holds MARCHAM itself. It always held it.
Before 1066 it answered for 20 hides; now for 10 hides.
Land for 10 ploughs. In lordship 3 ploughs;
    18 villagers and 10 smallholders with 10 ploughs.
    A church; 6 slaves; a mill at 15s; meadow, 100 acres.
    Askell holds 1 hide of this land; Alwin held it from
      the Abbot; in lordship 1 plough.
Value of the whole before 1066 £12 10s; now as much.

18 The Abbey holds FRILFORD itself. It always held it.
Before 1066 it answered for 10 hides, and does so now.
In lordship 4 hides. Land for 4 ploughs.
    8 villagers with 2 ploughs.
    Meadow, 40 acres.
The value is and was 40s.
    Reginald holds 4 hides of this land of this manor; Reinbald, 1 hide; Salvi, 1 hide. Five thanes held them from the Abbot; they could not withdraw. Land for 6 ploughs. 2½ ploughs there;
    6 villagers and 10 smallholders with 2 ploughs; 2 slaves.
    Meadow, 60 acres.
Value of the whole before 1066, 70s; later, the same; now £6.

19 Reinbald holds 1 hide from the Abbot in TUBNEY. Norman and Aelfric held it before 1066. Now it answers for 1 hide.
Land for 6 ploughs. In lordship nothing.
    2 villagers and 16 smallholders with 6 ploughs.
    2 slaves; meadow, 15 acres.
Value before 1066 and later 40s; now £4.

20 William holds (Bessels) LEIGH from the Abbot. Norman held from the Abbot before 1066. Then and now it answered for 1 hide.
Land for 5 ploughs. In lordship 2 ploughs;
    12 smallholders with 3 ploughs.
The value was 40s; now £4.

21 The Abbey holds GARFORD itself, and always held it.   59 a
Before 1066 it answered for 10 hides; now for 6 hides.
The Abbot has 8 hides thereof; Berner 2 (hides) of it.

Tra.ē.vii.car.In dnio funt.iii.car.7 x.uilti 7 x.bord.cū.iii.

car.Ibi molin de.vii.folid 7 vi.den.7 xxx.ac pti.

7 Berneri ht.i.car cū.vi.bord.7 vi.acs pti.

Tot T.R.E.ualb.xii.lib.7 poft:´x.lib.Modo:´tntd.

Ipfa abbatia ten HANLEI.7 femp tenuit.T.R.E.7 m̄ fe defd

p.x.hid.Tra.ē.vii.car.Ibi funt x.uilti cū.ii.car.7 c.ac

pti.De hac tra huj ꝏ ten Vluui.iii.hid que fuer de dnico

uictu monacho̗.T.R.E.7 Nicolaus ten.i.hid de abbe.quā te

nuit Eduuin pbr 7 n̄ potuit ab eo recede.In his.iiii.hid funt

.ii.car.7 ix.bord cū dim car.7 molin de.xii.folid.7 iiii.ferui.

7 lx.ac pti.

Tot T.R.E.ualb.viii.lib.7 poft:´vii.lib.Modo:´fimilit.

Ipfa abbatia ten GOSEI.7 femp tenuit.T.R.E.fe defd p xvii.

hid.modo p.xi.hid.Tra.ē.ix.car.In dnio funt.ii.car.

7 vi.uilti 7 iii.bord cū.ii.car.7 i.rachenefte cū fua car.

7 c.ac pti.7 de paftura.xvi.den.

De hac tra huj ꝏ ten Hermer.vii.hid.7 ē in dnico

uictu monacho̗.Ibi ht.i.car.7 vii.uilt cū dimid car.

7 xxxv.acs pti.

Tot T.R.E.ualb.ix.lib.7 poft.x.lib.Modo:´fimilit.

Walteri gifard ten de abbe LINFORD.T.R.E.tenuer filij

Eliert de abbe.nec poteray´ alias ire abfq; licentia.7 tam cō

mendauer fe Walterio fine abbis pcepto.Tc 7 m̄ fe defd

p.vii.hid.Tra.ē.iii.car.In dnio funt.ii.7 viii.uilti 7 vii.

bord cū.ii.car.7 ibi.iiii.ac pti´.Valuit.iiii.lib.modo:´c.fot.

Rainald ten de abbe.iii.hid in ead uilla.Linbald mo

nach tenuit de abbatia.7 p.iii.hid fe defd tc 7 m̄.Tra.ē

un car.7 dim.In dnio.ē car.7 iii.uilti 7 iii.bord cū dim car.

Ibi.i.feru.7 xxxvi.ac pti.Valuit.xx.folid.modo:´xl.fot.

Land for 7 ploughs. In lordship 3 ploughs;
   10 villagers and 10 smallholders with 3 ploughs.
   A mill at 7s 6d; meadow, 30 acres.
   Berner has 1 plough, with
      6 smallholders.
   Meadow, 6 acres.
Value of the whole before 1066 £12; later £10; now as much.

22 The Abbey holds (East) HANNEY itself, and always held it. Before
   1066 and now it answered for 10 hides. Land for 7 ploughs.
      10 villagers with 2 ploughs.
   Meadow, 100 acres.
   Wulfwin holds 3 hides of this land of this manor, which were for
   the monks' household supplies before 1066. Nicolas holds 1 hide
   from the Abbot, which Edwin the priest held; he could not
   withdraw from him. In these 4 hides are 2 ploughs;
      9 smallholders with ½ plough.
   A mill at 12s; 4 slaves; meadow, 60 acres.
   Value of the whole before 1066 £8; later £7; now the same.

23 The Abbey holds GOOSEY itself, and always held it.
   Before 1066 it answered for 17 hides, now for 11 hides.
   Land for 9 ploughs. In lordship 2 ploughs;
      6 villagers and 3 smallholders with 2 ploughs;
         1 riding man with his plough.
   Meadow, 100 acres; from pasture, 16d.
   Hermer holds 7 hides of this land of this manor.
   It is for the monks' household supplies. He has 1 plough;
      7 villagers with ½ plough.
   Meadow, 35 acres.
   Value of the whole before 1066 £9; later £10; now the same.

24 Walter Giffard holds LYFORD from the Abbot. Before 1066
   Alfyard's sons held it from the Abbot; they could not go
   elsewhere without permission; however they commended
   themselves to Walter without the Abbot's command. Then and
   now it answered for 7 hides. Land for 3 ploughs. In lordship 2;
      8 villagers and 7 smallholders with 2 ploughs.
   Meadow, 4 acres.
   The value was £4; now 100s.

25 Reginald holds 3 hides from the Abbot in the same village.
   Lindbald the monk held them from the Abbey. Then and now it
   answered for 3 hides. Land for 1½ ploughs. In lordship a plough;
      3 villagers and 3 smallholders with ½ plough.
      1 slave; meadow, 36 acres.
   The value was 20s; now 40s.

Ipſa abbatia teñ DRAICOTE.⁊ ſép tenuit.T.R.E.⁊ m̃ ſe defđ

⁊p.x.hiđ.Tra.ē.viii.cař.Ibi ſunt xvi.uilli cũ.vii.cař.

⁊ xl.ãc p̃ti.De hac t̃ra teñ Gillebt.i.hiđ.⁊ q̃đã anglic̃

dim̃ hiđ.⁊ ibi.ē.i.cař cũ.ii.uillis ⁊ ii.ſeruis.⁊ vi.ãc p̃ti.

⁊ piſcaria.Toť T.R.E.⁊ poſt:̃ualb.c.ſoliđ.modo.vi.lib.

Ipſa abbatia teñ MIDDELTVNE.⁊ ſép tenuit.IN SVDTVNE HĐ.

T.R.E.ſe defđ ⁊p.xxviii.hiđ.modo ⁊p xxiii.hiđ.Tra.ē xxiiii.

cař.In dñio ſunt.iiii.cař.⁊ xxxix.uilli ⁊ xxv.borđ.cũ xv.

cař.Ibi.iiii.ſerui.⁊ moliñ de.x.ſoliđ.⁊ ccc.xliiii.ãc p̃ti.

De eađ t̃ra teñ Azeliñ.ii.hiđ ⁊ unã v de abbe.⁊ Rainald

iii.hiđ.Ibi ſunt.iii.cař.⁊ v.uilli ⁊ xi.borđ.⁊ moliñ de xii.

ſol.⁊ vi.deñ.⁊ ii.ſerui.⁊ xxx.ãc p̃ti.   ⌐ ⁊ v.ſol.

Toť T.R.E.ualb xxv.lib.Modo tñtđ qđ hť abb.Qđ hões:̃iiii.lib.

Ipſa abbatia teñ in dñio APLEFORD.T.R.E.⁊ m̃ ſe defđ

⁊p.v.hiđ.Tra.ē.vi.cař ⁊ dim̃.In dñio ſunt.ii.⁊ xiiii.uilli

⁊ xx.borđ cũ.iiii.cař.Ibi.i.ſeru.⁊ ii.molini de xxv.ſoliđ.

⁊ piſcaria de.x.ſol.⁊ lx.ãc p̃ti.⁊ de lucro t̃ræ dñicæ.xxi.ſol.

De hac t̃ra teñ Robť.i.hiđ.⁊ ibi hť.ii.borđ.

Toť T.R.E.ualb.ix.lib.⁊ poſt.⁊ modo ſimiliť.

In SVDTVNE teñ Aluui p̃br.i.hidã de abbe.Pať ej̃ tenuit.

⁊ ⁊p tanto ſe defđ tc̃ ⁊ m̃.Ibi hť dim̃ cař cũ.iii.borđ.Val.xx.ſol.

★ Ipſa abbatia teñ WITEHA.⁊ ſép tenuit.T.R.E.ſe defđ

⁊p.x.hiđ.modo ⁊p.v.hiđ.Tra.ē.vi.cař.In dñio ſunt.ii.cař.

⁊ xi.uilli ⁊ ix.borđ.cũ.iii.cař.Ibi æccła ⁊ moliñ de.x.ſol.

⁊ l,iii.ãc p̃ti.T.R.E.ualb.xv.lib.⁊ poſt ⁊ m̃.xii.lib.

26 The Abbey holds DRAYCOTT (Moor) itself and always held it.
Before 1066 and now it answered for 10 hides. Land for 8 ploughs.
16 villagers with 7 ploughs.
Meadow, 40 acres.
Gilbert holds 1 hide of this land, and an Englishman ½ hide.
1 plough there, with
2 villagers and 2 slaves.
Meadow, 6 acres; a fishery.
Value of the whole before 1066 and later 100s; now £6.

In SUTTON Hundred
27 The Abbey holds MILTON itself, and always held it.
Before 1066 it answered for 28 hides; now for 23 hides.
Land for 24 ploughs. In lordship 4 ploughs;
39 villagers and 25 smallholders with 15 ploughs.
4 slaves; a mill at 10s; meadow, 344 acres.
Azelin holds 2 hides and 1 virgate of this land from the Abbot;
Reginald 3 hides. 3 ploughs there;
5 villagers and 11 smallholders.
A mill at 12s 6d; 2 slaves; meadow, 30 acres.
Value of the whole before 1066 £25; now, what the Abbot has,
as much; what the men (have), £4 5s.

28 The Abbey holds APPLEFORD itself, in lordship. Before 1066 and
now it answered for 5 hides. Land for 6½ ploughs. In lordship 2;
14 villagers and 20 smallholders with 4 ploughs.
1 slave; 2 mills at 25s; a fishery at 10s; meadow, 60 acres;
from profit of the lordship land, 21s.
Robert holds 1 hide of this land; he has
2 smallholders.
Value of the whole before 1066 £9; later and now, the same.

29 In SUTTON (Courtenay) Alwin the priest holds 1 hide from
the Abbot. His father held it; it answered for as much then
and now. He has ½ plough, with
3 smallholders.
Value 20s.

30 The Abbey holds (Little) WITTENHAM itself, and always held it.
Before 1066 it answered for 10 hides; now for 5 hides.
Land for 6 ploughs. In lordship 2 ploughs;
11 villagers and 9 smallholders with 3 ploughs.
A church; a mill at 10s; meadow, 53 acres.
Value before 1066 £15; later and now £12.

Ipſa abbatia teñ *WENESFELLE*.7 ſep *IN RIPLESMERE HD*.

tenuit.T.R.E.ſe defđ ᵱ.x.hid.modo ᵱ.iii.hiđ 7 dim.

Tra.ē.xx.car.Ibi ſunt xx.uilli cū.ix.car.7 uñ hō

teñ dimid hiđ.abſq̛ uoluntate abbis.7 injuſte facit.

De hac ira ſunt.iiii.hiđe in foreſta regis.

Val 7 ualuit ſep.iiii.lib.   *IN CERLEDONE HD*.

Ipſa abbatia teñ *WISELEI*.7 ſep tenuit.T.R.E.

ſe defđ ᵱ.x.hiđ.m̃ ᵱ.vii.hiđ.Tra.ē.xii.car.Ibi ſũɟ

xvi.uilli 7 uñ borđ cū.ix.car.7 moliñ de.v.ſol

7 ccl.anguill.7 x.ãc p̃ti.Silua de.l.porc.7 piſcaria

de.ccc.anguil.Valuit.x.lib.modo:ˊvi.lib.

Ipſa abbatia teñ *FERMEBERGE*. *IN NACHEDEDORNE HD*.

T.R.E.ſe defđ ᵱ.x.hiđ.modo ᵱ.iiii.hiđ 7 dim.

Tra.ē.x.car.In dñio ſunt.ii.car.7 viii.uilli 7 x.

borđ.cū.vi.car.Ibi.i.ſeru.7 v.ãc p̃ti.Silua ad

clauſurā.T.R.E.ualb.ix.lib.7 poſt:ˊvi.lib.Modo:ˊviii.lib.

Wenric̛ teñ de abbe *CILLETONE*.Blacheman te

nuit de Heraldo in alođ.7 potuit ire quo uoluit.

Tc 7 m̃ ᵱ.v.hid.Tra.ē.vi.car.In dñio.ē car 7 dim.

7 iii.uilli.7 xiii.borđ cū.ii.car 7 dim.Silua de.x.porc.

Hezeliñ teñ de abbe *LEWARTONE*.Blacheman   *IN CHENETE*

tenuit in feudo.T.R.E.Tc ſe defđᵱ.vi.hiđ 7 dimid.   *BERIE HD*

modo ᵱ.iiii.hiđ 7 dimiđ.Tra.ē.iiii.car.In dñio eſt

una.7 iiii.uilli 7 iii.borđ cū.ii.car.Ibi.ii.ſerui.

7 moliñ de.x.ſoliđ.Silua.de.ii.porc.

Valuit.lx.ſoliđ.Modo:ˊl.ſoliđ. *IN SERIVEHĀ HD*.

Ipſa abbatia teñ *WACHENESFELD*.7 tenuit T.R.E.

Tc ſe defđ ᵱ.xx.hiđ.modo ᵱ.x.hiđ.Tra.ē.xii.car.

In dñio ſunt.iii.car.7 xiiii.uilli 7 x.borđ cū.vi.car.

Ibi·.viii.ſerui.7 moliñ de.xxv.ſol.7 cl.ãc p̃ti.

In RIPPLESMERE Hundred
31 The Abbey holds WINKFIELD itself, and always held it. Before 1066
it answered for 10 hides; now for 3½ hides. Land for 20 ploughs.
   20 villagers with 9 ploughs; one man holds ½ hide
      without the Abbot's will, and does so wrongfully.
   4 hides of this land are in the King's Forest.
The value is and always was £4.

In CHARLTON Hundred
32 The Abbey holds WHISTLEY itself, and always held it. Before 1066
it answered for 10 hides; now for 7 hides. Land for 12 ploughs.
   16 villagers and 1 smallholder with 9 ploughs.
   A mill at 5s and 250 eels; meadow, 10 acres;
      woodland at 50 pigs; a fishery at 300 eels.
The value was £10; now £6.

In COMPTON Hundred
33 The Abbey holds FARNBOROUGH itself. Before 1066 it answered
for 10 hides; now for 4½ hides. Land for 10 ploughs.
In lordship 2 ploughs;
   8 villagers and 10 smallholders with 6 ploughs.
   1 slave; meadow, 5 acres; woodland for fencing.
Value before 1066 £9; later £6; now £8.

34 Wynric holds CHILTON from the Abbot. Blackman held it from
Earl Harold in freehold; he could go where he would.
Then and now for 5 hides. Land for 6 ploughs. In lordship
1½ ploughs;
   3 villagers and 13 smallholders with 2½ ploughs.
   Woodland at 10 pigs.
[Value ....]

In KINTBURY Hundred
35 Hezelin holds LEVERTON from the Abbot. Blackman held it
as a Holding before 1066. Then it answered for 6½ hides;
now for 4½ hides. Land for 4 ploughs. In lordship 1;
   4 villagers and 3 smallholders with 2 ploughs.
   2 slaves; a mill at 10s; woodland at 2 pigs.
The value was 60s; now 50s.

In SHRIVENHAM Hundred
36 The Abbey holds WATCHFIELD itself, and held it before 1066.
Then it answered for 20 hides; now for 10 hides.
Land for 12 ploughs. In lordship 3 ploughs;
   14 villagers and 10 smallholders with 6 ploughs.
   8 slaves; a mill at 25s; meadow, 150 acres.

De tra ista ten Gisłebt̄. III . hid 7 unā v̄ de abbe.

7 Wimund . I . hid. Ibi in dn̄io . I . car̄.7 II. uiłłi 7 VII.

bord . Tot̄ T.R.E.uałb̄ xv . łib.7 post . x . łib ̖ Modo

XII . łib . qd h̄ abb̄.Qd hōes: L . solid. IN *HILLESLAVE HD̄*.

Ipsa abbatia ten̄ *OFFENTONE*.7 sēp tenuit . T.R.E.

se defd ꝓ XL . hid . m̄ ꝓ XIIII . hid . Tra . ē . XIIII . car̄.

In dn̄io sunt. III. car̄.7 XVII . uiłłi 7 XVI . bord cū. VII.

car̄ ̖ Ibi . XI. serui.7 moliñ de . v . solid.7 q̄t x̄x̄ 7 v . ac̄ p̄ti.

De hac tra ten̄ Gisłebt̄. VI . hid de abb̄e.7 ibi h̄

.I.car̄.7 XVI . bord cū . I . car̄.

Tot̄ T.R.E. uałb̄. xv . łib.7 post xxI . łib . Modo: xxVI . łib.

Anschil ten̄ *SPERSOLD* de abb̄e . Edric tenuit in

alod de rege.E.7 potuit ire quó uoluit . Tc̄ 7 m̄ se

defd ꝓ . x . hid . Tra . ē . IIII . car̄ . In dn̄io sunt . II . car̄.

7 II. uiłłi 7 I. seru̅ cū . I . car̄.7 moliñ de . v . sol.7 L . ac̄

p̄ti . T.R.E.uałb̄. VII . łib.7 post . IIII . łib . Modo: VI . łib.

De hoc m̄ scira attestat̄ . qd·Edric qui eū tenebat

delibauit illū filio suo qui erat in abendone monach.

ut ad firmā illud teneret.7 sibi donec uiueret neces

saria uitæ inde donaret . post mortē u̅ ej̄ m̄ habet.

7 idō nesciun̄ hōes de scira qd abbatiæ ꝑtineat . Neq̄

enī inde uider̄ breuē regis ł sigillū . Abb̄ u̅ testat̄

qd in T.R.E. misit ille m̄ ad æccłam unde erat.7 inde

h̄ breuē 7 sigillū . R.E. attestantib; om̄ib; mona

chis suis.   IN *GAMENESFELLE HD̄*.

Ipsa abbatia ten̄ in dn̄io *ORDAM*.7 T.R.E.tenuit.

Tc̄ ꝓ.xxx . hid ̖ modo ꝓ̖VIII . hid . Tra . ē . VIII . car̄.

In dn̄io sunt. III . car̄.7 VIII.uiłłi 7 XIIII . cot̄ cū . VI . car̄.

Ibi æccła 7 VIII . serui.7 piscaria de . II . sol.7 c . acræ p̄ti ̖

Vał 7 ualuit semp . xv . łib.

Gilbert holds 3 hides and 1 virgate of this land from the Abbot;
Wimund 1 hide. In lordship 1 plough;
  2 villagers and 7 smallholders.
Value of the whole before 1066 £15; later £10; now what the
Abbot has, £12; what the men (have), 50s.

In HILLSLOW Hundred

37 The Abbey holds UFFINGTON itself, and always held it.
Before 1066 it answered for 40 hides; now for 14 hides.
Land for 14 ploughs. In lordship 3 ploughs;
  17 villagers and 16 smallholders with 7 ploughs.
  11 slaves; a mill at 5s; meadow, 85 acres.
Gilbert holds 6 hides of this land from the Abbot; he has 1 plough and
  16 smallholders with 1 plough.
Value of the whole before 1066 £15; later £21; now £26.

38 Askell holds FAWLER from the Abbot. Edric held it in freehold
from King Edward; he could go where he would. Then and now it
answered for 10 hides. Land for 4 ploughs. In lordship 2 ploughs;
  2 villagers and 1 slave with 1 plough.
  A mill at 5s; meadow, 50 acres.
Value before 1066 £7; later £4; now £6.
  Of this manor, the Shire confirms that Edric, who held it,
delivered it to his son, who was a monk in Abingdon, to hold
at a revenue and to provide him with the necessities of life
for as long as he lived; but that after his death, he should
have the manor. Therefore the men of the Shire do not know
what belongs to the Abbey, for they have not seen the King's
writ or seal. But the Abbot testifies that before 1066 he put the
manor in the (lands of the) church where it was, and has King
Edward's writ and seal for it, which all his monks confirm.

In GANFIELD Hundred

39 The Abbey holds LONGWORTH itself, in lordship, and held it
before 1066. Then for 30 hides; now for 8 hides. Land for 8
ploughs. In lordship 3 ploughs;   59 c
  8 villagers and 14 cottagers with 6 ploughs.
  A church; 8 slaves; a fishery at 2s; meadow, 100 acres.
The value is and always was £15.

Ipſa abbatia teñ CERNEI.7 T.R.E.7 m̃ ſe defđ pro
duab.v.Tra.ē.v.car̃.In dñio ſunt.ii.car̃.7 xiii.
cot cũ.v.car̃.7 iiii.ſerui ibi.   Val 7 ualuit.vi.lib.
Warin teñ de abbatia dim̃ hiđ.Vluuiñ tenuit
T.R.E.de abbe.Tc̃ 7 m̃ ᵱ dim̃ hida.Ibi.ē.i.car̃ cũ
ii.cot 7 uno ſeruo.7 xvi.ãc p̃ti.Val 7 ualuit.xii.ſol.
Ipſa abbatia teñ SERENGEFORD.7 ſep̃ tenuit.
T.R.E.ᵱ xii.hiđ.m̃ ᵱ.ii.hiđ 7 una v̄.Tra.ē.ix.
car̃.In dñio ſunt.iii.car̃.7 xiii.uilti 7 uñ cot cũ
iiii.car̃.Ibi.vi.ſerui.7 moliñ de.xxx.deñ.7 c.iiii.ãc
p̃ti.7 de alijs p̃tis.xii.ſolid 7 vi.deñ.7 de c̃ſuetuđ
caſeoȝ.iiii.lib.7 xvi.ſolid 7 viii.deñ.
De hoc ⊕ teñ Giſlebt̃.ii.hiđ de abbe.7 Wimund
unā hiđ.Ibi una car̃ 7 dimiđ.cũ uno ſeruo.
Toť T.R.E.7 poſt.ualb.xii.lib.Modo:ʼix.lib qđ teñ
abb.Qđ hões:ʼlx.ſolid.
Giſlebt̃ teñ de abbe PESEI.Alured tenuit de abbe
T.R.E.Tc̃ 7 m̃ ᵱ.ii.hiđ.Tra.ē.iii.car̃.In dñio
ſunt.ii.car̃.7 uñ cot.7 ii.ſerui.Valuit.iiii.lib.Modo:ʼ
Ipſa abbatia teñ   IN WANETINZ HD̃. ᚠ iii.lib.
LACHINGES.7 T.R.E.tenuit.Tc̃ ᵱ x.hiđ.m̃ ᵱ vi.
hiđ.7 una v̄.Tra.ē.viii.car̃.In dñio.ē una car̃.
7 viii.uilti 7 xi.cot cũ.iiii.car̃.Ibi.iii.ſerui.
7 moliñ de.xxx.deñ.7 xxx.iiii.ãc p̃ti.
De hac tra teñ Giſlebt̃.i.hiđ de abbe.7 unā æcclam̃
cũ dimiđ hiđ.7 ibi hť.i.car̃ cũ uno uillo.
Toť T.R.E.ualb.ix.lib.Modo dñium abbatiæ:ʼ
ual.vii.lib.Giſlebti:ʼxxxvi.ſolid.
Ipſa abbatia teñ GAINZ.7 ſep̃ tenuit T.R.E.ſe
defđ ᵱ.x.hiđ.Modo ᵱ.ii.hiđ 7 una v̄.Tra.ē.v.car̃.

40 The Abbey holds CHARNEY (Bassett) itself. Before 1066 and now
it answered for 2 virgates. Land for 5 ploughs.
In lordship 2 ploughs;
13 cottagers with 5 ploughs; 4 slaves.
The value is and was £6.

41 Warin holds ½ hide from the Abbey. Wulfwin held from the
Abbot before 1066. Then and now for ½ hide. 1 plough, with
2 cottagers and 1 slave.
Meadow, 16 acres.
The value is and was 12s.

42 The Abbey holds SHELLINGFORD itself, and always held it.
Before 1066 for 12 hides; now for 2 hides and 1 virgate.
Land for 9 ploughs. In lordship 3 ploughs;
13 villagers and 1 cottager with 4 ploughs.
6 slaves; a mill at 30d; meadow, 104 acres; from other
meadows 12s 6d; from customary dues of cheeses
£4 16s 8d.
Gilbert holds 2 hides of this manor from the Abbot.
Wimund 1 hide. 1½ ploughs there, with 1 slave.
Value of the whole before 1066 and later £12; now, what
the Abbot holds, £9; what the men (hold), 60s.

43 Gilbert holds PUSEY from the Abbot. Alfred held from
the Abbot before 1066. Then and now for 2 hides.
Land for 3 ploughs. In lordship 2 ploughs;
1 cottager and 2 slaves.
The value was £4; now £3.

In WANTAGE Hundred
44 The Abbey holds (East) LOCKINGE itself, and held it before 1066.
Then for 10 hides; now for 6 hides and 1 virgate.
Land for 8 ploughs. In lordship 1 plough;
8 villagers and 11 cottagers with 4 ploughs.
3 slaves; a mill at 30d; meadow, 34 acres.
Gilbert holds 1 hide of this land from the Abbot, and
a church, with ½ hide. He has 1 plough there, with
1 villager.
Value of the whole before 1066 £9; now, the value of the Abbot's
lordship, £7; Gilbert's, 36s.

45 The Abbey holds (West) GINGE itself, and always held it.
Before 1066 it answered for 10 hides; now for 2 hides and
1 virgate. Land for 5 ploughs. In lordship 2 ploughs;

In dñio ſųṇt . ii . cař . 7 iiii . uiłłi 7 xviii . cot cũ . ii . cař.

Ibi . v . ſerui . 7 molñ de . vi . ſoł 7 vi . denař . 7 iii . ãc p̃ti.

Valuit . viii . liƀ . Modo: vii . liƀ.

Rainald ten de ạƀƀe . ii . hiđ . Norman tenuit

T.R.E . de ạƀƀe . Tc̃ 7 m̃ ꝑ . ii . hiđ . Tra . ē . i . cař . Ibi ſuɴ
ii . cot 7 ii . ãc p̃ti . Valuit xl . ſoł . Modo: xxx . ſoliđ.

Ipſa abbatia ten BOCHELANDE . Ælmar tenuit

T.R.E . Tc̃ 7 m̃ ꝑ . v . hiđ . Tra . ē . ii . cař . In dñio . ē . i . cař.
7 iiii . uiłłi 7 un cot 7 un ſeru . cũ . i . cař . 7 dimiđ
piſcaria de . iii . ſoł . 7 xv . ãc p̃ti.

T.R.E . uałƀ . c . ſoł . 7 poſt: xl . ſoł . Modo: lx . ſoliđ.

TERRA ÆCCLÆ GLASTINGBEŘ . IN HILLESLAVE HĎ.
.VIII. Abbatia de GLASTINGEBERIE ten EISSESBERIE.

7 ſep̃ tenuit . T.R.E . ſe defđ ꝑ . xl . hiđ . m̃ ꝑ . xvi . hiđ.

7 ii . uirg 7 dimiđ . Tra . ē . xx . cař . In dñio ſunt . iii . cař.

7 xiii . uiłłi 7 xxvi . borđ cũ . v . cař . Ibi . v . ſerui . 7 mo
linũ de . x . ſoliđ . 7 cc . ãc p̃ti . 7 parua ſilua.

De hac tra huj M̃ ten Roƀt de olgi . iiii . hiđ 7 dimiđ
de aƀƀe . 7 Aluuin . iii . hiđ . 7 Eduuard . ii . hiđ.

Ibi in dñio ſunt . v . cař . 7 ii . uiłłi 7 vii . borđ cũ . i . cař . Ibi
æccła 7 pƀr hñs . i . hiđ . 7 iiii . ſerui ibi . 7 molñ de xii . ſoł
7 vi . denař.

Tot T.R.E . uałƀ . xxxv . liƀ . 7 poſt . xx . liƀ . Modo qđ aƀƀ
★ ten: xx . liƀ . Qđ hões: xx . liƀ.

TERRA SC̃I PETRI WESMONAST . IN RIPLESMERE HĎ.
.IX. Abbatia de WESTMONAST . ten LACHENESTEDE . T.R.E . te
nuit 7 tc̃ ſe defđ ꝑ . x . hiđ . m̃ ꝑ . v . hiđ . Tra . ē . viii . cař . Ibi
ſunt . xiiii . uiłłi cũ . v . cař . 7 Silua de . x . porc.

T.R.E . uałƀ . c . ſoliđ . 7 poſt: l . ſoliđ . Modo: lx . ſoliđ.

4 villagers and 18 cottagers with 2 ploughs.
5 slaves; a mill at 6s 6d; meadow, 3 acres.
The value was £8; now £7.

46 Reginald holds 2 hides from the Abbot. Norman held from the Abbot
before 1066. Then and now for 2 hides. Land for 1 plough.
2 cottagers.
Meadow, 2 acres.
The value was 40s; now 30s.

47 The Abbey holds BUCKLAND itself. Aelmer held it before 1066.
Then and now for 5 hides. Land for 2 ploughs.
In lordship 1 plough;
4 villagers, 1 cottager and 1 slave with 1 plough.
½ a fishery at 3s; meadow, 15 acres.
Value before 1066, 100s; later 40s; now 60s.

8   LAND OF GLASTONBURY CHURCH

In HILLSLOW Hundred
1 Glastonbury Abbey holds ASHBURY, and always held it.
Before 1066 it answered for 40 hides; now for 16 hides
and 2½ virgates. Land for 20 ploughs. In lordship 3 ploughs;
13 villagers and 26 smallholders with 5 ploughs.
5 slaves; a mill at 10s; meadow, 200 acres; a small wood.
Of this land of this manor Robert d'Oilly holds 4½ hides
from the Abbot; Alwin, 3 hides; Edward, 2 hides.
In lordship 5 ploughs;
2 villagers and 7 smallholders with 1 plough. A church and
a priest who has 1 hide.
4 slaves; a mill at 12s 6d.
Value of the whole before 1066 £35; later £20; now, what the
Abbot holds, £20; what the men (hold), £12.

9   LAND OF ST. PETER'S OF WESTMINSTER   59 d

In RIPPLESMERE Hundred
1 Westminster Abbey holds EASTHAMPSTEAD; it held it before 1066.
Then it answered for 10 hides; now for 5 hides.
Land for 8 ploughs.
14 villagers with 5 ploughs.
Woodland at 10 pigs.
Value before 1066, 100s; later 50s; now 60s.

TERRA ABBATIÆ S PETRI WINTONIENS. IN EGLEI HD.

.X. ABBATIA de WINCESTRE ten CEDENEORD. Duo libi hões
tenuer de Gida comitiſſa 7 de Guert filio ej p. II. manerijs.
Tc ſe defd p. XVI. hid. modo p. x. hid. Tra. e. x. car. In dnio. e
una car. 7 v. uilti 7 v. bord. cu. IIII. car. Ibi. VI. ſerui. 7 II. ac
pti. Silua de. xx. porc.
T.R.E. ualb. XIIII. lib. 7 poſt: x. lib. Modo: xii. lib.
Hoc M ded Oda de Winceſtre Robto dapifero Hugon de port.
quom ht abbatia neſciunt hões de ſcira. IN HESLITESFORD HD.
Ipſa abbatia tenuit SOTWELLE in dnio de uictu monachoz T.R.E.
Modo ten Hugo de Port de abbe in feudo. Tc 7 m ſe defd p x.
hid. Tra. e. v. car. In dnio ſunt. II. car. 7 IX. uilti cu. III. car.
Ibi molin de. XV. ſol. 7 xxx. ac pti. 7 IX. cot. 7 in Walengeford
VIII. hagæ de XIIII. ſol 7 IIII. den.
Vn hõ ten de ead tra. I. hid. 7 ibi ht. I. car cu. III. cot.
Tot T.R.E ualb VIII. lib. 7 poſt: tntd. Modo: xii. lib.

TERRA ÆCCLÆ DE CERTESYGE.   IN BENERS HVND.

.XI. ABBATIA de CERTESYG ten WALTHAM. de dnico uictu mo
nachoz. T.R.E. tenuit. Tc 7 m ſe defd p. x. hid. Tra. e. XII. car.
In dnio ſunt. II. car. 7 XVIII. uilti cu. x. car. Ibi. I. ſeru. 7 æcctola.
7 IX. ac pti. Silua de. v. porc.   [cu. II. cot.
De ead tra ten Turold. I. hid 7 una v de abbe. 7 ibi ht. II. car.
Tot. T.R.E. ualb. VIII. lib. Modo pars abbis: VI. lib. Turoldi: x. ſol.

TERRA ÆCCLÆ SCI ALBANI.   IN WANETINZ HD.

.XII. ABBATIA de S ALBANO ten HENRET. Nigellus de Albengi
ded æcctæ. Tres taini tenuer. T.R.E. 7 poteraɴ ire quo uoleb.
Tc ſe defd p. x. hid. m p. IIII. Tra. e. IIII. car. In dnio ſunt. II. car.

10   LAND OF ST. PETER'S ABBEY, WINCHESTER

In EAGLE Hundred

1 Winchester Abbey holds CHADDLEWORTH. Two free men held it
from Countess Gytha and from her son (Earl) Gyrth, as two manors.
Then it answered for 16 hides; now for 10 hides.
Land for 10 ploughs. In lordship 1 plough;
    5 villagers and 5 smallholders with 4 ploughs.
    6 slaves; meadow, 2 acres; woodland at 20 pigs.
Value before 1066 £14; later £10; now £12.
    Odo of Winchester gave this manor to Robert, Hugh of Port's
steward; the men of the Shire do not know how the Abbey has it.

In SLOTISFORD Hundred

2 The Abbey held SOTWELL itself in lordship for the supplies of the
monks before 1066. Now Hugh of Port holds it from the Abbot
as a Holding. Then and now it answered for 10 hides.
Land for 5 ploughs. In lordship 2 ploughs;
    9 villagers with 3 ploughs.
    A mill at 15s; meadow, 30 acres; 9 cottagers;
        in Wallingford 8 sites at 14s 4d.
A man holds 1 hide of this land; he has 1 plough there, with
    3 cottagers.
Value of the whole before 1066 £8; later, as much; now £12.

11   LAND OF CHERTSEY CHURCH

In BEYNHURST Hundred

1 Chertsey Abbey holds (White) WALTHAM for the household supplies
of the monks; it held it before 1066. Then and now it answered
for 10 hides. Land for 12 ploughs. In lordship 2 ploughs;
    18 villagers with 10 ploughs.
    1 slave; a small church; meadow, 9 acres; woodland at 5 pigs.
Thorold holds 1 hide and 1 virgate of this land from the Abbot;
he has 2 ploughs there, with
    2 cottagers.
Value of the whole before 1066 £8; now the Abbot's part, £6;
Thorold's, 10s.

12   LAND OF ST. ALBAN'S CHURCH

In WANTAGE Hundred

1 St. Alban's Abbey holds (West) HENDRED. Nigel of Aubigny gave it
to the church. Three thanes held it before 1066; they could go
where they would. Then it answered for 10 hides; now for 4.
Land for 4 ploughs. In lordship 2 ploughs;

7 III . uilli 7 III . cot . cū . I . car̄ . 7 ibi XL.V . ac p̃ti.

De hac t̃ra ten̄ Ernuzon . II . hid de abɓe . 7 ibi hr̄ . I . car̄

cū . IIII . cot . Ibi æccla 7 v . ac p̃ti.

Tot̄ T.R.E. 7 poſt.́ ualɓ . x . liɓ . Modo ſimilir̄ totū.́ x . liɓ.

TERRA ÆCCLÆ DE SVPDIVE.   *In GAMENESFELLE HD̄.*

.XIII. ABBAS de ſupdiua ten̄ de rege . *PEISE* . Duo alodiarij

tenuer̄ . 7 potuer̄ ire quo uoluer̄ . Tc̄ ſe defd ꝓ . II . hid

7 dimid . modo ꝓ nichilo . Ibi . ē una car̄ . 7 II . uilli.

Val 7 ualuit . XXXII . ſolid . 7 uñ denar̄ . *In TACEHĀ HD̄.*

Ipſe abɓ ten̄ . II . hid in *COSERIGE* . Eduuard tenuit de rege . E.

ꝓ m̃ . Tc̄ ꝓ . II . hid . modo ꝓ nichilo . Ibi . ē un uilɬs cū . III . boɓ.

TERRA SC̄Æ MARIÆ WINTONIENSIS.   Val 7 ualuit . x . ſol.

.XII ABBATISSA de WINTONIA ten̄ *COLESELLE* . *In WILFOL HD̄.*

Edmund tenuit de rege . E . in alod . Walteri de Laci

ded æcclæ cū filia ſua . Scira neſcit quom̃ . T . R . E . ſe defd

ꝓ VIII . hid . m̃ ꝓ . II . hid 7 dim . Tra . ē   In dñio

funt . II . car̄ . 7 VI . uilli 7 III . bord . cū . I car̄ . Ibi . II . ſerui.

7 tcia pars molini de . x . ſol . 7 LXIX . ac p̃ti.

Valuit . VII . liɓ . 7 pôſt.́ VI . liɓ . Modo.́ c . ſolid.

TERRA ÆCCLÆ DE LABATAILGE . *In NACHEDEDORNE HD̄.*

.XV. ABBAS De Labatailge ten̄ de rege *BRISTOLDESTONE*.

Herald tenuit . Tc̄ ꝓ . x . hid . Quidā tain qui ante eū

tenuit.́ geldɓ ꝓ . XV . hid . Modo ꝓ nichilo . Tra . ē

In dñio funt . II . car̄ . 7 x . uilli 7 XIII . bord . cū . VII . car̄.

Ibi . III . ſerui . 7 æccla cū pɓro . Silua de xx . porc̄ . In Walen

geford . v . hagæ.   Valuit . x . liɓ . Modo.́ IX . liɓ.

3 villagers and 3 cottagers with 1 plough.
Meadow, 45 acres.
Ernucion holds 2 hides of this land from the Abbot; he has
1 plough there, with
4 cottagers.
A church; meadow, 5 acres.
Value of the whole before 1066 and later £10; now the same,
the whole £10.

13 LAND OF THE CHURCH OF (ST. PIERRE) -SUR-DIVES

In GANFIELD Hundred
1 The Abbot of (St. Pierre) - sur - Dives holds PUSEY from the King.
Two freeholders held it; they could go where they would.
Then it answered for 2½ hides; now for nothing. 1 plough.
2 villagers.
The value is and was 32s 1d.

In THATCHAM Hundred
2 The Abbot holds 2 hides in CURRIDGE himself. Edward held
from King Edward as a manor. Then for 2 hides; now for nothing.
1 villager with 3 oxen.
The value is and was 10s.

14 LAND OF ST. MARY'S OF WINCHESTER

In WYFOLD Hundred
1 The Abbess of Winchester holds COLESHILL. Edmund held it from
King Edward in freehold. Walter of Lacy gave it to the church
with his daughter; the Shire does not know how.
Before 1066 it answered for 8 hides; now for 2½ hides.
Land for .... In lordship 2 ploughs;
6 villagers and 3 smallholders with 1 plough.
2 slaves; the third part of a mill at 10s; meadow, 69 acres.
The value was £7; later £6; now 100s.

15 LAND OF THE CHURCH OF BATTLE

In COMPTON Hundred
1 The Abbot of Battle holds BRIGHTWALTON from the King. Earl
Harold held it. Then for 10 hides. A thane who held it before
him paid tax at 15 hides; now for nothing. Land for ......
In lordship 2 ploughs;
10 villagers and 13 smallholders with 7 ploughs.
3 slaves; a church with a priest; woodland at 20 pigs;
in Wallingford 5 sites.
The value was £10; now £9.

Ipfe abb ten in Reddinges æcclam cū. viii. hid ibi ptin.

Lcueua abbatiffa tenuit   de rege. E. Tc fe defd

ꝑ viii. hid. modo ꝑ. iii. hid. Tra. e. vii. car. In dnio

eft una. 7 ix. uilli 7 viii. bord cū. v. car. Ibi. ii. molini

de. xl. folid. 7 ii. pifcarie 7 dimid de. v. folid. In Red

dinges. xxix. mafuræ de xxviii. folid. 7 viii. denar.

7 xii. ac pti. Silua de. v. porc. De æccla. iii. lib.

T.R.E. ualb. ix. lib. 7 poft. viii. lib. Modo: xi. lib.

TERRA ÆCCLÆ DE AMBRESBERIE. *IN CHENETEBERIE HD.*

.XVI ABBATISSA de AMBRESBERIE ten *CHENETEBERIE*. Sep æccla

tenuit. T.R.E. fe defd ꝑ. xi. hid. m̂ ꝑ. viii. hid. Tra. e. x. car.

In dnio funt. iiii. car. 7 xii. uilli 7 xviii. bord. cū. viii. car.

Ibi. xi. ferui. 7 molin de. iiii. fol. 7 lx. ac pti. Silua de x. porc.

Valuit xii. lib. Modo: xi. lib.   *IN EGLEI HVND.*

Ipfa abbatia ten *CEVESLANE*. 7 fep tenuit. T.R..E. fe defd ꝑ. vii.

hid. Modo ꝑ. iii. hid 7 dim. Tra. e. v. car. In dnio funt. ii. car.

7 x. uilli 7 viii. bord. cū. ii. car. Ibi. ii. ferui. 7 xl. ac pti.

Val 7 ualuit fep. vii. lib.

Ipfa abbatia ten *FARELLEI*. T.R.E. defd fe ꝑ. x. hid. modo ꝑ. v.

hid. Tra. e. v. car. In dnio funt. ii. car. 7 viii. uilli. 7 iiii. ferui.

cū. iii. car. 7 xx. ac pti. Val 7 ualuit fep. vi. lib.

TERRA COMITIS EBROICENSIS *IN RADINGES HD.*

.XVII. COMES Ebroicenfis ten de rege *SEWELLE*. Coleman 7 Bric

★ tuuard tenuer de rege. E. 7 potuer ire quo uoluer. Tc 7 m̂

fe defd ꝑ. ii. hid. Tra. e. iii. car. In dnio nichil. Ibi funt. v.

uilli. 7 v. bord. cū. ii. car. 7 iiii. ferui. 7 molin de. x. folid.

7 xx. ac pti. Silua de. x. porc. Val 7 ualuit. xl. fol.

2 The Abbot holds a church in READING himself with 8 hides   60 a
which belong to it. Abbess Leofeva held it from King Edward.
Then it answered for 8 hides; now for 3 hides.
Land for 7 ploughs. In lordship 1;
   9 villagers and 8 smallholders with 5 ploughs.
   2 mills at 40s; 2½ fisheries at 5s.
   In Reading, 29 dwellings at 28s 8d; meadow, 12 acres;
     woodland at 5 pigs; from the church £3.
Value before 1066 £9; later £8; now £11.

16   LAND OF AMESBURY CHURCH

In KINTBURY Hundred
1 The Abbess of Amesbury holds KINTBURY. The Church always
held it. Before 1066 it answered for 11 hides; now for 8 hides.
Land for 10 ploughs. In lordship 4 ploughs;
   12 villagers and 18 smallholders with 8 ploughs.
   11 slaves; a mill at 4s; meadow, 60 acres;
     woodland at 10 pigs.
The value was £12; now £11.

In EAGLE Hundred
2 The Abbey holds (West) CHALLOW itself and always held it.
Before 1066 it answered for 7 hides; now for 3½ hides.
Land for 5 ploughs. In lordship 2 ploughs;
   10 villagers and 8 smallholders with 2 ploughs.
   2 slaves; meadow, 40 acres.
The value is and was always £7.

3 The Abbey holds (Great) FAWLEY itself. Before 1066 it answered
for 10 hides; now for 5 hides. Land for 5 ploughs.
In lordship 2 ploughs;
   8 villagers and 4 slaves with 3 ploughs.
   Meadow, 20 acres.
The value is and was always £6.

17   LAND OF THE COUNT OF EVREUX

In READING Hundred
1 The Count of Evreux holds SHEFFIELD from the King.
Colman and Brictward held from King Edward; they could go
where they would. Then and now it answered for 2 hides.
Land for 3 ploughs. In lordship nothing.
   5 villagers and 5 smallholders with 2 ploughs; 4 slaves.
   A mill at 10s; meadow, 20 acres; woodland at 10 pigs.
The value is and was 40s.

Ifd com̃ ten̊ . i . hid in PRAXEMERE . Aluuin̊ tenuit in paragio.

7 p una hida fe defd tc̃.7 m̃ p nichilo . Ibi . e un̊ bord cũ dim̃ car̊.

Ifd com̃ ten̊ BORGEDEBERIE . IN BORGEDEBERIE HĎ. ∫ Val.x.fol.

Leuuin̊ tenuit de rege . E . Tc̃ p . iiii . hid . m̃ p . i . hida 7 una v̊.

Tr̊a . ē . iiii . car̊ . In dñio funt . ii . 7 iii . uilli 7 iiii . bord cũ . ii .

★ car̊ . Ibi . vii . ferui . 7 molin̄ de . iiii . fol . Val 7 ualuit . iiii . liƀ.

Ifd com̃ ten̊ CROCHESTROPE . Quattuor libi hōes tenuer̊

de rege . E . Tc̃ 7 m̃ p una hida . Nil . ē in dñio . Ibi . iii . uilli

hñt . i . car̊ . 7 iiii . ac̄ p̃ti . Val 7 ualuit . x . fol. IN CHENETE

Ifd com̃ ten COLECOTE . Briĉuard tenuit de rege . E . ∫ BERIE HĎ.

p ω . Tc̃ p . iii . hid . m̃ p una hida . Tr̊a . ē . ii . car̊ . In dñio . ē una

car̊ . 7 iii . uilli 7 iiii . bord . cũ una car̊ . Ibi molin̄ de . iiii . folid.

7 v . ac̄ p̃ti . Silua ad claufurā . Valuit . xxx . folid . Modo: xx . fol.

Ipfe com̃ ten̊ BECOTE . Duo libi hōes tenuer̊ de rege . E . in alod IN SERI

p . ii . ω . Tc̃ fe defd p . v . hid . Modo p . ii . hid 7 iiii . acris.   VEHĀ HĎ.

Tr̊a . ē . iiii . car̊ . In dñio funt . ii . car̊ . 7 ii . uilli 7 xiii . bord . cũ

una car̊ . 7 dim̊ . 7 c . ac̄ p̃ti . vii . min̊ . Valuit . iiii . liƀ . 7 m̃ fimilit̊.

Ipfe com̃ ten̊ BLITBERIE . Briĉuard   IN BLITBERIE HĎ.

tenuit T . R . E . Tc̃ p . ii . hid . modo p una v̊ . Tr̊a . ē . i . car̊ . Ibi fun̊

iiii . cot . 7 molin̄ de . iiii . fol . 7 x . ac̄ p̃ti . Valuit . xl . fol . m̃ . xx . fol.

Ifd com̃ ten̊ HANLEI . Duo libi hōes   IN WANETINZ HĎ.

tenuer̊ . T . R . E . Tc̃ fe defd p . vi . hid . modo p . ii . hid . Tr̊a . ē . v . car̊.

In dñio . ē una car̊ . 7 xx . cot cũ . i . car̊ . Ibi un̊ feruus . 7 ii . mo

lini de . xxvii . folid . 7 vi . den̊ . 7 lxx . ac̄ p̃ti . Valuit . c . fol . m̃: vi . liƀ.

2 The Count also holds 1 hide in PEASEMORE. Alwin held it, jointly.
Then it answered for 1 hide; now for nothing.
    1 smallholder with ½ plough.
Value 10s.

In BUCKLEBURY Hundred
3 The Count also holds BUCKLEBURY. Leofwin held it from King
Edward. Then for 4 hides; now for 1 hide and 1 virgate.
Land for 4 ploughs. In lordship 2;
    3 villagers and 4 smallholders with 2 ploughs.
    8 slaves; a mill at 4s.
The value is and was £4.

4 The Count also holds CROCHESTROPE. Four free men held it from King
Edward. Then and now it answered for 1 hide. Nothing in lordship.
    3 villagers have 1 plough.
    Meadow, 4 acres.
The value is and was 10s.

In KINTBURY Hundred
5 The Count also holds 'CALCOT'. Brictward held it from King Edward
as a manor. Then for 3 hides; now for 1 hide. Land for 2 ploughs.
In lordship 1 plough;
    3 villagers and 4 smallholders with 1 plough.
    A mill at 4s; meadow, 5 acres; woodland for fencing.
The value was 30s; now 20s.

In SHRIVENHAM Hundred
6 The Count holds BECKETT himself. Two free men held it from
King Edward in freehold as two manors. Then it answered
for 5 hides; now for 2 hides and 4 acres. Land for 4 ploughs.
In lordship 2 ploughs;
    2 villagers and 13 smallholders with 1½ ploughs.
    Meadow, 100 acres less 7.
The value was £4; now the same.

In BLEWBURY Hundred
7 The Count holds BLEWBURY himself. Brictward held it before 1066.
Then for 2 hides; now for 1 virgate. Land for 1 plough.
    4 cottagers.
    A mill at 4s; meadow, 10 acres.
The value was 40s; now 20s.

In WANTAGE Hundred
8 The Count also holds (East) HANNEY. Two free men held it
before 1066. Then it answered for 6 hides; now for 2 hides.
Land for 5 ploughs. In lordship 1 plough;
    20 cottagers with 1 plough.
    1 slave; 2 mills at 27s 6d; meadow, 70 acres.
The value was 100s; now £6.

Ifd com ten HENRET. Aluuin tenuit T.R.E.Tc ꝑ.v.hid.

Modo ꝑ.II.hid.Tra.e.II.caɼ.Ibi.e una caɼ.7 vi.cot cu.i.caɼ.

Ibi æccła 7 un feru.7 v.ãc ꝑti.Valuit.lx.foł.Modoʾlxx.foł.

Ifd com ten.v.hid.quas tenueɼ.vii.liberi hões T.R.E.Tc fe
defd ꝑ.v.hid.m̃ ꝑ.xxx.acris tre.Tra.e.ii.caɼ 7 dim̃.Ibi
funt.vi.cot cu.i.caɼ.7 v.ãc ꝑti.Vał 7 ualuit.xxx.foł.

60 b

Ifd com hɼ in eod HVND.i.hid.Vlgar q̃dã tenuit.T.R.E.

Tc ꝑ.i.hida.m̃ ꝑ.vi.acris.Tra.e.i.caɼ.Ibi funt.ii.cot
7 xii.ãc ꝑti.Vał 7 ualuit.x.folid. IN GAMESFELLE HD.

Ifd com hɼ.i.hid 7 iii.v.7 ii.acs.Vluuin q̃dã tenuit.T.R.E.
7 ꝑ tanto fe defd.modo ꝑ nichilo.Ibi.iiii.cot.Ibi.vii.ãc ꝑti.

Ifd com ten.ii.hid 7 ii.acs træ. ⌐Valuit.xxx.foł.m̃.xv.foł.

Has tenueɼ.iiii.łibi hões.T.R.E.7 ꝑ tanto fe tc defd.modo
ꝑ.v.uirg.Ibi.e un uiłłs 7 iiii.cot.7 xii.ãc ꝑti.

T.R.E.uałb.xxxvii.foł.7 vi.den.Modo.xxii.foł.

TERRA HVGONIS COMITIS. IN SVDTVNE HD.

.XVIII Comes Hvgo ten DRAITVNE.7 Wiłłs de eo.Ednod
tenuit de Heraldo.7 ñ potuit ire q̃libet.Tc fe defd ꝑ.ii.hid.

modo ꝑ nichilo.Tra.e.i.caɼ 7 dimid.In dñio.e una caɼ.

7 iiii.bord 7 ii.ferui.7 xiii.ãc ꝑti.Vał 7 ualuit.l.folid.

Ipfe com ten BOROARDESCOTE.7 Robt de eo. IN WIFOLD HD.
Herald com tenuit.Tc fe defd ꝑ xl.hid.modo ꝑ.vi.hid.

9 The Count also holds (East) HENDRED. Alwin held it before 1066.
Then for 5 hides; now for 2 hides.
Land for 2 ploughs. 1 plough there;
  6 cottagers with 1 plough.
  A church; 1 slave; meadow, 5 acres.
The value was 60s; now 70s.

10 The Count also holds 5 hides which 7 free men held before 1066.
Then they answered for 5 hides; now for 30 acres of land.
Land for 2½ ploughs.
  6 cottagers with 1 plough.
  Meadow, 5 acres.
The value is and was 30s.

11 The Count also has 1 hide in the same Hundred. One Wulfgar held 60 b
it before 1066. Then for 1 hide; now for 6 acres. Land for 1 plough.
  2 cottagers.
  Meadow, 12 acres.
The value is and was 10s.

In GANFIELD Hundred
12 The Count also has 1 hide, 3 virgates and 2 acres.
One Wulfwin held them before 1066; they answered for as much;
now for nothing.
  4 cottagers.
  Meadow, 7 acres.
The value was 30s; now 15s.

13 The Count also holds 2 hides and 2 acres of land. Four free men
held them before 1066; they answered for as much; now for 5 virgates.
  1 villager and 4 cottagers.
  Meadow, 12 acres.
Value before 1066, 37s 6d; now 22s.

18   LAND OF EARL HUGH

In SUTTON Hundred
1 Earl Hugh holds DRAYTON and William from him. Ednoth held from
Harold; he could not go where he would. Then it answered for 2 hides;
now for nothing. Land for 1½ ploughs. In lordship 1 plough;
  4 smallholders and 2 slaves.
  Meadow, 13 acres.
The value is and was 50s.

In WYFOLD Hundred
2 The Earl holds BUSCOT himself and Robert from him. Earl Harold
held it. Then it answered for 40 hides; now for 6 hides.

Ṫra . ē . xx . caṝ . In dñio ſunt . iiii . caṝ .7 xxv . uiłłi 7 xxv.
borđ cū . viii . caṝ . Ibi . vi . ſerui.7 piſcaria de xviii . ſoliđ.
7 viii . den.7 ccc . ac p̄ti.
De hac ṫra teñ Drogo . viii . hiđ.7 Rannulf. iiii . hiđ.
7 ibi in dñio . ii . caṝ.7 ii . uiłłi 7 vi . borđ
Toṫ . T . R . E . ualb . xx . lib.7 poſt: xvii . lib . Modo: xxvi . lib.

TERRA COMITIS MORITON̄. *IN BLITBERIE HD̄.*

.XIX Comes MORITON̄ teñ ESTONE .7 abbatia de pratellis
teñ de eo . Anſchil tenuit . T . R . E . Tc̄ ꝑ . v . hiđ . m̄ ꝑ . ii . hiđ.
Ṫra . ē . ii . caṝ . In dñio . ē una caṝ.7 iii . uiłłi 7 iii . cot̄ 7 vi . ſerui.
7 una æccła . Valuit 7 ual . iii . lib.

TERRA WALTERIJ GIFARD. *IN WANETINZ HD̄.*

.XX. WALTERIVS Gifard teñ HANNEI Oſbn̄ 7 Teodric teñ
de eo . Eduuin un̄ lib hō tenuit de rege . E . Tc̄ 7 m̄ ꝑ . ii . hiđ.
Ṫra . ē . i . caṝ . Ibi . ē una caṝ.7 xi . cot̄.7 xxiiii . ac p̄ti.
Val 7 ualuit . xl . ſoliđ.
Ipſe Walteri teñ HANNEI . Toſti tenuit . Tc̄ ꝑ xiiii . hiđ
modo ꝑ.vii . hiđ . Ṫra . ē . viii . caṝ . In dñio ſunt . ii . caṝ.7 xiiii.
uiłłi 7 viii . cot̄ cū . iii . caṝ . Ibi . iiii . ſerui.7 moliñ de.xii . ſoliđ
7 vi . denaṝ.7 aliud moliñ de . vii . ſoliđ 7 vi . denaṝ . qđ
ꝑtiñ ad M̄ de Cerletone ſic dicit HVND̄.
Huj uillæ æcclam teñ de Walterio Turolđ p̄br . i . hida
quæ ſep gelda̅t . Valuit . x . lib.7 poſt . viii . lib . Modo: xiiii . lib. ☞

.XXI. TERRA HENRICI DE FERIERES. *IN NACHEDEDORNE HD̄.*

HENRICVS de Ferreres teñ CATMERE .7 Henric de eo.
Ezui tenuit de rege . E . Tc̄ ꝑ . v . hiđ . modo ꝑ . iii . hiđ . Ṫra . ē
vi . caṝ . In dñio . ē una.7 v . uiłłi 7 xii . borđ . cū . iii . caṝ.
Valuit . vii . lib.7 poſt . xl . ſol . Modo: lxx . ſoliđ.

Land for 20 ploughs. In lordship 4 ploughs;
25 villagers and 25 smallholders with 8 ploughs.
6 slaves; a fishery at 18s 8d; meadow, 300 acres.
Of this land Drogo holds 8 hides and Ranulf 4 hides;
in lordship 2 ploughs;
2 villagers and 6 smallholders.
Value of the whole before 1066 £20; later £17; now £26.

19   LAND OF THE COUNT OF MORTAIN

In BLEWBURY Hundred
1 The Count of Mortain holds ASTON (Tirrold). The Abbey of Preaux
holds from him. Askell held it before 1066.
Then for 5 hides; now for 2 hides. Land for 2 ploughs.
In lordship 1 plough;
3 villagers and 3 cottagers; 6 slaves; a church.
The value was and is £3.

20   LAND OF WALTER GIFFARD

In WANTAGE Hundred
1 Walter Giffard holds (West) HANNEY. Osbern and Theodoric hold
from him. Edwin, a free man, held it from King Edward. Then and
now for 2 hides. Land for 1 plough. 1 plough there;
11 cottagers.
Meadow, 24 acres.
The value is and was 40s.

2 Walter holds (West) HANNEY himself. Earl Tosti held it.
Then for 14 hides; now for 7 hides. Land for 8 ploughs.
In lordship 2 ploughs;
14 villagers and 8 cottagers with 3 ploughs.
4 slaves; a mill at 12s 6d; another mill at 7s 6d which
belongs to the manor of Charlton, as the Hundred states.
Thorold the priest holds the church of this village from Walter,
1 hide which always pays tax.
The value was £10; later £8; now £14.

†3 is entered after 21, 4 at the foot of col. 60b

21   LAND OF HENRY OF FERRERS

In COMPTON Hundred
1 Henry of Ferrers holds CATMORE and Henry from him. Edsi held it
from King Edward. Then for 5 hides; now for 3 hides.
Land for 6 ploughs. In lordship 1;
5 villagers and 12 smallholders with 3 ploughs.
The value was £7; later 40s; now 70s.

Iſd Henric teñ *HISLELEI*.7 Rogeꝛ de eo. Algar tenuit
de rege. E. Tꝛ 7 m̄ .p. III . hid 7 dimid . Tra . ē . II . caꝛ . In
dñio. ē dim caꝛ. cū. II. bord 7 uñ ſeruus. Valuit. LX. ſoł:´m̄:´XL . ſoł.
Iſd Henric teñ *ASSEDONE*. 7 Radulf de eo. Bundi
tenuit de rege. E. Tꝛ ꝑ x . hid 7 una v̄ . Modo ꝑ. IX . hid.
Tra. ē. x . caꝛ. In dñio ſunt . IIII . caꝛ. 7 VIII . uiłłi 7 VIII .
bord. Ibi. IX . ſerui. 7 VI . ā̆c p̄ti . Silua de. v. porc.
Toꝛ. T. R. E. uałb . XII . lib. 7 poſt:´VI . lib . Modo:´x . lib.
Iſd Henric teñ *FRILESHA*:7 Rogeꝛ IN *BORGEDEBERIE HD̄*
de eo. Duo libi hōes tenueꝛ de rege. E. Tꝛ 7 m̄ ſe defd
ꝑ. VII. hid 7 dimid . Tra . ē   In dñio. ē una caꝛ 7 dim.

IN *SVTTVNE HD̄*. Ipſe. W. teñ *WITEHA*. Eddid regina tenuit .
Tꝛ ſe defd ꝑ. xx. hid.   Modo ꝑ XIII . hid 7 una v̄ . Tra. ē. XVI. caꝛ.
In dñio ſunt. III. caꝛ. 7 XXIX. uiłłi. 7 XVI. bord. cū. IX. caꝛ. Ibi. VI. ſerui.
7 CLXIII. ā̆c p̄ti. 7 In Warengeford. VIII. hagæ. de. IIII. ſoł. ꝑ herbagio.
v. ſolid . T. R. E. uałb . xx . lib. 7 poſt. xv . lib . Modo:´xx. lib.

60 c
7 v. uiłłi 7 XI. bord cū . VI . caꝛ 7 dim . Ibi. III . ſerui. 7 moliñ
de . IIII . ſolid. 7 x . ā̆c p̄ti . Silua. de . x. porc.
Vał 7 ualuit ſep . VI . lib.   IN *TACEHA HD̄*.
Ipſe HENRIC teñ *GRENEHA*. Seuuard tenuit de
rege. E. in alod. Tꝛ ꝑ. v. hid . modo ꝑ. II . hid 7 dimid.
Tra. ē. x . caꝛ. In dñio ſunt. II . caꝛ. 7 XI . uiłłi 7 XIX.
bord cū . VII . caꝛ. Ibi æccła 7 IIII . ſerui. 7 moliñ ∫ de
XI. ſolid. 7 II. deñ miñ. 7 XL una. ā̆c p̄ti . 7 q̄t xx . ā̆c p̄ti.
T. R. E. 7 poſt. uałb . VIII . lib . Modo:´VI . lib.

2 Henry also holds (East) ILSLEY and Roger from him.
Algar held it from King Edward. Then and now for 3½ hides.
Land for 2 ploughs. In lordship ½ plough, with
    2 smallholders and 1 slave.
The value was 60s; now 40s.

3 Henry also holds 'ASHDEN' and Ralph (of Bagpuize) from him.
Bondi held it from King Edward. Then for 10 hides and 1 virgate.
Now for 9 hides. Land for 10 ploughs. In lordship 4 ploughs;
    8 villagers and 8 smallholders.
    9 slaves; meadow, 6 acres; woodland at 5 pigs.
Value of the whole before 1066 £12; later £6; now £10.

In BUCKLEBURY Hundred
4 Henry also holds FRILSHAM and Roger from him. Two free men
held it from King Edward. Then and now it answered for 7½ hides.
Land for .... In lordship 1½ ploughs;

† (Directed to its proper place, after 20,2, by transposition signs)

(20)
† In SUTTON Hundred
3 Walter holds (Long) WITTENHAM himself. Queen Edith held it.
Then it answered for 20 hides; now for 13 hides and 1 virgate.
Land for 16 ploughs. In lordship 3 ploughs;
    29 villagers and 16 smallholders with 9 ploughs.
    6 slaves; meadow, 163 acres.
    In Wallingford 8 sites at 4s; for grazing, 5s.
Value before 1066 £20; later £15; now £20.

(21,4 continued)
    5 villagers and 11 smallholders with 6½ ploughs.   60 c
    3 slaves; a mill at 4s; meadow, 10 acres;
        woodland at 10 pigs.
The value is and was always £6.

In THATCHAM Hundred
5 Henry holds GREENHAM himself. Siward (Bairn) held it from
King Edward in freehold. Then for 5 hides; now for 2½ hides.
Land for 10 ploughs. In lordship 2 ploughs;
    11 villagers and 19 smallholders with 7 ploughs.
    A church; 4 slaves; 1½ mills at 11s less 2d.
        meadow, 41 acres; meadow, 80 acres.
Value before 1066 and later £8; now £6.

Iſd . H . tcñ *Bechesgete* . Godric　*In Cheneteberie Hᴰ.*

tcnuit de rege . E . ꝑ Ṁ. Duæ hidæ . ñ geldaƀ . q̇a de firma
regis craꞩ .7 ad oꝑ regis calũniatæ ſunt . Ṫra . ē . iiii . caꞃ.
Ibi ſunt . ix . uiłłi 7 x . bord . cũ . iiii . car . Ibi . iii . ſerui.
7 moliñ de . xi . foliđ .7 viii . aͨ p̊ti . Silua ad clauſurã.
Valuit . xxx . foliđ . modo ꞉ xl . foliđ . *In Benes Hᴰ.*

Iſđ HenricꞋ teñ Ꞌ *Bistesha* . Bondi tenuit de rege . E.
Ṫc 7 m̃ ꝑ . viii . hiđ . Ṫra . ē . x . caꞃ . In dñio ſunt . ii . caꞃ.
7 xvii . uiłłi 7 ii . cot cũ . viii . caꞃ . Ibi æccła 7 ii . ſerui.
7 xxvi . aͨ p̊ti .7 xii . arpendi uineæ.
Valuit . viii . liƀ . Modo ꞉ xii . liƀ . *In Blitberie Hᴰ.*

Iſđ . H . teñ Ꞌ *Wibalditone* .7 NigełłꞋ de eo . Turchil
uñ liƀ hõ tenuit de rege . E . Ṫra . ē . vi . caꞃ . Ṫc ꝑ . viii.
hiđ . Modo ꝑ . iiii . hiđ 7 una v̄ . Ibi æccła 7 ix . ſerui.
7 ii . caꞃ in dñio .7 x . uiłłi 7 ii . cot . cũ . viii . caꞃ .7 xl.
aͨ p̊ti . Valuit . vi . liƀ . Modo ꞉ ix . liƀ. *In Wanetinz*

Iſđ . H . teñ Ꞌ *Denchesworde* .7 Rayner꜖ ꞗ Hvnᴰ.
de eo . ÆilricꞋ tenuit T.R.E. Ṫc ꝑ . vii . hiđ . Modo
ꝑ . v . hiđ 7 dimiđ . Ṫra . ē . v . caꞃ . In dñio . ē una caꞃ
7 v . uiłłi 7 v . cot . cũ . i . caꞃ .7 xxx . aͨ p̊ti .7 ibi æccła.
T.R.E. uałƀ . lxx . ſoł .7 poſt . lx . ſoł . Modo ꞉ iiii . liƀ.

Iſđ . H . teñ *Cerletone* .7 Roƀt de eo . Toui uñ
liƀ hõ tenuit . Ṫc 7 m̃ ꝑ . ii . hiđ 7 dimiđ . Ṫra . ē . i . caꞃ.
In dñio . ē una caꞃ . cũ . vii . cot .7 dimiđ moliñ de . v.
foliđ .7 viii . aͨ p̊ti . Vał 7 ualuit . l . foliđ.

Ipſe . H . teñ Ꞌ *Lachinge* .7 HuƀtꞋ de Henrico . Siuuarđ
tenuit de rege . E. Ṫc 7 m̃ ꝑ . x . hiđ . Ṫra . ē . vi . caꞃ.
In dñio ſunt . ii . caꞃ .7 iii . uiłłi 7 xiiii . cot . cũ . ii . caꞃ ̦
Ibi uñ ſeruus .7 xl una aͨ p̊ti . Valuit . x . liƀ . m̃ . viii . liƀ.

Henry also holds
in KINTBURY Hundred
6 BAGSHOT. Godric held it from King Edward as a manor. 2 hides.
They did not pay tax because they were of the King's revenue;
they are claimed for the King's work. Land for 4 ploughs.
9 villagers and 10 smallholders with 4 ploughs.
3 slaves; a mill at 11s; meadow, 8 acres; woodland for fencing.
The value was 30s; now 40s.

in BEYNHURST Hundred
7 BISHAM. Bondi held it from King Edward. Then and now
for 8 hides. Land for 10 ploughs. In lordship 2 ploughs;
17 villagers and 2 cottagers with 8 ploughs.
A church; 2 slaves; meadow, 26 acres; 12 arpents of vines.
The value was £8; now £12.

in BLEWBURY Hundred
8 WILLINGTON. Nigel holds from him. Thorkell, a free man, held it
from King Edward. Land for 6 ploughs. Then for 8 hides;
now for 4 hides and 1 virgate.
A church; 9 slaves; 2 ploughs in lordship;
10 villagers; 2 cottagers with 8 ploughs.
Meadow, 40 acres.
The value was £6; now £9.

in WANTAGE Hundred
9 (South) DENCHWORTH. Rayner holds from him. Alric held it before 1066.
Then for 7 hides; now for 5½ hides. Land for 5 ploughs.
In lordship 1 plough;
5 villagers and 5 cottagers with 1 plough.
Meadow, 30 acres. A church.
Value before 1066, 70s; later 60s; now £4.

10 CHARLTON. Robert holds from him. Tovi, a free man, held it.
Then and now for 2½ hides. Land for 1 plough.
In lordship 1 plough, with
7 cottagers.
Half a mill at 5s; meadow, 8 acres.
The value is and was 50s.

11 Henry holds (West) LOCKINGE himself, and Hubert (of Curzon) from
Henry. Siward (Bairn) held it from King Edward. Then and now
for 10 hides. Land for 6 ploughs. In lordship 2 ploughs;
3 villagers and 14 cottagers with 2 ploughs.
1 slave; meadow, 41 acres.
The value was £10; now £8.

Iſd . H . ten SPERSOLT .7 Polcehard de eo . Godric

un lib hō tenuit . Tc 7 m̄ ᵽ una hida 7 dimid . Tra . ē

uni caſ . Ibi ſunt . II . uilti 7 II . cot .7 IIII . ſerui.

Valuit . XL . ſolid . Modo: xxx . ſolid.

Iſd . H . ten . III . hid 7 unā v . Quattuor libi hōes tenueⁿ

T . R . E . Tc ſe defd ᵽ . III . hid 7 una v . Modo ᵽ una hida.

Tra . ē . II . caſ . Ibi ſunt . VIII . cot cū . I . caſ .7 III . ac pti.

T . R . E . ualb . LX . ſot .7 poſt 7 modo: XL . ſolid.

Hanc trā dic Henric fuiſſe Godrici Anteceſſoris ſui.

ſed ſic Hund teſtaͭ Godric eā occupauit ſuᵽ W . regē.

poſt bellū de Haſtinges . nec unq̄ tenuit . T . E . regis.

Ipſe . H . ten CHINGESTVNE 7 Radulf IN MERCEHĀ HD.

de eo . Stanchil tenuit T . R . E .7 tc 7 m̄ ſe defd ᵽ . v . hid.

Tra . ē . IIII . caſ . In dnio ſunt . II . caſ .7 XI . uilti 7 VI.

bord . cū . II . caſ . Ibi . III . ſerui .7 XXX . ac pti.

Valuit . LX . ſolid . Modo: L . ſolid.

Iſd . H . ten FIVEHIDE .7 alt Henric de eo . Godric

tenuit de abbe .7 n̄ potuit ire q̄libet cū iſta tra . Tc

7 m̄ ſe defd ᵽ . x . hid . Tra . ē . VIII . caſ . In dnio ſunt . II . caſ.

7 XIII . uilti 7 v . bord . cū . III . caſ . Ibi æccta 7 VII . ſerui.

7 c . ac pti . T . R . E .7 poſt: ualb . x . lib .7 m̄: VI . lib.

60 d

Iſd . H . ten FIVEHIDE . Godric tenuit de rege . E .7 tc ſe defd

ᵽ . x . hid .7 modo ᵽ . v . hid . q̄a rex . E . ſic condonauit.

ut hund teſtat . Tra . ē . VI . caſ . In dnio ſunt . II . caſ .7 VIII.

uilti 7 III . bord cū . II . caſ .7 dimid piſcaſ de . XI . ſot 7 VIII . den.

Ibi . IIII . ſerui .7 XII . ac pti . Valuit . VI . lib . Modo: c . ſolid.

Iſd . H . ten HENRET .7 alt Henric de eo . IN SVDTVNE HD

Godric uicecom tenuit de rege . E . Tc ſe defd ᵽ una hida.

modo ᵽ nichilo . H eſt illa hida quæ jacuit in firma regis.

de qua Aluric detulit teſtimon . Tra . ē . II . caſ . Ibi ſunt in dnio

12 Henry also holds SPARSHOLT and Fulchard from him. Godric,
a free man, held it. Then and now for 1½ hides. Land for 1 plough.
2 villagers; 2 cottagers; 4 slaves.
The value was 40s; now 30s.

13 Henry also holds 3 hides and 1 virgate. Four free men held them
before 1066. Then they answered for 3 hides and 1 virgate;
now for 1 hide. Land for 2 ploughs.
8 cottagers with 1 plough.
Meadow, 3 acres.
Value before 1066, 60s; later and now 40s.
Henry states that this land belonged to Godric, his predecessor,
but the Hundred testifies that Godric appropriated it in
King William's despite, after the Battle of Hastings, and that
he never held it before 1066.

In MARCHAM Hundred
14 Henry holds KINGSTON (Bagpuize) himself and Ralph (of Bagpuize)
from him. Stankell held it before 1066. Then and now it answered
for 5 hides. Land for 4 ploughs. In lordship 2 ploughs;
11 villagers and 6 smallholders with 2 ploughs.
3 slaves; meadow, 30 acres.
The value was 60s; now 50s.

Henry also holds
15 FYFIELD. A second Henry holds from him. Godric the Sheriff held it
from the Abbot. He could not go wherever he would with this land.
Then and now it answered for 10 hides. Land for 8 ploughs. In
lordship 2 ploughs;
13 villagers and 5 smallholders with 3 ploughs.
A church; 7 slaves; meadow, 100 acres.
Value before 1066 and later £10; now £6.

16 FYFIELD. Godric held it from King Edward. Then it answered   60 d
for 10 hides; now for 5 hides, because King Edward so remitted it,
as the Hundred testifies. Land for 6 ploughs. In lordship 2 ploughs;
8 villagers and 3 smallholders with 2 ploughs.
Half a fishery at 11s 8d. 4 slaves; meadow, 12 acres.
The value was £6; now 100s.

in SUTTON Hundred
17 (East) HENDRED. A second Henry holds from him. Godric the Sheriff
held it from King Edward. Then it answered for 1 hide;
now for nothing. This is the hide which lay in the King's
revenue of which Aelfric bore witness. Land for 2 ploughs;
they are there, in lordship, with

cū . viii . bord . ỿ vi . ãc p̃ti . Valuit . c . fol . ỿ m̃ fimilit.

Ifđ . H . teñ STANFORD . Siuuard tenuit de rege . E: Tc̄ fe

defđ .p . xl . hiđ . ỿ ut dn̄t rex . E . condonauit .p xxx . hiđ.

Modo gelđ .p . vi . hid . Tra . ē . xx . cař . In dn̄io funt . iii . cař.

ỿ xxi . uilłs . ỿ xxii . borđ cū . ix . cař . Ibi . vii . ferui . ỿ ii . molini

de . vii . fol ỿ viii . den̄ . ỿ ccc.xviii . ãc p̃ti . .p paftura . xxxii.

denař . De hac tra teñ Henric dim̄ car . ỿ ibi ht̄ . i . borđ.

Tot̄ T . R . E . ualb . xxx . lib . ỿ poft . xxiiii . lib . Modo:́xx.lib ỿ x . fol.

Ifđ . H . teñ PEISE . ỿ alt Henric de eo . Domniz tenuit

de rege . E . ỿ potuit ire quo uoluit . Tc̄ fe defđ .p . ii . hiđ ỿ dim̄

ỿ ii . acris træ . Modo .p . ii . hiđ . Tra . ē . i . cař . ỿ ibi . ē in dn̄io.

cū . iiii . borđ . T . R . E . ualb . xl . fol . ỿ poft:́xx . fol . Modo:́xxx . fol.

Ifđ . H . teñ . i . hiđ ỿ dim̄ in BORGEFELLE . IN REDINGES HĎ.

Duo alodiarij tenuer̄ T . R . E . ỿ .p tanto fe defđr . Vn̄ feruiuit

reginæ . ỿ alt Bundino . Qui tc̄ teneb:́adhuc teñ de Henrico.

fed hund nefcit quare . Tra . ē . vi . cař . In dn̄io funt . ii . cař.

ỿ ii . uilłi ỿ ii . borđ cū . i . cař . ỿ molin̄ de . v . fol ỿ . x . denař.

ỿ pifcaria de . lxviii . den̄ . ỿ xl . ãc p̃ti . Silua . de . xv . porc̄.

Valuit . xl . fol . Modo:́l . foliđ.

Ifđ . H . teñ in BVRLEI . i . hiđ . Leuuin tenuit de rege . E.

ỿ potuit ire quo uoluit . Ifđ adhuc teñ . ỿ .p una hiđ fe defđ tc̄ ỿ m̃.

Ibi . ē un uilłs ỿ i . borđ cū . i . cař . ỿ pifcaria de . viii . den̄.

ỿ ii . ãc p̃ti . Silua de . v . porc̄ . Valuit . x . fol . modo:́xx . foliđ.

Ifđ . H . teñ OLLAVINTONE . Godric tenuit de rege . E.

ỿ defđ fe .p . iii . hiđ tc̄ ỿ m̃ . Tra . ē . v . cař . Ibi funt . xii . uilłi

ỿ iiii . borđ . cū . v . cař . ỿ iiii . ferui . ỿ molin̄ de xv . fol . ỿ xl.

ãc p̃ti . Valuit . vi . lib . ỿ poft ỿ m̃:́iiii . lib.

8 smallholders.
Meadow, 6 acres.
The value was 100s; now the same.

[in GANFIELD Hundred]

18 STANFORD (in the Vale). Siward (Bairn) held it from King Edward.
Then it answered for 40 hides, but as they state, King Edward
remitted it for 30 hides; now it pays tax for 6 hides.
Land for 20 ploughs. In lordship 3 ploughs;
  21 villagers and 22 smallholders with 9 ploughs.
  7 slaves; 2 mills at 7s 8d; meadow, 318 acres;
  for pasture, 32d.
Henry the Steward holds ½ [hide?] of this land. He has
  1 smallholder.
Value of the whole before 1066 £30; later £24; now £20 10s.

19 PUSEY. A second Henry holds from him. Domnic held it from
King Edward. He could go wherever he would. Then it answered
for 2½ hides and 2 acres of land; now for 2 hides. Land for
1 plough; it is there, in lordship, with
  4 smallholders.
Value before 1066, 40s; later 20s; now 30s.

in READING Hundred

20 in BURGHFIELD 1½ hides. Two freeholders held it before 1066
and it answered for as much. One served the Queen and the
other (served) Bondi. Its holders then still hold from Henry,
but the Hundred do not know why. Land for 6 ploughs.
In lordship 2 ploughs;
  2 villagers and 2 smallholders with 1 plough.
  A mill at 5s 10d; a fishery at 68d; meadow, 40 acres;
    woodland at 15 pigs.
The value was 40s; now 50s.

21 in 'BURLEY' 1 hide. Leofwin held it from King Edward. He could
go wherever he would. He still holds it. Then and now it
answered for 1 hide.
  1 villager and 1 smallholder with 1 plough.
  A fishery at 8d; meadow, 2 acres; woodland at 5 pigs.
The value was 10s; now 20s.

22 WOOLHAMPTON. Godric the Sheriff held from King Edward.
It answered for 3 hides, then and now. Land for 5 ploughs.
  12 villagers and 4 smallholders with 5 ploughs; 4 slaves.
  A mill at 15s; meadow, 40 acres.
The value was £6; later and now £4.

Hanc t̃ra ded̃ rex .E. de ſua firma Godrico .7 inde uider̃
ſigillũ ej hõẽs de comitatu .P̃t iſtas hid̃ accep̃ ipſe Godric̃
de firma regis unā v̊ træ .de qua ñ uider̃ ſigillũ regis.

TERRA WILLI FILIJ ANSCVLFI. *IN RADINGES HD̃.*

.XXII. **W**ILLS filius Anſcul ten̊ *INGLEFELLE* .7 Giſlebt̊ de eo.
Aluuin̊ tenuit de rege .E. T̃c 7 m̊ ſe deſd̃ ℈p.x.hid̃.T̊ra.ē.xIII.
car̃.In dñio funt.II.car̃.7 xvII.uiłłi 7 III.bord̃.cũ xI.car̃.
Ibi.IIII.ſerui.7 moliñ de.x.ſolid̃.7 Lx.ãc p̊ti.
T.R.E.ualb̃.x.lib̃.7 poſt.vII.lib̃.Modo:̊vII.ſoł plus.

Iſd̃ Wiłłs ten̊ *BRADEFELT*.Horling tenuit de rege.E.
T̃c ſe deſd̃ ℈p.Ix.hid̃.Modo ℈p.vI.hid̃.T̊ra.ē.xxx.car̊.
In dñio funt.II.car̃.7 xx.uiłłi 7 xxxI.bord̃.cũ.xvIII.car̃.
Ibi.Ix.ſerui.7 III.moliñi de.LIII.ſolid̃.7 xx.ãc p̊ti.Silua.
de.c.porc̊.T.R.E.7 poſt:̊ualb̃ xxIIII.lib̃.Modo:̊xvI.lib̃.

Iſd̃.W.ten̊ *HVRTERIGE*.Alured tenuit de rege.E.7 nc̃
ten̊ de.W.T̃c 7 m̊ ſe deſd̃ ℈p una hida.T̊ra.ē.v.car̊.In
dñio.ē una car̃.7 II.uiłłi 7 II.bord̃.cũ.I.car̃.Ibi.III.ſerui̊.
7 ſilua de.III.porc̊.Valuit.Lx.ſoł.Modo:̊xxx.ſolid̃.

Iſd̃.W.ten̊ *ENGLEFEL*.Vlmer tenuit de rege.E.T̃c
7 m̊ ſe deſd̃ ℈p una hida.T̊ra.ē.I.car̃.Ibi funt.II.bord̃.

       £ 7 IIII.ãc p̊ti.

61 a
Hanc t̃ra ten̊ Stefan̊ de Wiłło:Valuit.xx.ſoł.m̊.vII.ſolid̃.

Iſd̃.W.ten̊ *OFFETVNE*.7 q̊dā miles de eo.Horling tenuit
de rege.E.T̃c ſe deſd̃ ℈p.v.hid̃.modo ℈p.IIII.hid̃ 7 dimid̃.T̊ra.ē
.v.car̊.In dñio.ē una.7 vIII.uiłłi 7 v.bord̃ cũ.v.car̃.Ibi
un̊ ſerù.7 xL.IIII.ãc p̊ti.7 ſilua de.I.porc̊.
De hac t̊ra ten̊ alt̊ miles.III.uirg̊.7 ibi h̃t̊.I.car̃.
Tot̊ T.R.E.ualb̃.c.ſolid̃.7 poſt 7 modo:̊Lx.ſolid̃.

King Edward gave this land, from his revenue, to Godric
and the men of the County have seen his seal for it. Besides
these hides, Godric also received from the King's revenue
1 virgate of land for which they have not seen the King's seal.

22   LAND OF WILLIAM SON OF ANSCULF

In READING Hundred
1 William son of Ansculf holds ENGLEFIELD and Gilbert from him.
Alwin held from King Edward. Then and now it answered for
10 hides. Land for 13 ploughs. In lordship 2 ploughs;
    17 villagers and 3 smallholders with 11 ploughs.
    4 slaves; a mill at 10s; meadow, 60 acres.
Value before 1066 £10; later £7; now 7s more.

William also holds
2 BRADFIELD. Horling held it from King Edward. Then it answered
for 9 hides; now for 6 hides. Land for 30 ploughs.
In lordship 2 ploughs.
    20 villagers and 31 smallholders with 18 ploughs.
    9 slaves; 3 mills at 53s; meadow, 20 acres;
        woodland at 100 pigs.
Value before 1066 and later £24; now £16.

3 HARTRIDGE. Alfred held it from King Edward; now he holds from
William. Then and now it answered for 1 hide. Land for 5 ploughs.
In lordship 1 plough.
    2 villagers and 2 smallholders with 1 plough.
    3 slaves; woodland at 3 pigs.
The value was 60s; now 30s.

4 ENGLEFIELD. Wulfmer held it from King Edward. Then and now it
answered for 1 hide. Land for 1 plough.
    2 smallholders.
    Meadow, 4 acres.
    Stephen holds this land from William.
The value was 20s; now 7s.

61 a

5 UFTON (Robert). A man-at-arms holds from him. Horling
held it from King Edward. Then it answered for 5 hides;
now for 4½ hides. Land for 5 ploughs. In lordship 1;
    8 villagers and 5 smallholders with 5 ploughs.
    1 slave; meadow, 44 acres; woodland at 1 pig.
    Another man-at-arms holds 3 virgates of this land; he has
        1 plough.
Value of the whole before 1066, 100s; later and now 60s.

Iſd.W.ten HODICOTE.7 Stefan de eo. IN NACHEDEDORN HD.

Balduin tenuit de rege.E. Tc 7 m ꝓ.v.hid.Tra.e.iii.car.

In dnio.e una.cu.iii.bord.

Valuit.vi.lib.7 poſt.xxx.ſol.Modo.Lx.ſolid.

Iſd.W.ten HISLELEV.7 Stefan de eo.Balduin tenuit

de rege.E. Tc 7 m ſe defd ꝓ.vi.hid 7 dim.Tra.e.iii.car.

In dnio.e.i.car.7 iiii.uiłłi 7 ii.bord cu.ii.car.Ibi.vii.

ſerui.Valuit.vii.lib.7 poſt.7 modo.iiii.lib.

Iſd.W.ten ETINGEDENE.7 Godebold de eo.Balduin te

nuit de rege.E.in alod.Tc 7 m ꝓ.viii.hid.Hoc ſcira teſtat.

In dnio ſunt.ii.car.7 iiii.uiłłi 7 vi.bord.cu.iii.car.Ibi.ix.

ſerui.7 molin de.v.ſolid.7 v.ac ꝑti.Silua ad clauſura.

Valuit.vii.lib.modo.viii.lib.

Iſd.W.ten STANWORDE.Edric tenuit de rege.E.in alod.

Tc 7 m ꝓ.v.hid.Tra.e.iiii.car.In dnio ſunt.ii.car.7 viii.

uiłłi 7 ii.bord cu.iii.car.Ibi.iii.ſerui.7 molin de.xii.ſolid.

Val 7 ualuit ſep.iiii.lib.Giſlebt ten de Witło.

Iſd.W.ten HINGEPENE.Duo libi hoes IN CHENETEBERIE HD.

tenuer de rege.E.ꝓ.ii.M in alod.Tc ꝓ.v.hid.Modo

ꝓ.ii.hid 7 dim.Tra.e.   In dnio ſunt.iiii.car.

7 x.uiłłi.7 xv.bord cu.vii.car.Ibi.xx.ſerui.7 molin

de.xii.ſolid 7 vi.den.7 xvi.ac ꝑti.Silua ad clauſura.

Valuit.xiiii.lib.7 poſt 7 modo.xii.lib. IN HILLESLAV HD.

Iſd.W.ten CONTONE.Almar tenuit in alod de rege.E.

Tc 7 m ſe defd ꝓ.v.hid.Tra.e.iiii.car.In dnio ſunt.ii.car.

7 un uiłłs 7 ix.bord cu.i.car.Ibi.æccła cu dim hida de hac

tra.7 Lx.ac ꝑti.Valuit.viii.lib.7 poſt.c.ſol.Modo.vi.lib.

in COMPTON Hundred

6 HODCOTT. Stephen holds from him. Baldwin held it from
King Edward. Then and now for 5 hides. Land for 3 ploughs.
In lordship 1, with
   3 smallholders.
The value was £6; later 30s; now 60s.

7 (East) ILSLEY. Stephen holds from him. Baldwin held it from
King Edward. Then and now it answered for 6½ hides.
Land for 3 ploughs. In lordship 1 plough;
   4 villagers and 2 smallholders with 2 ploughs.
   7 slaves.
The value was £7; later and now £4.

8. YATTENDON. Godbald holds from him. Baldwin held it from
King Edward in freehold. Then and now for 8 hides. This the Shire
testifies. In lordship 2 ploughs;
   4 villagers and 6 smallholders with 3 ploughs.
   9 slaves; a mill at 5s; meadow, 5 acres; woodland for fencing.
The value was £7; now £8.

9 STANFORD (Dingley). Edric held it from King Edward in freehold.
Then and now for 5 hides. Land for 4 ploughs.
In lordship 2 ploughs;
   8 villagers and 2 smallholders with 3 ploughs.
   3 slaves; a mill at 12s.
The value is and was always £4.
   Gilbert holds from William.

in KINTBURY Hundred

10 INKPEN. Two free men held it from King Edward as two manors in
freehold. Then for 5 hides; now for 2½ hides. Land for ....
In lordship 4 ploughs;
   10 villagers and 15 smallholders with 7 ploughs.
   20 slaves; a mill at 12s 6d; meadow, 16 acres;
     woodland for fencing.
The value was £14; later and now £12.

in HILLSLOW Hundred

11 COMPTON (Beauchamp). Aelmer held in freehold from
King Edward. Then and now it answered for 5 hides.
Land for 4 ploughs. In lordship 2 ploughs;
   1 villager and 9 smallholders with 1 plough.
   A church with ½ hide of this land; meadow, 60 acres.
The value was £8; later 100s; now £6.

Iſđ.W.ten CHINGESTVNE.7 Adelelm IN MERCEHĀ HĐ.

de eo.Turchil tenuit de rege.E.7 potuit ire quo uoluit.Tc

ſe defđ ꝑ.v.hiđ.modo ꝑ.iiii.hiđ.Tra.e.iiii.caꝛ.In dnio

ſunt.ii.caꝛ.7 vi.uiłłi 7 ix.borđ cū.i.caꝛ.Ibi.v.ſerui.

7 piſcaria de.v.ſoł.7 xxx.ac ꝑti.Valuit.c.ſoł.Modoːʟx.ſoł.

TERRA WILLI DE OW   IN REDINGES HĐ.

.XXII. WILLs de Ow.ten de rege PETEORDE.7 Gozelin de eo.

Aleſtan tenuit de rege.E.7 tc 7 m̄ ſe defđ ꝑ.ii.hiđ 7 dim̄.

Tra.e.ii.caꝛ.In dnio.e una.7 iii.uiłłi 7 iiii.borđ.cū.i.caꝛ.

Ibi dimiđ moliñ de.vii.ſoł 7 vi.deñ.7 xvi.ac ꝑti.

Valuit.ʟ.ſoliđ.Modoːxʟ.ſoliđ. IN CHENETEBERIE HĐ.

Iſđ.W.ten DANEFORD.Aluuard tenuit in alođ de rege.E.

Tc ꝑ.x.hiđ.modo ꝑ.v.hiđ.Tra.e.   In dnio.e.i.caꝛ.

7 iiii.uiłłi 7 iiii.borđ cū.ii.caꝛ 7 dim̄.Ibi.iii.ſerui.7 æcc̵a.

Valuit.c.ſoliđ.m̄.iiii.liƀ.Cū iſto M̄ ten.W.dim̄ hidā

quæ duoꝛ liberoꝛ hōum fuit.7 nunꝗ M̄ huic ꝑtiñ.ut ſcira dicit.

Iſđ.W.ten DENCHESWORDE.7 Gozelin IN WANETINZ HĐ.

de eo.Aluuard un lib hō tenuit de rege.E.Tc 7 m̄ ꝑ.v.hiđ.

Tra.e.ii.caꝛ.In dnio.e una.7 ii.uiłłi 7 vi.cot cū.i.caꝛ.Ibi.ii.

ſerui.7 xxvii.ac ꝑti.Valuit.ʟ.ſoł.7 poſtːxʟ.ſoł.Modoːʟx.ſoł.

TERRA WILLI PEVREL.   IN EGLEI HĐ.

.XX. WILLs peurel ten de rege OLVELEI.Radulf tenuit de rege.E.

Tc ſe defđ ꝑ x.hiđ.m̄ ꝑ.iii.hiđ 7 dimiđ.Tra.e.vi.caꝛ.In dnio

ſunt.ii.caꝛ.7 x.uiłłi 7 viii.borđ.cū.iiii.caꝛ.Ibi.iiii.ſerui.

Valuit.x.liƀ.modo.vi.liƀ.

in MARCHAM Hundred

12 KINGSTON (Bagpuize). Aethelhelm holds from him. Thorkell held
it from King Edward; he could go where he would. Then it
answered for 5 hides; now for 4 hides. Land for 4 ploughs.
In lordship 2 ploughs;
6 villagers and 9 smallholders with 1 plough.
5 slaves; a fishery at 5s; meadow, 30 acres.
The value was 100s; now 60s.

23 LAND OF WILLIAM OF EU

In READING Hundred

1 William of Eu holds PADWORTH from the King and Jocelyn from him.
Alstan held it from King Edward. Then and now it answered
for 2½ hides. Land for 2 ploughs. In lordship 1;
3 villagers and 4 smallholders with 1 plough.
Half a mill at 7s 6d; meadow, 16 acres.
The value was 50s; now 40s.

In KINTBURY Hundred

2 Willam also holds DENFORD. Alfward held it in freehold from
King Edward. Then for 10 hides; now for 5 hides. Land for ....
In lordship 1 plough;
4 villagers and 4 smallholders with 2½ ploughs.
3 slaves; a church.
The value was 100s; now £4.
With this manor William holds ½ hide which was two free
men's. It never belonged to this manor, as the Shire states.

In WANTAGE Hundred

3 William also holds (North) DENCHWORTH and Jocelyn from him.
Alfward, a free man, held it from King Edward. Then and now
for 5 hides. Land for 2 ploughs. In lordship 1;
2 villagers and 6 cottagers with 1 plough.
2 slaves; meadow, 27 acres.
The value was 50s; later 40s; now 60s.

24 LAND OF WILLIAM PEVEREL

In EAGLE Hundred

1 William Peverel holds WOOLLEY from the King. Earl Ralph held it
from King Edward. Then it answered for 10 hides; now for
3½ hides. Land for 6 ploughs. In lordship 2 ploughs;
10 villagers and 8 smallholders with 4 ploughs.
4 slaves.
The value was £10; now £6.

TERRA WILLI DE BRAIOSE. *IN REDINGES HD̄.*

.XXV WILLS de Braiofe ten̄ de rege *SVDCOTE*.Brictuard̄

tenuit de rege .E. Tc̄ fe defd̄ ꝑ . II . hid̄ . Modo ꝑ una hida.

Tra . ē . III . car̄ . In dn̄io . ē una .7 v . uitti 7 VIII . bord̄ cū . II .

car̄ . Ibi molin̄ de . XVIII . folid̄ .7 pifcaria de . L . denar̄.

Valuit . IIII . lib̄ . Modo: c . folid̄.

TERRA WILLELMI LOVET   *IN TACEHA HD̄.*

.XXVI. WILLS Louet ten̄ de rege *DERITONE* . Toti tenuit de rege .E.

in alod̄ . Tc̄ fe defd̄ ꝑ . VIII . hid̄ . modo ꝑ . I . hida 7 una v̄.

Tra . ē . v . car̄ . In dn̄io dim̄ car̄ .7 IIII . uitti 7 III . bord̄ cū . II .

car̄ . Ibi . II . ferui .7 molin̄ de . XV . folid̄ .7 IIII . āc p̊ti.

Silua de . v . porc̄ . Valuit VIII . lib̄ .7 poft: c . fot . Modo: LXX . fot.

Ifd̄ . W . ten̄ *ANEBORNE* . Toti tenuit   *IN CHENETEBERIE.HD̄.*

de rege .E. in alod̄ ꝑ cō̄ . Tc̄ 7 m̄ ꝑ . III . hid̄ 7 una v̄.

Tra . ē . II . car̄ . Ibi funt . II . uitti 7 VII . bord̄ cū . II . car̄.

7 XIII . āc p̊ti . Silua ad claufurā . Valuit . XL . fot . modo: XXX . folid̄.

Ifd̄ . W . ten̄ *MORTVNE* . Toti tenuit   *IN BLITBERIE HD̄.*

de rege .E. Tc̄ ꝑ . v . hid̄ . m̄ ꝑ . II . hid̄ 7 dimid̄ . Tra . ē

IIII . car̄ . In dn̄io . ē una .7 III . uitti 7.IIII . cot̄ . cū . I . car̄

7 dimid̄ . Ibi molin̄ de . XII . fot 7 VI . den̄ .7 XL . āc p̊ti.

Valuit . VI . lib̄ 7 ualet . quis redd̄ . VII . lib̄.

TERRA WILLI FILIJ CORBVCION *IN CHENETEBERIE HD̄.*

.XXVII. WILLS fili Corbuzon ten̄ de rege . x . hid̄ in *TANEBVRNE*.

Toui tenuit ꝑ cō̄ in alod̄ de rege . E . Tc̄ ꝑ x . hid̄ . modo

ꝑ . VIII . hid̄ . Tra . ē . III . car̄ . In dn̄io . ē una .7 IIII . uitti

7 VII . bord̄ cū . II . car̄ . Ibi . II . ferui .7 molin̄ de . XX . folid̄.

7 XX . āc p̊ti . Silua de . x . porc̄ . Valuit . c . fot . modo: IIII . lib̄.

25   LAND OF WILLIAM OF BRAOSE   61 b

In READING Hundred

1 William of Braose holds SOUTHCOTE from the King. Brictward held it from King Edward. Then it answered for 2 hides; now for 1 hide. Land for 3 ploughs. In lordship 1;
     5 villagers and 8 smallholders with 2 ploughs.
     A mill at 18s; a fishery at 50d.
The value was £4; now 100s.

26   LAND OF WILLIAM LOVETT

In THATCHAM Hundred

1 William Lovett holds DONNINGTON from the King. Toti held it from King Edward in freehold. Then it answered for 8 hides; now for 1 hide and 1 virgate. Land for 5 ploughs.
In lordship ½ plough;
     4 villagers and 3 smallholders with 2 ploughs.
     2 slaves; a mill at 15s; meadow, 4 acres; woodland at 5 pigs.
The value was £8; later 100s; now 70s.

In KINTBURY Hundred

2 William also holds ENBORNE. Toti held it from King Edward in freehold as a manor. Then and now for 3 hides and 1 virgate. Land for 2 ploughs.
     2 villagers and 7 smallholders with 2 ploughs.
     Meadow, 13 acres; woodland for fencing.
The value was 40s; now 30s.

In BLEWBURY Hundred

3 William also holds (South) MORETON. Toti held it from King Edward. Then for 5 hides; now for 2½ hides. Land for 4 ploughs.
In lordship 1;
     3 villagers and 4 cottagers with 1½ ploughs.
     A mill at 12s 6d; meadow, 40 acres.
The value was and is £6; nevertheless it pays £7.

27   LAND OF WILLIAM SON OF CORBUCION

In KINTBURY Hundred

1 William son of Corbucion holds 10 hides in ENBORNE from the King. Tovi held it as a manor in freehold from King Edward. Then for 10 hides; now for 8 hides.
Land for 3 ploughs. In lordship 1;
     4 villagers and 7 smallholders with 2 ploughs.
     2 slaves; a mill at 20s; meadow, 20 acres;
         woodland at 10 pigs.
The value was 100s; now £4.

Iſđ.W.teñ MORTVNE .7 Radulf⁹de eo. IN BLITBERIE HD̄.

Quidā liƀ hō tenuit.T.R.E. Tc̄ 7 m̊ ֱp.x.hiđ.Tra.e̅.vii.car̅.

In dñio ſunt.ii.car̅.7 xiiii.uiłłi 7 viii.cot cū.vi.car̅.

7 moliñ de xii.ſoliđ.7 vi.den̊.Ibi æcc̄ła 7 iii.ſerui.7 in

Walengeford.v.hagæ de.l.denar̊.Valuit.x.liƀ.Modo⸴xii.liƀ.

Iſđ.W.ten̊ CERLETONE 7 Goiffriđ IN WANETINZ HD̄.

de eo.Toui q̇đā liƀ hō tenuit.T.R.E.Tc̄ 7 m̊.ֱp.ii.hiđ 7 dim̊.

Tra.e̅.i.car̅.In dñio.e̅ una.7 uñ uiłłs.7 v.cot cū dim̊ car̅.

Valuit.xl.ſoł.Modo⸴l.ſoliđ.

TERRA WILLI FILIJ RICARDI. IN WIFOL HD̄.

.XXVI Wᴵᴵ ILLs fili⁹ Ricardi ten̊ COLESHALLE .Oſgot tenuit in

alođ de rege ⸴ E.Tc̄ ſe deſđ ֱp viii.hiđ.Modo ֱp.v.hiđ.

Tra.e̅.iii.car̅.In dñio ſunt.ii.car̅.7 ii.uiłłi 7 v.borđ.

Ibi.iiii.ſerui.7 tcia pars uni⁹ molini de.x.ſoliđ.7 lxix.

ac̄ ṗti.Valuit.vii.liƀ.7 poſt⸴vi.liƀ.Modo⸴iiii.liƀ.

Iſđ.W.ten̊ CELREA.Oſgot q̇đā liƀ hō IN WANETINZ HD̄.

tenuit T.R.E. Tc̄ ֱp xii.hiđ.modo ֱp.viii.hiđ.Tra.e̅.iiii.

car̅.In dñio h̅t Wiłłs.ii.hiđ.7 ibi h̅t.ii.uiłłos.7 iii.cot

cū dim̊ car̅.7 Godefriđ ten̊ de eo.x.hiđ.7 ibi ſunt.vi.uiłłi

7 viii.cot cū dim̊ car̅.7 moliñ de.iiii.ſoł.7 xxx.vi.ac̄ ṗti.

Tot̄ T.R.E.7 poſt⸴uałƀ.ix.liƀ.Modo⸴vi.liƀ 7 xii.ſoł.   ☞

TERRA WILLI DE CAILGI. IN REDINGES HD.

.XXIX. Wᴵᴵ ILLs de calgi.ten̊ de rege SOLEHA̅.7 q̇đā miles de eo.

Godric⁹ tenuit de rege.E.Tc̄ 7 m̊ ſe deſđ ֱp.ii.hiđ.Tra.e̅

v.car̅.In dñio ſunt.ii.car̅.7 iiii.uiłłi 7 vi.borđ cū.ii.car̅.

Ibi.æcc̄ła 7 ii.ſerui.7 iiii.ac̄ ṗti.Valuit.iiii.liƀ.7 poſt.iii.liƀ.

⌐ Modo⸴c.ſoł.

In BLEWBURY Hundred
2 William also holds (North) MORETON and Ralph from him.
A free man held it before 1066. Then and now for 10 hides.
Land for 7 ploughs. In lordship 2 ploughs;
14 villagers and 8 cottagers with 6 ploughs.
A mill at 12s 6d. A church; 3 slaves; in Wallingford,
5 sites at 50d.
The value was £10; now £12.

In WANTAGE Hundred
3 William also holds CHARLTON and Geoffrey from him. Tovi,
a free man, held it before 1066. Then and now for 2½ hides.
Land for 1 plough. In lordship 1;
1 villager and 5 cottagers with ½ plough.
The value was 40s; now 50s.

28   LAND OF WILLIAM SON OF RICHARD

In WYFOLD Hundred
1 William son of Richard holds COLESHILL. Osgot held it in
freehold from King Edward. Then it answered for 8 hides; now
for 5 hides. Land for 3 ploughs. In lordship 2 ploughs;
2 villagers and 5 smallholders.
4 slaves; the third part of 1 mill at 10s;
meadow, 69 acres.
The value was £7; later £6; now £4.

In WANTAGE Hundred
2 William also holds CHILDREY. Osgot, a free man, held it
before 1066. Then for 12 hides, now for 8 hides. Land for
4 ploughs. In lordship William has 2 hides. He has there
2 villagers and 3 cottagers with ½ plough.
Godfrey holds 10 hides from him.
6 villagers and 8 cottagers with ½ plough.
A mill at 4s; meadow, 36 acres.
Value of the whole before 1066 and later £9; now £6 12s.

(3 is entered after 30,1, at the foot of col. 61 b.)

29   LAND OF WILLIAM OF CAILLY

In READING Hundred
1 William of Cailly holds SULHAM from the King. A man-at-arms
holds from him. Godric held it from King Edward. Then and now it
answered for 2 hides. Land for 5 ploughs. In lordship 2 ploughs;
4 villagers and 6 smallholders with 2 ploughs.
A church; 2 slaves; meadow, 4 acres.
The value was £4; later £3; now 100s.

TERRA WALTERIJ FILIJ PONZ.

.XXX. WALTERI⁹ fili⁹ ponz teñ de rege . ETONE . Guert tenuit in

alod de rege . E . Tc̄ ſe defđ ᵱ . xx . hiđ . Modo ᵱ . vi . hiđ . T̄ra . ē

Iɴ dñio ſunt . iii . car̄ .7 xiii . uiłłi 7 v . borđ . cū . iiii . car̄ . Ibi . vii.

ſerui . ñ deder̄ gelđ . Ibi . ii . piſcariæ de . xvi . ſoł .7 cxlviii . ac̄ p̄ti.

T . R . E . uałb . x . lib .7 poſt : c . ſoł . Modo : ix . lib.

De iſto ꝏ . iii . hiđ deđ Ponz ᚹ petro de Weſtmonaſt ᵱ anima ſua.

7 ibi . ē una car̄ cū . iiii . borđ .7 iii . bob . Vał . xx . ſoliđ.

☞ Iɴ *HILLESLAV HD̄* Iſđ . W . teñ *ORDEGESTON* .

   Oſgot tenuit de rege . E . in alođ.

   Tc̄ ſe defđ ᵱ . x . hiđ . m̄ ᵱ . v . hiđ . T̄ra . ē . vii . car̄.

   In dñio ſunt . ii . car̄ .7 xviii . borđ.

   cū . iii . car̄ . Ibi . v . ſerui .7 cc . ac̄ p̄ti . T . R . E . ualuit . xii . lib.

   7 poſt . viii . lib . Modo : x . lib.

61 c
TERRA WALTERIJ . F . OTHER *IN RIPLESMER HD̄.*

.XXXI. WALTERIVꞩ filius Otherij teñ *ORTONE* . Godric

tenuit de rege . E . Tc̄ ſe defđ | ᵱ una hida 7 dimiđ.

T̄ra . ē .   In dñio ſunt . ii . car̄ .7 iii . borđ .7 una

ac̄ p̄ti . Silua de . ii . porc̄ . Valuit . xl . ſoł . m̄ xl . ſoł.

Iſđ . W . teñ *CILTONE* . Weneſi *IN NACHEDEDORN HD̄.*

tenuit de rege . E . Tc̄ 7 m̄ ſe defđ ᵱ . v . hiđ . T̄ra . ē

In dñio ſunt . ii . car̄ .7 vii . uiłłi 7 . ix . borđ . cū car̄ 7 dim̄.

Ibi . iiii . ſerui .7 vi . hagæ in Warengeford de . ii . ſoliđ.

Iſđ . W . teñ *BORCHELDEBERIE* . i . hiđ . *IN BORCHELDEBERIE*

7 q̇đā ſuus hō de eo . In foreſta jacet .7 nunꝙ   ⌐ HVND.

geldaū ſic̄ ſcira dicit . Aluiladeſe tenuit de rege . E.

Ibi . ē . i . car̄ in dñio . Vał 7 ualuit . vii . ſoł 7 vi . deñ.

30   LAND OF WALTER SON OF POYNTZ

[In WYFOLD Hundred]
1 Walter son of Poyntz holds EATON (Hastings) from the King.
Gyrth held it in freehold from King Edward. Then it answered
for 20 hides; now for 6 hides. Land for ...
In lordship 3 ploughs;
    13 villagers and 5 smallholders with 4 ploughs.
    7 slaves. They have not paid tax. 2 fisheries at 16s;
        meadow, 148 acres.
Value before 1066 £10; later 100s; now £9.
    Poyntz gave 3 hides of this manor to St. Peter's of Westminster
for his soul's sake. 1 plough there, with
    4 smallholders and 3 oxen.
Value 20s.

(Directed to its proper place by transposition signs)
(28)
    In   HILLSLOW Hundred
3 William also holds ODSTONE. Osgot held it from King Edward
in freehold. Then it answered for 10 hides; now for 5 hides.
Land for 7 ploughs. In lordship 2 ploughs;
    18 smallholders with 3 ploughs.
    5 slaves; meadow, 200 acres.
Value before 1066 £12; later £8; now £10.

31   LAND OF WALTER SON OF OTHERE   61 c

In RIPPLESMERE Hundred
1 Walter son of Othere holds ORTONE. Godric held it from
King Edward. Then and now it answered for 1½ hides. Land for ....
In lordship 2 ploughs;
    3 smallholders.
    Meadow, 1 acre; woodland at 2 pigs.
The value was 40s; now 30s.

In COMPTON Hundred
2 Walter also holds CHILTON. Wynsi held it from King Edward.
Then and now it answered for 5 hides. Land for ....
In lordship 2 ploughs;
    7 villagers and 9 smallholders with 1½ ploughs.
    4 slaves. 6 sites in Wallingford at 2s.

In BUCKLEBURY Hundred
3 Walter also holds BUCKLEBURY. 1 hide. One of his men holds from
him. It lies in the Forest and never paid tax as the Shire
states. Aelfhild Dese held it from King Edward. 1 plough in lordship.
The value is and was 7s 6d.

In CHENETEBERIE teñ iſd . W . dimid hid . quã rex .E.
ded ej antecefſori de firma ſua .7 ſolutã ab omĩ con
ſuetudine ‚ppt foreſtã cuſtodiendã . excepta forisfac
tura regis ſic̃. e̅ Latrociniũ 7 homicidiũ 7 Heinfara.
7 fracta pax . Val̃ . v . ſolid . *IN BLITBERIE HD̃.*

Iſd . W . teñ *HACHEBORNE* . Aluuiñ uñ lib̃ ho̅ te
nuit . Tc̃ 7 m̃ . x . hidæ ibi . ſed ‚p . vi . hid 7 dim̃ ſe defd.
Tra . e̅ . vi . car̃ . In dñio ſunt . ii . car̃.7 xiiii . uilli 7 x.
cot̃ . cu̅ . v . car̃ . Ibi . iiii . ſerui.7 moliñ de . xii . ſolid.
7 xx.iiii . ac̃ p̃ti . De hac tra teñ Robt̃ . i . hid de Walto.
7 ibi ht̃ . i . car̃ cu̅ . i . cot̃.7 iiii . ac̃ p̃ti.
Tot̃ T.R.E.7 poſt.́ual̃b . xiii . lib̃.7 modo:́xiii . lib̃.

Iſd . W . teñ *OFFELLE* 7 q̣dã miles de eo . *IN REDINGES HD̃.*
Wicſtric̃ tenuit de rege .E. Tc̃ 7 m̃ ſe defd ‚p una hida
7 dimid . Tra . e̅ . ii . car̃. In dñio . e̅ una.7 vi . bord̃ cu̅ . i . car̃.
Ibi . iiii . ac̃ p̃ti . Silua . de . xv . porc̃ . Valuit . xx . ſot . m̃ . xxx . ſot̃.

XXX.ii. TERRA EVDONIS FILIJ HVBTI. *IN RIPLESMERE HD̃.*

Evdo Dapifer teñ *LOSFELLE* de rege . Aluric tenuit
de rege .E. Tc̃ ‚p . ii . hid . modo ‚p una hida.
In dñio ſunt . ii . car̃.7 vii . uilli cu̅ . ii . car̃.7 vii . ac̃ p̃ti.
Silua de . v . porc̃ . Valuit . iiii . lib̃ . modo:́xxx . ſolid.

.XXXIII. TERRA MILONIS CRISPIN. *IN RADINGES HD̃.*

Milo criſpin teñ *PANGEBORNE*.7 Will̃s de eo . Bal
duin tenuit de rege .E. Ibi . vi . hidæ 7 una v̄.7 non
geldau T.R.E.7 m̃ niſi ‚p.v. hid . Nil ibi in dñio.7 iii.uilli
7 v. bord̃.cu̅.ii. car̃.7 moliñ de . x . ſol.7 xii . ac̃ p̃ti.
De hac tra teñ uñ miles . i . hid.7 ibi ht̃ . i . car̃.7 ii . ac̃s
p̃ti . Valuit tot̃ . vi . lib̃.7 poſt . v . lib̃ . Modo:́iiii . lib̃.

61 c

[In KINTBURY Hundred]
4 In KINTBURY Walter also holds ½ hide which King Edward gave to
his predecessor from his revenue, absolved from all customary dues,
because of Keeping the Forest, except for the King's fines, as for
robbery, homicide, house-breaking and breach of the peace.
Value 5s.

In BLEWBURY Hundred
5 Walter also holds (West) HAGBOURNE. Alwin, a free man, held it.
Then and now 10 hides there, but it answers for 6½ hides.
Land for 6 ploughs. In lordship 2 ploughs;
14 villagers and 10 cottagers with 5 ploughs.
4 slaves; a mill at 12s; meadow, 24 acres.
Robert holds 1 hide of this land from Walter; he has
1 plough,with
1 cottager; meadow, 4 acres.
Value of the whole before 1066 and later £13; now £13.

In READING Hundred
6 Walter also holds WOKEFIELD and a man-at-arms from him.
Wictric held it from King Edward. Then and now it answered for
1½ hides. Land for 2 ploughs. In lordship 1;
6 smallholders with 1 plough.
Meadow, 4 acres; woodland at 15 pigs.
The value was 20s; now 30s.

32   LAND OF EUDO SON OF HUBERT
In RIPPLE MERE Hundred
1 Eudo the Steward holds 'LOSFIELD' from the King. Aelfric
held it from King Edward. Then for 2 hides; now for 1 hide.
In lordship 2 ploughs;
7 villagers with 2 ploughs.
Meadow, 7 acres; woodland at 5 pigs.
The value was £4; now 30s.

33   LAND OF MILES CRISPIN
In READING Hundred
1 Miles Crispin holds PANGBOURNE and William from him.
Baldwin held it from King Edward. 6 hides and 1 virgate. They
did not pay tax before 1066 and now only for 5 hides.
Nothing in lordship.
3 villagers and 5 smallholders with 2 ploughs.
A mill at 10s; meadow, 12 acres.
A man-at-arms holds 1 hide of this land. He has 1 plough;
meadow, 2 acres.
The value of the whole was £6; later £5; now £4.

Isđ Witts teñ de Milone . I . hiđ in *SOLEHĀ* . Balduiñ
tenuit de rege . E . 7 p̧ tanto se defđ tc̄ 7 m̊ . Ibi . ē . I . car̄
in dn̄io . 7 III . borđ cū dim̄ car̄ . Valuit . xx . sot . modo: xxx.

Ipse Milo teñ *CLOPECOTE*. *IN ELETESFORD HD̄*.
Vlnod uñ lib hō tenuit . T . R . E . Tc̄ p̧ . VII . hiđ . Modo
p̧ una hida 7 una v̄ . Tra . ē . III . car̄ . In dn̄io . ē una car̄
7 dim̄ . 7 VII . uitti 7 II . cot cū . II . car̄ . 7 molin̄ de . XXVI.
solid . 7 xxv . ac p̄ti.
Valuit . VII . lib . 7 post: IIII . lib . modo: c . solid.

Isđ Milo teñ *CLOPECOTE* . Safford uñ lib hō tenuit
T . R . E . 7 tc̄ p̧ . VII . hiđ . m̊ p̧ una hida 7 una v̄ . Tra . ē . III.
car̄ . In dn̄io . ē una car̄ 7 dim̄ . 7 II . uitti 7 VI . cot cū . III . car̄.
Ibi . xxv . ac p̄ti . De isto M teñ Herold unā v̄ 7 dimid
de Milone . Tot valuit VII . lib . 7 post: IIII . lib . M: c . solid.
H duo M teñ Milo p̧ uno M. *IN WANETINZ HD̄*.

Isđ Milo teñ *BEDRETONE* . 7 Witts de eo . Leuric monac̄
tenuit T . R . E . 7 potuit ire quo uoluit . Tc̄ p̧ . x . hiđ . Modo
p̧ . v . hiđ . Tra . ē . IIII . car̄ . Ibi . ē uñ uitts 7 v . cot cū dim̄ car̄.
7 II . serui . 7 molin̄ de . v . sot . 7 x . ac p̄ti.
Valuit . VIII . lib . 7 post . IIII . lib . Modo: III . lib.

61 d

Isđ Milo teñ *APLETVNE* . 7 Ricarđ de eo. *IN MERCEHĀ HD̄*.
Halden tenuit T . R . E . Tc̄ se defđ p̧ . v . hiđ . Modo p̧ . II . hiđ
7 dimid . Tra . ē . VI . car̄ . In dn̄io . ē una . 7 IIII . uilli 7 v . borđ
cū . I . car̄ . Ibi . III . serui . 7 piscaria de . XXXIIII . sot 7 II . deñ.
Valuit . c . solid . 7 post: LXX . solid . Modo: LX . solid.

Isđ Milo teñ *ELTVNE* . 7 Ricarđ de eo . Halden tenuit
de rege . E . Tc̄ 7 m̊ se defđ p̧ . v . hiđ . Tra . ē . IIII . car̄ . In dn̄io
sunt . II . car̄ . 7 III . uitti 7 IIII . borđ cū . III . car̄ . 7 piscaria
de . v . sot . 7 xx . v . ac p̄ti . Valuit . LX . solid . Modo: L . solid.

2 William also holds 1 hide from Miles in SULHAM. Baldwin held it
from King Edward. It answered for as much, then and now.
1 plough in lordship;
   3 smallholders with ½ plough.
The value was 20s; now 30[s].

In SLOTISFORD Hundred
3 Miles holds CLAPCOT himself. Wulfnoth, a free man, held it
before 1066. Then for 7 hides; now for 1 hide and 1 virgate.
Land for 3 ploughs. In lordship 1½ ploughs;
   7 villagers and 2 cottagers with 2 ploughs.
A mill at 26s; meadow, 25 acres.
The value was £7; later £4; now 100s.

Miles also holds

4 CLAPCOT. Saxfrid, a free man, held it before 1066.
Then for 7 hides; now for 1 hide and 1 virgate.
Land for 3 ploughs. In lordship 1½ ploughs.
   2 villagers and 6 cottagers with 3 ploughs.
   Meadow, 25 acres.
   Harold holds 1½ virgates of this manor from Miles.
Value of the whole £7; later £4; now 100s.
Miles holds these two manors as one manor.

in WANTAGE Hundred
5 BETTERTON. William holds from him. Leofric, a monk, held it
before 1066. He could go where he would. Then for 10 hides;
now for 5 hides. Land for 4 ploughs.
   1 villager and 5 cottagers with ½ plough; 2 slaves.
A mill at 5s; meadow, 10 acres.
The value was £8; later £4; now £3.

in MARCHAM Hundred   61 d
6 APPLETON. Richard holds from him. Haldane held it before 1066.
Then it answered for 5 hides; now for 2½ hides.
Land for 6 ploughs. In lordship 1;
   4 villagers and 5 smallholders with 1 plough.
   3 slaves; a fishery at 34s 2d.
The value was 100s; later 70s; now 60s.

7 EATON. Richard holds from him. Haldane held it from King Edward.
Then and now it answered for 5 hides. Land for 4 ploughs.
In lordship 2 ploughs;
   3 villagers and 4 smallholders with 3 ploughs.
   A fishery at 5s; meadow, 25 acres.
The value was 60s; now 50s.

Iſd Milo teñ *EDTVNE* .7 Alured de eo . Boſi tenuit de
rege . E . Tc̄ 7 m̄ ſe defd̄ p . v . hid̄ . Ťra . ē . IIII . car̄ . In dñio
ſunt . II . car̄ . 7 III . uiłłi 7 VI . bord̄ cū . I . car̄ 7 II . piſcarie de . XVIII .
ſoł . 7 xxv . ãc p̃ti . Valuit . LX . ſoł . modo . LXX . ſoł .
In *RADINGES* hd̄ teñ Leuuard in *LONCHELEI* . I . hid̄ de Milone .
7 ñ potuit ire q̃libet abſq̃ licentia Wigoti . H̄ ťra jacet 7 ap
p̃ciata . ē in *GRATENTVN* qd̄ . ē in Oxenefordſcire . 7 tam̄ dat
ſcotū in Berchefcire .

TERRA GILONIS FŘIS ANSCVLFI . *IN ŤACEHĀ HD̄.*

.IIII.
.XXX. Gᴴɪʟᴏ teñ de rege *MIGEHĀ* . Quinq̃ libi hōēs de rege . E .
p m̄ . Tc̄ ſe defd̄ p . v . hid̄ . modo p . II . hid̄ . Ťra . ē . x . car̄ .
In dñio nil ibi . ē . ſed . IX . uiłłi 7 v . bord̄ cū . v . car̄ . 7 moliñ
de . XIIII . ſoł . De hac ťra teñ Almær . III . virg̃ . Raẏner
unā v̄ . Giſłebt . I . hid̄ 7 unā v̄ 7 dim̄ . 7 ibi ſunt . II . car̄ 7 dim̄ .
7 v . uiłłi 7 VIII . bord̄ cū . I . car̄ 7 dimid̄ . 7 q̃t xx . ãc p̃ti in m̄ .
Toť T . R . E . ualb̄ . c . ſoł . Modo inť totū : VI . lib̄ . *IN BENES HD̄.*
Iſd Ghilo teñ *ELENTONE* . Siuuard tenuit T . R . E . Tc̄ 7 modo
p . III . hid̄ . Ťra . ē . IIII . car̄ . Duo hōēs teñ de Gilone . Hugo
7 Landri . Ibi hñt . II . car̄ . 7 VI . uiłłi 7 IIII . coť . cū . I . car̄ . Ibi
xvi . ãc p̃ti . Silua . de . x . porc̄ . Valuit . LX . ſoł . modo : XL . ſoł .
Iſd Ghilo teñ *OFFETVNE* . Saulf tenuit *IN REDINGES HVND̄.*
de rege . E . Tc̄ ſe defd̄ p . v . hid̄ . modo p . III . hid̄ 7 dim̄ . Ťra . ē . v . car̄ .
Ibi ſunt . VIII . uiłłi 7 v . bord̄ cū . III . car̄ . 7 xxxvi . ãc p̃ti .
☞ Valuit . c . ſolid̄ : Modo : LX . ſolid̄ .

8 EATON. Alfred holds from him. Bosi held it from King Edward.
Then and now it answered for 5 hides. Land for 4 ploughs.
In lordship 2 ploughs;
    3 villagers and 6 smallholders with 1 plough.
    2 fisheries at 18s; meadow, 25 acres.
The value was 60s; now 70s.

In READING Hundred
9 Leofward holds 1 hide from Miles in LANGLEY(?). He could not
go wherever he would without Wigot's permission.
This land lies and is assessed in *GRATENTUN*, which is in
Oxfordshire; however it pays the levy in Berkshire.

34   LAND OF GILES BROTHER OF ANSCULF

In THATCHAM Hundred
1 Giles holds MIDGHAM from the King. 5 free men held it
from King Edward as a manor. Then it answered for 5 hides; now
for 2 hides. Land for 10 ploughs. In lordship nothing; but
    9 villagers and 5 smallholders with 5 ploughs.
    A mill at 14s.
Aelmer holds 3 virgates of this land; Rayner 1 virgate;
Gilbert 1 hide and 1½ virgates. 2½ ploughs there;
    5 villagers and 8 smallholders with 1½ ploughs.
    Meadow, 80 acres in the manor.
Value of the whole before 1066, 100s; now in total £6.

In BEYNHURST Hundred
2 Giles also holds MAIDENHEAD. Siward held it before 1066.
Then and now for 3 hides. Land for 4 ploughs. Two men,
Hugh and Landri, hold from Giles; they have 2 ploughs;
    6 villagers and 4 cottagers with 1 plough.
    Meadow, 16 acres; woodland at 10 pigs.
The value was 60s; now 40s.

In READING Hundred
3 Giles also holds UFTON (Nervet). Saewulf held it from King
Edward. Then it answered for 5 hides; now for 3½ hides.
Land for 5 ploughs.
    8 villagers and 5 smallholders with 3 ploughs.
    Meadow, 36 acres.
The value was 100s; now 60s.

(4 is entered after 36,1, at the foot of col. 61 d)

.XXXV. TERRA HASCOITH. _IN ROËBERG HD̄._

Hᴀꜱᴄᴏɪᴛ teñ de rege _WINTREBVRNE_.7 Chemarhuec de eo.
Briſtec tenuit T.R.E.7 potuit ire quo uoluit. Tc̄ ſe defd ᵽ.ɪɪ.hid.
Modo ᵽ una hid 7 ɪɪɪ.uirg. In dñio.ē.ɪ.car.7 uñ uiłłs 7 ɪɪ.bord
cū dimid car. Val 7 ualuit. xx.ſolid.

In ead uilla teñ Norman de Haſcoit.v.hid.has tenuit Briſtec
de rege.E. Tc̄ ſe defd ᵽ.v.hid.modo ᵽ.ɪɪ.hid 7 una v̄.Tra.ē.vɪ.
car. In dñio ſunt.ɪɪ.car.7 v.uiłłi 7 vɪɪɪ.bord.cū.ɪɪɪɪ.car.Ibi.ɪɪ.
ſerui.7 ɪɪ.āc p̄ti.7 ſilua de.ɪɪɪɪ.porc. Valuit.vɪɪɪ.lib.m̄.ɪɪɪɪ.lib.

Iſd Haſcoit teñ _LANBORNE_.Briſtec _IN LAMBORNE HVND̄._
tenuit de rege.E.in alod. Tc̄ ſe defd ᵽ.vɪɪɪ.hid. modo ᵽ.ɪɪ.hid
7 una v̄.Tra.ē.v.car. In dñio ſunt.ɪɪ.7 ɪɪɪɪ.uiłłi 7 vɪ.bord
cū.ɪɪ.car 7 dim.Ibi.vɪɪɪ.ſerui. Valuit xɪɪ.lib.Modo.vɪ.lib.

Iſd Haſcoit teñ _DRAITONE_.Goduiñ tenuit in alod de rege.E.
ᵽ m̄.Tc̄ ᵽ.ɪɪɪ.hid 7 dim.modo ᵽ una hida.Tra.ē.ɪ.car.Ibi ſuꝥ
ɪɪɪɪ.uiłłi cū una car.Valuit.ʟx.ſolid.Modo.xx.ſolid.

Iſd Haſcoit teñ _SPERSOLT_.Briſtric _IN WANETINZ HD̄._
uñ lib hō tenuit.T.R.E.Tc̄ 7 m̄ ᵽ.ɪɪ.hid.Tra.ē.ɪɪɪɪ.car.In dñio
ē una car.7 vɪɪɪ.uiłłi 7 v.cot.cū.ɪɪ.car.Ibi.ɪɪ.ſerui.
Val 7 ualuit.vɪɪɪ.lib.

.XXXVI. TERRA GISLEBTI DE BRETEVILE. _IN BORGELDEBERIE HD̄._

Gɪꜱʟᴇʙᴇʀᴛ de Breteuile teñ _WILLE_.7 Wiłłs de eo. Eluinus
tenuit de rege.E.Tc̄ 7 m̄ ᵽ una hida.Tra.ē.ɪɪ.car. In dñio ſuꝥ
.ɪɪ.car.7 ɪɪ.uiłłi 7 ɪɪ.bord cū.ɪ.car.Ibi.ɪɪ.ſerui.Valuit.xxx.ſol.

Iſd Giſlebt teñ _HANNEI_.7 Gozeliñ de eo.Godricus ⎰ m̄.xʟ.ſol.
q̄dā lib hō tenuit.T.R.E.Tc̄ 7 m̄ ſe defd ᵽ.vɪ.hid.Tra.ē.ɪɪɪ.c ł.

35   LAND OF HASCOIT (MUSARD)

In ROWBURY Hundred
1 Hascoit holds WINTERBOURNE from the King, and Kenmarchuc
   from him. Brictheah held it before 1066. He could go where he
   would. Then it answered for 2 hides; now for 1 hide and 3
   virgates. In lordship 1 plough;
      1 villager and 2 smallholders with ½ plough.
   The value is and was 20s.

2 In the same village Norman holds 5 hides from Hascoit.
   Brictheah held them from King Edward. Then they answered
   for 5 hides; now for 2 hides and 1 virgate. Land for 6 ploughs.
   In lordship 2 ploughs;
      5 villagers and 8 smallholders with 4 ploughs.
      2 slaves; meadow, 2 acres; woodland at 4 pigs.
   The value was £8; now £4.

In LAMBOURN Hundred
3 Hascoit also holds LAMBOURN. Brictheah held it from King Edward
   in freehold. Then it answered for 8 hides; now for 2 hides
   and 1 virgate. Land for 5 ploughs. In lordship 2;
      4 villagers and 6 smallholders with 2½ ploughs. 8 slaves.
   The value was £12; now £6.

[In SUTTON Hundred]
4 Hascoit also holds DRAYTON. Godwin held it in freehold from
   King Edward as a manor. Then for 3½ hides; now for 1 hide.
   Land for 1 plough.
      4 villagers with 1 plough.
   The value was 60s; now 20s.

In WANTAGE Hundred
5 Hascoit also holds SPARSHOLT. Brictric, a free man, held it
   before 1066. Then and now for 2 hides. Land for 4 ploughs.
   In lordship 1 plough;
      8 villagers and 5 cottagers with 2 ploughs. 2 slaves.
   The value is and was £8.

36   LAND OF GILBERT OF BRETTEVILLE

In BUCKLEBURY Hundred
1 Gilbert of Bretteville holds WYLD and William from him.
   Alwin held it from King Edward. Then and now for 1 hide.
   Land for 2 ploughs. In lordship 2 ploughs;
      2 villagers and 2 smallholders with 1 plough. 2 slaves.
   The value was 30s; now 40s.

[In WANTAGE Hundred]
2 Gilbert also holds (East?) HANNEY and Jocelyn from him.
   Godric, a free man, held it before 1066. Then and now it answered

In dñio funt . II . cař. 7 XII . cot cũ dim cař . Ibi . II . molini de.xxx.fol.

$\lceil$ In Cheneteberie Hð. Ifð Ghilo teñ Aneborne.

Saulf tenuit de rege. E . ‿p ꝃ)

in aloð. Tc fe defð ‿p . III . hið 7 dim . m̂ ‿p una hida.

Tra .ē.II.cař. In dñio . ē dim cař.

7 II . uilli 7 II . borð .7 XIII . ac p̃ti.Villi . II . cař .

Valuit.XL.fol.Modo⁚xx.fol.

62 a
7 xxxvIII ‹ ac p̃ti . Valuit 7 uaÍ ‹ vI . liƀ.7 tam redð ‹ vI ‹ liƀ 7 uñciã ⌐auri.
Ifð Gifleƀt teñ dimið hið . Aluric uñ hõ liƀ tenuit.Tc 7 m̂
‿p dimið hida. Ibi . ē uñ uilÍs 7 uñ ferũ 7 vIII ‹ ac p̃ti . Vaí . x . fol.
Ifð Gifleƀt teñ Hevaford‹7 Pagañ de eo‹ In Merceha Hð.

★ Duo f̃s tenuer in paragio . q̃fq̃ habuit Haulã.7 potuer ire
quo uoluer . Tc 7 m̂ fe defð ‿p . x . hið . Tra .ē . vI . cař . In dñio
funt . II . cař.7 III ‹ uilli 7 XI . borð . cũ . II . cař . Ibi æccla 7 III . ferui.
7 c. ac p̃ti . Valuit . vIII . liƀ.7 poft⁚c . folið . Modo⁚x . liƀ.
Ifð Gifleƀt teñ Niwetone‹7 Pagañ de eo . Alric tenuit
7 potuit ire quo uoluit. Tc 7 m̂ fe defð ‿p . II . hið.Tra .ē ‹ I . cař‹
7 ibi. ē in dñio ‹ cũ ‹ IIII . borð 7 II .feruis.7 XIII ‹ ac p̃ti‹Vaí xxx.fol‹
Ifð Gifleƀt teñ Praxemere.7 Ricarð de eo . In Merceha Hð.
Goduiñ 7 Vrleuuine tenuer T.R‹E.7 potuer ire quo uoluer.
Tc fe defð ‿p . vII . hið . Modo ‿p . IIII . hið ‹ Duæ hallæ fuer ‹ m̂ una.
Tra .ē . III . cař . In dñio eft una 7 dim‹7 II‹uilli 7 v‹ borð cũ
dim cař . Silua.de . II . porc . Valuit 7 uaÍ ‹ IIII ‹ liƀ.

for 6 hides. Land for 3 ploughs. In lordship 2 ploughs;
   12 cottagers with ½ plough.
   2 mills at 30s.
(Directed to its proper place by transposition signs.)

(34) In KINTBURY Hundred
4 Giles also holds ENBORNE. Saewulf held it from King Edward
as a manor in freehold. Then it answered for 3½ hides; now
for 1 hide. Land for 2 ploughs. In lordship ½ plough.
   2 villagers and 2 smallholders.
   Meadow, 13 acres. The villagers, 2 ploughs.
The value was 40s; now 20s.

(36,2 *continued*)
   Meadow, 38 acres.
   The value was and is £6; however it pays £6 and
an ounce of gold.

3 Gilbert also holds ½ hide. Aelfric, a free man, held it.
Then and now for ½ hide.
   1 villager; 1 slave.
   Meadow, 8 acres.
Value 10s.

In MARCHAM Hundred
4 Gilbert also holds HATFORD and Payne from him. Two brothers
held it jointly; each had a Hall. They could go where they would.
Then and now it answered for 10 hides. Land for 6 ploughs.
In lordship 2 ploughs;
   3 villagers and 11 smallholders with 2 ploughs.
   A church; 3 slaves;
     meadow, 100 acres.
The value was £8; later 100s; now £10.

[In GANFIELD Hundred]
5 Gilbert also holds NEWTON and Payne from him. Alric held it;
he could go where he would. Then and now it answered
for 2 hides. Land for 1 plough. It is there, in lordship, with
   4 smallholders and 2 slaves.
   Meadow, 13 acres.
Value 30s.

In MARCHAM [ROWBURY] Hundred
6 Gilbert also holds PEASEMORE and Richard from him. Godwin and
Herlwin held it before 1066; they could go where they would.
Then it answered for 7 hides; now for 4 hides. There were
two Halls, now one. Land for 3 ploughs. In lordship 1½.
   2 villagers and 5 smallholders with ½ plough.
   Woodland at 2 pigs.
The value was and is £4.

62 a

.XXXVII. TERRA GISLEBERTI DE GAND. *IN ROEBERGE HD.*

GISLEBERT de Gand hr de rege uñ Maneriũ.7 Robt de eo.

Tunna tenuit T.R.E.7 tc fe defd ,p . vi . hid . Modo ,p . iii . hid.

Tra.e.vi.car.In dñio.e una.7 ii.uitti 7 iiii . bord cũ .iiii.car.

Ibi . iii . ferui.7 filua de . xx . porc.

De hac tra ten Algolt . iii . hid.7 ibi hr . i . car.7 ii . uitti 7 vi.

bord cũ .ii . car. Valebat . vi . lib.7 poft . lx . fot. Modo:' fimilit.

.XXXVIII. TERRA GOISFRIDI DE MANNEVILE. *IN CHENETEBERIE HD.*

GOISFRID de Manneuile ten HILDESLEI.7 Safuualo de eo.

Ordolf tenuit ,p M in alod de rege . E . Tc 7 m ,p una hida.

Tra.e. ii . car . In dñio.e una car.7 un uitts 7 vii . bord cũ.i.car.

Ibi.iii.ferui.7 vii.ac pti . Silua ad claufurã. Vat 7 ualuit.xx.fot.

Ifd Goiffrid ten HILDESLEI.7 Safuualo de eo.Ordolf tenuit

in alod de rege.E.Tc 7 m ,p . x . hid . Tra.e. vi.car . In dñio funt

.ii . car.7 vii . uitti 7 xii . bord . cũ . iii.car . Ibi·. iiii . ferui.

Valuit . viii . lib.7 poft.v. lib . Modo:'vi .lib. *IN LABORNE HD.*

Ifd Goiffrid ten LAMBORNE . Efgar tenuit de rege . E . Tc

,p xxx.hid . Modo ,p.x . hid . Tra.e. xx . car . In dñio funt

iiii.car.7 xxiii . uitti 7 xii . bord cũ . x . car . Ibi . iii.ferui.

7 ii .molini de . xv . fot.7 v . ac pti . Silua de . xl . porc.

Valeb.xx . lib.7 poft 7 modo:'xii . lib. *IN EGLEI HVND.*

Ifd Goiffrid ten WATECVBE . Seuuard tenuit in alod de rege.E.

Tc 7 m fe defd ,p . ii . hid . Tra.e. iii . car . In dñio.e una car.cũ.iii.

bord.7 dim car . Valuit . xxx . folid . Modo:'xx . folid.

Ifd Gouffrid ten HERLEI . Efgar tenuit *IN BENES HD.*

de rege . E . Tc 7 m ,p . xiiii . hid . una v min . Tra . e . xviii . car.

In dñio funt . iiii.car.7 xxv . uitti 7 xii . cot . cũ . xv . car.

37   LAND OF GILBERT OF GHENT

In ROWBURY Hundred
1 Gilbert of Ghent has one manor from the King and Robert
   from him. Tonni held it before 1066. Then it answered for
   6 hides; now for 3 hides. Land for 6 ploughs. In lordship 1;
      2 villagers and 4 smallholders with 4 ploughs.
      3 slaves; woodland at 20 pigs.
   Algot holds 3 hides of this land. He has 1 plough;
      2 villagers and 6 smallholders with 2 ploughs.
   The value was £6; later 60s; now the same.

38   LAND OF GEOFFREY DE MANDEVILLE

In KINTBURY [COMPTON] Hundred
1 Geoffrey de Mandeville holds (East) ILSLEY, and Saswalo
   from him. Ordwulf held it as a manor in freehold from
   King Edward. Then and now for 1 hide. Land for 2 ploughs.
   In lordship 1 plough;
      1 villager and 7 smallholders with 1 plough.
      3 slaves; meadow, 7 acres; woodland for fencing.
   The value is and was 20s.

Geoffrey also holds

2 (West) ILSLEY and Saswalo from him. Ordwulf
   held it in freehold from King Edward. Then and now for 10 hides.
   Land for 6 ploughs. In lordship 2 ploughs;
      7 villagers and 12 smallholders with 3 ploughs. 4 slaves.
   The value was £8; later £5; now £6.

in LAMBOURN Hundred
3 EAST GARSTON. Asgar held it from King Edward. Then for 30 hides;
   now for 10 hides. Land for 20 ploughs. In lordship 4 ploughs;
      23 villagers and 12 smallholders with 10 ploughs.
      3 slaves; 2 mills at 15s; meadow, 5 acres; woodland at 40 pigs.
   The value was £20; later and now £12.

in EAGLE Hundred
4 WHATCOMBE. Siward held it in freehold from King Edward.
   Then and now it answered for 2 hides. Land for 3 ploughs.
   In lordship 1 plough, with
      3 smallholders and ½ plough.
   The value was 30s; now 20s.

in BEYNHURST Hundred
5 HURLEY. Asgar held it from King Edward. Then and now for
   14 hides less 1 virgate. Land for 18 ploughs. In lordship 4 ploughs;
      25 villagers and 12 cottagers with 15 ploughs.

Ibi.x.ſerui.7 moliñ de.xx.ſolid.Ibi æccła 7 11.piſcariæ de.xii.

ſolid.7 xx.ãc p̃ti.Silua:ʹde.v.porc̃.Val 7 ualuit.xii.liƀ.

Iſd Goiffrid teñ Estralei.Eſgaɼ *In Eletesford* HD̃.

tenuit de rege.E.Tc̃ ᵭp.xxv.hid.Modo ᵭp.x.hid.T́ra.ē.xv.

caɼ.In dñio ſunt.111.caɼ.7 xviii.uiłłi 7 x.cot́.cũ.xii.caɼ.

Ibi.vii.ſerui.7 moliñ de.xxii.ſolid.7 11.piſcariæ de.xi.ſoł.

7 xx.11.ãc p̃ti.In Oxineford.1.haga de.x.denaɼ.

T.R.E.7 poſt:ʹualuit.xx.liƀ.Modo:ʹxxiiii.liƀ.

Æcclam huj c̃ teñ Wiƀt p̃br de Goiſſrido.cũ,1.hida.

7 ibi ht̃.1.caɼ.cũ uno cot́.7 1111.ãc p̃ti.Val 7 ualuit.l.ſoł.

.XXXIX. TERRA OSBERNI GIFARD. *In Cerledone* HD̃.

OSBERN⁹ Gifard teñ de rege Herlei.Don tenuit de rege.E.

in alod.Tc̃ ᵭp.v.hid.modo ᵭp.11.hid.T́ra.ē.vii.caɼ.In dñio.ē una

caɼ 7 dim̃.7 1111.uiłłi.7 vii.bord cũ.11.caɼ 7 dim̃.Ibi uñ ſeruus.

62 b

7 11.piſcariæ de ilxviii.deñ:7 xx.ãc p̃ti.Silua de ixxx.

porc̃.Valuit.c.ſolid.7 poſt:ʹlx.ſolid.Modo:ʹ1111.liƀ.

TERRA ROBERTI FILIJ GIROLD *In Taceha* HD̃.

iXL ROTBERT⁹ fili⁹ Giroldi teñ Brintone.Briſtric te

nuit in alod de rege iE.Tc̃ ᵭp.ʹ1111.hid 7 dimid imodo

ᵭp.111.hid 7 dim.T́ra.ē.1111.caɼ.In dñio.ē una caɼ ᠆ dim.

7 v.uiłłi 7 111 ibord 7 uñ⁹ miles anglic⁹ cũ.111.caɼ.Ibi

uñ ſeruus.7 æccła:7 11.molini de.xxvi.ſoł.7 111.deñi

7 xxxv.ãc p̃ti.   Val 7 ualuit.1111.liƀ 7 x.ſoł.

Iſd Roƀt teñ Inglefol.Duo liƀi *In Cheneteberie* HD̃.

hões tenueɼ de rege.E.ᵭp.ii͡.c̃.Tc̃ 7 m̃ ᵭp.111.hid.

T́ra.ē   In dñio.ē.1 caɼ.7 vii.bord cũ.1.caɼ.Ibi

uñ⁹ ſeru⁹.7 1111.ãc p̃ti.7 parua ſilua.Valuit.xxx.ſoł.m̃:ʹxx.ſoł.

10 slaves; a mill at 20s. A church; 2 fisheries at 12s;
meadow, 20 acres; woodland at 5 pigs.
The value is and was £12.

in SLOTISFORD Hundred

6 STREATLEY. Asgar held it from King Edward. Then for 25 hides;
now for 10 hides. Land for 15 ploughs. In lordship 3 ploughs;
18 villagers and 10 cottagers with 12 ploughs.
7 slaves; a mill at 22s; 2 fisheries at 11s;
meadow, 22 acres.
In Oxford 1 site at 10d.
Value before 1066 and later £20; now £24.
Wibert the priest holds the church of this manor from Geoffrey,
with 1 hide. He has 1 plough, with
1 cottager.
Meadow, 4 acres.
The value is and was 50s.

39 LAND OF OSBERN GIFFARD

In CHARLTON Hundred

1 Osbern Giffard holds EARLEY from the King. Dunn held it from
King Edward in freehold. Then for 5 hides; now for 2 hides. Land
for 7 ploughs. In lordship 1½ ploughs;
4 villagers and 7 smallholders with 2½ ploughs.
1 slave; 2 fisheries at 68d; meadow, 20 acres;
woodland at 30 pigs.   62 b
The value was 100s; later 60s; now £4.

40 LAND OF ROBERT SON OF GERALD

In THATCHAM Hundred

1 Robert son of Gerald holds BRIMPTON. Brictric held it in
freehold from King Edward. Then for 4½ hides; now for 3½ hides.
Land for 4 ploughs. In lordship 1½ ploughs;
5 villagers, 3 smallholders and an English man-at-arms
with 3 ploughs.
1 slave; a church; 2 mills at 26s 3d; meadow, 35 acres.
The value is and was £4 10s.

In KINTBURY Hundred

2 Robert also holds INGLEWOOD. Two freemen held it from
King Edward as two manors. Then and now for 3 hides.
Land for .... In lordship 1 plough;
7 smallholders with 1 plough.
1 slave; meadow, 4 acres; a little woodland.
The value was 30s; now 20s.

.XLI. Rotbert de Olgi ten *CEDELEDORDE* . Eduuard tenuit
de rege . E . in alod ꝑ ꝺ̃ . Tc̄ 7 m̄ ſe defd ꝑ . IIII . hid . Tra . e̅ . II .
car̄ . In dñio . e̅ una car̄ . 7 II . uiłłi . 7 II . bord . cū dim̄ car̄ .
7 III . ſerui . 7 una ac̄ p̃ti . Silūa de . x . porc̄ .

Valuit , LX . ſoł . 7 poſt; xxx . ſoł . Modo; XL . ſoł;

Iſd Robt ten *LEDECVBE* . Wigot tenuit de rege . E.

Tc̄ ſe defd ꝑ . x . hid . Modo ꝑ . VII . hid . Tra . e̅ . VII . car̄ .

In dñio ſunt . II . car̄ . 7 XIIII . uiłłi 7 VIII . bord . cū . v . car̄ .

Ibi . IIII . ſerui . 7 II . molini de . III . liƀ . 7 xxxvi . ac̄ p̃ti .

T.R.E. 7 poſt . uałƀ . xv . liƀ . Modo; xvi . liƀ .

Iſd Robt ten in *SIFORD* . unā hid 7 dim̄ . de feudo ep̃i
baiocc̄ſis . Briſtei tenuit de rege . E . 7 potuit ire q̃ uoluit .

Tc̄ 7 m̄ ſe defd ꝑ una hida 7 dimid . In dñio . e̅ . I . car̄ .
7 IIII . bord 7 II . ſerui . 7 molin̄ de . VIII . ſolid . 7 una ac̄ p̃ti .

Silua ad clauſurā . Valuit . xxx . ſoł . Modo; xx . ſolid .

Iſd . R . ten *ARDINTONE* . Eduin̄ un̄ *IN WANETINZ HD.*

liƀ ho̅ tenuit . T.R.E. Tc̄ ꝑ . v . hid . modo ꝑ . II . hid 7 una v̄ .

Tra . e̅ . II . car̄ . In dñio . e̅ una . 7 III . uiłłi 7 VIII . cot . cū dim̄ car̄ .

Ibi . II . ſerui . 7 molin̄ de . XI . ſolid . 7 xxvi . ac̄ p̃ti .

Vał 7 ualuit . IIII . liƀ .

Iſd . R . ten *ARDINTONE* . Sauuin̄ un̄ liƀ ho̅ tenuit T.R.E.

Tc̄ ꝑ . IX . hid . modo ꝑ . IIII . hid . 7 III . uirg̃ . Tra . e̅ . v . car̄ .

In dñio . e̅ una . 7 vi . uiłłi 7 v . ſerui . 7 II . molini de . xxv .
ſolid . Cola anglic calūniat̄ un̄ ex his molinis . ſed Aluuin
7 Goduin̄ 7 Aluric̄ teſtificant̄ qd̄ ſep̄ jacuit in Ardintone .

Valuit . xvi . liƀ . 7 poſt; xii . liƀ . Modo; xvi . liƀ .

Iſd . R . ten unā hid . quā Azor diſpenſator . R.E. tenuit .

7 cū ea ire potuit quo uoluit . Tc̄ ꝑ una hida . m̄ ꝑ nichilo .

Tra . e̅ . II . car̄ . In dñio . e̅ una . 7 xi . cot cū dim̄ car̄ . 7 x . ac̄ p̃ti .

LAND OF ROBERT D'OILLY

In EAGLE Hundred
1 Robert d'Oilly holds CHADDLEWORTH. Edward held it from King Edward in freehold as a manor. Then and now it answered for 4 hides. Land for 2 ploughs. In lordship 1 plough;
   2 villagers and 2 smallholders with ½ plough; 3 slaves.
   Meadow, 1 acre; woodland at 10 pigs.
The value was 60s; later 30s; now 40s.

Robert also holds
2 LETCOMBE (Bassett). Wigot held it from King Edward. Then it answered for 10 hides; now for 7 hides. Land for 7 ploughs.
In lordship 2 ploughs;
   14 villagers and 8 smallholders with 5 ploughs.
   4 slaves; 2 mills at £3; meadow, 36 acres.
Value before 1066 and later £15; now £16.

3 in (Great) SHEFFORD 1½ hides from the Bishop of Bayeux's Holding. Brictheah held it from King Edward and could go where he would. Then and now it answered for 1½ hides. In lordship 1 plough;
   4 smallholders and 2 slaves.
   A mill at 8s; meadow, 1 acre; woodland for fencing.
The value was 30s; now 20s.

in WANTAGE Hundred
4 ARDINGTON. Edwin, a free man, held it before 1066.
Then for 5 hides; now for 2 hides and 1 virgate.
Land for 2 ploughs. In lordship 1;
   3 villagers and 8 cottagers with ½ plough.
   2 slaves; a mill at 11s; meadow, 26 acres.
The value is and was £4.

5 ARDINGTON. Saewin, a free man, held it before 1066.
Then for 9 hides; now for 4 hides and 3 virgates.
Land for 5 ploughs. In lordship 1;
   6 villagers and 5 slaves.
   2 mills at 25s. Cola, an Englishman, claims one of
      these mills, but Alwin, Godwin and Aelfric testify
      that it always lay in Ardington (lands).
The value was £16; later £12; now £16.

6 Robert also holds 1 hide which Azor, King Edward's Bursar, held; he could go where he would with it. Then for 1 hide; now for nothing. Land for 2 ploughs. In lordship 1;
   11 cottagers with ½ plough.
   Meadow, 10 acres.

Hanc t̃ra teñ iſɗ Azor de . Roɓto . ſ; hões de hunɗ teſti
ficant̃ eū de rege debere tenere . qm̃ rex . W . ap̃ Win
deſores ei reddidit . 7 breuē ſuū inde ei deɗ.
Roɓt̃ ū teñ injuſte . Nemo enĩ eoꝗ uidit breuē regis
uel ex parte ej hõem qui eū inde ſaiſiſſet.
Val̃ 7 ualuit . iii . liɓ . quāuis reddat . iiii . liɓ.

TERRA ROBERTI DE STATFORD *In WANETINZ HD̄.*

.XLII. Rotbert̃ de Stadford teñ de rege *DENCHESWORDE.*
7 Laurentĩ de eo . Leueua quedā liɓa femina T . R . E.
Tc̃ ᵱ . vi . hiɗ . modo ᵱ iiii . hiɗ 7 dimiɗ . Tra . ē . ii . car̃.
In dñio . ē una . 7 iiii . uiłłi 7 v . cot cū . i . car̃ . 7 xxiiii . ⋆
ãc p̃ti . Val̃ 7 ualuit . iii . liɓ.

.XLIII. TERRA RICARDI PVINGIANT. *In ELETESFORD HD̄.*

Ricarɗ pungiant teñ *LOLINDONE* . Elmærus
un hõ liɓ tenuit . T . R . E . Tc̃ ᵱ iii . hiɗ . modo ᵱ nichilo.
62 c
Tra . ē . ii . car̃ . In dñio . ē una . 7 iii . uiłłi 7 iii . cot cū . i . car̃.
7 xii . ãc p̃ti . Valuit . c . ſoliɗ . 7 poſt . xl . ſol . Modo ꞉ lx . ſol.
Qɗo Ricarɗ hoc m̃ accep̃꞉ in firma de Celſei inuenit.
Nc̃ eſt foris.
Iſɗ Ricarɗ teñ *AVINTONE* . Gunnere tenuit de rege . E.
Tc̃ ſe defɗ ᵱ . x . hiɗ . Modo ᵱ . ii . hiɗ . Tra . ē
In dñio ſunt . iii . car̃ . 7 vi . uiłłi 7 vii . borɗ . cū . iii . car̃ . Ibi
iiii . ſerui . 7 moliñ de . x . ſol . 7 xx . ãc p̃ti . Silua de . x . porc̃.
Val̃ 7 ualuit . c . ſoliɗ.

TERRA ROGERIJ DE IVERI. *In BORGELDEBERIE HD̄.*

XLII. Rogerivs de Jurei teñ de rege . i . uirg in *ELINGE.*
Sauuiñ tenuit de rege . E . in Enrede m̃ ſuo . Hic Roger̃
miſit in Hareuuelle m̃ ſuo . ubi nunꝗ jacuit ſic̃ ſcira dicit.

Azor also holds this land from Robert, but the men of the
Hundred testify that he ought to hold from the King as
King William restored it to him at Windsor and gave him
his writ for it. Robert therefore holds it wrongfully;
for none of them has seen the King's writ, or a man
who put him in possession of it on his behalf.
The value is and was £3, although it pays £4.

42   LAND OF ROBERT OF STAFFORD

In WANTAGE Hundred
1   Robert of Stafford holds (South) DENCHWORTH from the
King and Lawrence from him. Leofeva, a free woman,
(held it) before 1066. Then for 6 hides; now for 4½ hides.
Land for 2 ploughs. In lordship 1;
     4 villagers and 5 cottagers with 1 plough.
     Meadow, 24 acres.
The value is and was £3.

43   LAND OF RICHARD POYNANT

In SLOTISFORD Hundred
1   Richard Poynant holds LOLLINGDON. Aelmer, a free man,
held it before 1066. Then for 3 hides; now for nothing.
Land for 2 ploughs. In lordship 1;
     3 villagers and 3 cottagers with 1 plough.
     Meadow, 12 acres.
The value was 100s; later 40s; now 60s.
     When Richard received this manor he found it in the
revenue of Cholsey; now it is outside it.

62 c

[In KINTBURY Hundred]
2   Richard also holds AVINGTON. Gunnar held from King Edward.
Then it answered for 10 hides; now for 2 hides. Land for ...
In lordship 3 ploughs;
     6 villagers and 7 smallholders with 3 ploughs.
     4 slaves; a mill at 10s; meadow, 20 acres; woodland at 10 pigs.
The value is and was 100s.

44   LAND OF ROGER OF IVRY

In BUCKLEBURY Hundred
1   Roger of Ivry holds 1 virgate from the King in ELING.
Saewin held it from King Edward in his manor of Hendred.
This Roger placed it in his manor of Harwell, where it
never lay, as the Shire states, nor has it ever paid tax.

nec unq̃ geldaũ . Ibi funt . iiii . uilti cũ . ii . caŕ . Silua . de xxx . porc̃ . Val . xx . folid̃. *IN EGLEI HVND̃.*

Iſd Rog ten in *SIFORD* . i . hid 7 dim̃ . de feudo epĩ baioc̃. Bricſtec de rege . E . tenuit ꝑ m̃ in alod̃ . Tc̃ 7 m̃ ſe defd̃ ꝑ una hida 7 dim̃ . Tra . ē . i . caŕ . 7 ibi . ē in dñio . 7 un uilts 7 iii . bord̃ . 7 dimid̃ molin̄ de . vii . fol 7 vi . den̄ . 7 una ac̃ p̃ti . 7 parua ſilua . Valuit . xxx . folid̃ . Modo.' xx . folid̃.

Iſd Rog ten *HAROWELLE* . Vluric̃ *IN BLITBERIE HD̃.* un lib̃ hõ tenuit . T . R . E . Tc̃ ꝑ . vi . hid̃ . Modo.' ꝑ . iii . hid̃ . Tra . ē . v . caŕ . In dñio funt . ii . caŕ . 7 vii . uilti 7 vii . cot̃ cũ . ii . caŕ . Ibi . ii . ſerui . 7 capella . Valuit . xii . lib̃ . M̊ . xv . lib̃.

Iſd Rog ten *HAROWELLE* de feudo Wilti comitis. Achi un lib̃ hõ tenuit . T . R . E . Tc̃ ꝑ . v . hid̃ . m̃ ꝑ . ii . hid̃ 7 dimid̃ . Tra . ē . iiii . caŕ . In dñio . ē una . 7 v . uilti . 7 v . cot̃ cũ . i . caŕ . 7 iii . ſerui ibi . Valuit . v . lib̃ . Modo.' vi . lib̃.

Iſd Rog ten *PESEI* . Aluric un *IN GAMESFELLE HVND̃.* lib̃ hõ tenuit T . R . E . Tc̃ 7 m̃ ꝑ . vi . hid̃ . Tra . ē . v . caŕ . In dñio funt ii . 7 iiii . uilti 7 iiii . cot̃ cũ . i . caŕ . Ibi æccta 7 iiii . ſerui . 7 v . ac̃ p̃ti . Val 7 ualuit . iiii . lib̃ . De feudo epĩ baioc̃ . ē.

TERRA ROGERIJ DE LACI. *IN CHENETEBERIE HD̃.*
.XLV ROGERIVS De Laci ten de rege *TANEBVRNE* . Edmund̃ tenuit de rege . E . in alod̃ . Tc̃ ꝑ . iii . hid̃ 7 una v . m̃ ꝑ una hida . Tra . ē . ii . caŕ . Ibi funt . vi . uilti 7 viii . bord̃ . cũ . iii . caŕ . 7 xiii . ac̃ p̃ti . Silua de . i . porc̃ . Valuit . xl . fol . Modo.' l . fol.

Iſd Rog ten *CELREA* . Edmund̃ *IN WANETINZ HD̃.* un lib̃ hõ tenuit T . R . E . Tc̃ ꝑ . xiii . hid̃ . Modo ꝑ . viii . hid̃

4 villagers with 2 ploughs. •
Woodland at 30 pigs.
Value 20s.

In EAGLE Hundred
2 Roger also holds in SHEFFORD 1½ hides of the Bishop of
Bayeux's Holding. Brictheah held it from King Edward as
a manor in freehold. Then and now it answered for 1½ hides.
Land for 1 plough. It is there in lordship;
1 villager and 3 smallholders.
½ mill at 7s 6d; meadow, 1 acre; a little woodland.
The value was 30s; now 20s.

In BLEWBURY Hundred
3 Roger also holds HARWELL. Wulfric, a free man, held it
before 1066. Then for 6 hides; now for 3 hides.
Land for 5 ploughs. In lordship 2 ploughs;
7 villagers and 7 cottagers with 2 ploughs.
2 slaves; a chapel.
The value was £12; now £15.

4 Roger also holds HARWELL of Earl William's Holding.
Aki, a free man, held it before 1066. Then for 5 hides;
now for 2½ hides. Land for 4 ploughs. In lordship 1;
5 villagers and 5 cottagers with 1 plough.
3 slaves.
The value was £5; now £6.

In GANFIELD Hundred
5 Roger also holds PUSEY. Aelfric, a free man, held it before 1066.
Then and now for 6 hides. Land for 5 ploughs. In lordship 2;
4 villagers and 4 cottagers with 1 plough.
A church; 4 slaves; meadow, 5 acres.
The value is and was £4.
It is of the Bishop of Bayeux's Holding.

45   LAND OF ROGER OF LACY

In KINTBURY Hundred
1 Roger of Lacy holds ENBORNE from the King. Edmund held it
from King Edward in freehold. Then for 3 hides and 1 virgate;
now for 1 hide. Land for 2 ploughs.
6 villagers and 8 smallholders with 3 ploughs.
Meadow, 13 acres; woodland at 1 pig.
The value was 40s; now 50s.

In WANTAGE Hundred
2 Roger also holds CHILDREY. Edmund, a free man, held it.
before 1066. Then for 13 hides; now for 8½ hides.

7 dim. Tra . e̅ . v . car. In dn̅io funt . ii . car.7 x . uiłłi 7 ix . cot

cū . iii . car. Ibi . ii . ferui.7 moliñ de . l . denar.

Vał 7 ualuit femp. viii . lib 7 . x . folid.

Ifd Rog ten . ii . hid. Leuuiñ uñ lib ho̅ tenuit . T . R . E . Tc̅ ,p . ii.

hid. m̅ ,p una hida 7 dim. Ibi . iii . uiłłi . cū dim car. Vał. xxx . fot.

TERRA RADVLFI DE MORTEMER *IN TACEHAM HVND.*

XLVI RADVLF de Mortemer ten BRINTONE. Goduin tenuit

de rege. E. in alod. Tc̅ ,p . iii . hid 7 dim. Modo ,p . ii . hid 7 dim.

Tra . e̅ . iiii . car. In dn̅io . e̅ una car 7 dim.7 vi . uiłłi.7 iii . bord

cū . iii . car. Ibi æccła 7 vi . ferui.7 moliñ de . xii . folid.

7 xxx . ac̅ p̅ti. Vał 7 ualuit . lxx . folid.

Ifd Radulf ten COSERIGE.7 Balduin de eo. Duo libi ho̅es

tenueř de rege. E. ,p . ii. M̅. Modo . e̅ in uno M̅. Tc̅ ,p . vii . hid.

modo. ,p . iii . hid una v̅ miñ. Tra . e̅ . ii . car. In dn̅io . e̅ . i . car.

7 uñ uiłłs 7 iiii . bord . cū . i . car. Valuit . lx . fot. modo: l . fot.

Ifd Ra . ten STRADFELD. Duo taini tenu IN REDINGES HVND.

eř in paragio . T . R . E. Cheping 7 Eduuiñ. Tc̅ ,p vi . hid . modo

,p . iii . hid. Tra . e̅ . xxi . car. In dn̅io funt . ii . car.7 xiiii . uiłłi

7 xiii . bord.cū . viii . car. Ibi . x . ferui.7 moliñ fine cenfu.

7 . vii . ac̅ p̅ti. Silua de . xl . porc.

De hac tra ten uñ miles dim hid.7 ibi hř . i . car . eccłam

cū.iiii.bord.Valuit.xviii.lib.7 poft: x.lib.Modo.x.lib 7 x.fot.

62 d

Ifd Radulf ten BORGEFEL.7 q̅dā miles de eo . Elfi abb tenuit

de ueteri monafterio Winton æcclæ . teftimonio fcire . T . R . E.

7 poftea donec Vtlage fuit. Tc̅ 7 m̅ ,p una hida 7 dim. Tra . e̅ . vi.

car. In dn̅io . e̅ una car.7 vi.uiłłi 7 viii . bord cū . v . car. Ibi æccła

dimid
7 moliñ de.v. folid 7 x . denar.7 pifcaria de . lxviii . denar.

7 xl.iii. ac̅ p̅ti. Silua de . xv . porc. Valuit . xl . fot. Modo: l . fot.

Land for 5 ploughs. In lordship 2 ploughs;
10 villagers and 9 cottagers with 3 ploughs.
2 slaves; a mill at 50d.
The value is and always was £8 10s.

3 Roger also holds 2 hides. Leofwin, a free man, held them
before 1066. Then for 2 hides; now for 1½ hides.
3 villagers with ½ plough.
Value 30s.

46   LAND OF RALPH OF MORTIMER

In THATCHAM Hundred
1 Ralph of Mortimer holds BRIMPTON. Godwin held it from King
Edward in freehold. Then for 3½ hides; now for 2½ hides.
Land for 4 ploughs. In lordship 1½ ploughs;
6 villagers and 3 smallholders with 3 ploughs.
A church; 6 slaves; a mill at 12s; meadow, 30 acres.
The value is and was 70s.

Ralph also holds
2 CURRIDGE. Baldwin holds from him. Two free men held it
from King Edward as two manors; now it is in one manor.
Then for 7 hides; now for 3 hides less 1 virgate.
Land for 2 ploughs. In lordship 1 plough;
1 villager and 4 smallholders with 1 plough.
The value was 60s; now 50s.

in READING Hundred
3 STRATFIELD (Mortimer). Two thanes, Chipping and Edwin,
held it jointly before 1066. Then for 6 hides; now for 3 hides.
Land for 21 ploughs. In lordship 2 ploughs;
14 villagers and 13 smallholders with 8 ploughs.
10 slaves; a mill without dues; meadow, 7 acres;
woodland at 40 pigs.
A man-at-arms holds ½ hide of this land; he has 1 plough;
a church, with 4 smallholders.
The value was £18; later £10; now £10 10s.

4 BURGHFIELD. A man-at-arms holds from him. Abbot Alfsi   62 d
held it from the old monastery of Winchester church,
as the Shire witnesses, before 1066 and afterwards, until
he was an outlaw. Then and now for 1½ hides.
Land for 6 ploughs. In lordship 1 plough;
6 villagers and 8 smallholders with 5 ploughs.
A church; ½ mill at 5s 10d; a fishery at 68d;
meadow, 43 acres; woodland at 15 pigs.
The value was 40s; now 50s.

Iſd Rað ten̄ *HVRLEI*. Rachenild tenuit de rege .E. Tc̄ ſe
defð ꝑ. ii. hið. Modo ꝑ una hida. Tra. ē. ii. car̄. Nil. ē in dn̄io.
ſed. ii. uiłłi 7 iii. borð hn̄t. ii. car̄. Ibi ſilua de. xv. porc̄. Vł. xl. ſoł.
Iſd Rað ten̄ *PRAXEMERE*. 7 Oidelarð *IN ROEBERG HD̄.*
de co. Duo taini tenuer̄. T.R.E. 7 ii. hallæ fuer̄ ibi. 7 q̊ uoluer̄
ire potuer̄. Tc̄ ſe defð ꝑ. viii. hið. m̄ ꝑ. iii. hið. Tra. ē. vi. car̄.
In dn̄io ſunt. ii. car̄. 7 iiii. uiłłi 7 xi. borð cū. iii. car̄. Silua
de. vi. porc̄. Valuit. vi. liƀ. 7 poſt. lx. ſoł. Modo: c. ſolið.
Iſd Rað ten̄ Hodicote. 7 Oidelarð *IN NACHEDEDORNE HD̄.*
de eo. Aluuin̄ tenuit de rege. E. Tc̄ 7 m̄ ꝑ. v. hið. Tra. ē
In dn̄io ſunt. ii. car̄. 7 v. borð cū dimið car̄. Valuit. vii. liƀ.
⎰ Modo: iiii. liƀ.

TERRA RADVLFI DE TODENI. *IN WANETINZ HD̄.*
.XLVII Radvlf̄ de Todeni ten̄ de rege *CERLETONE*. 7 Drogo de eo.
Tres liƀi hões tenuer̄ T.R.E. Tc̄ 7 m̄ ꝑ. vii. hið. Tra. ē. vii. car̄.
In dn̄io. ē una car̄. 7 iiii. uiłłi 7 xiii. cot cū. i. car̄. Ibi dimið
molin̄ de. v. ſolið. 7 xxi. ac̄ p̄ti. Valuit. c. ſolið. Modo: vi. liƀ.
H̄ tra. ē de feudo Rog comitis.

TERRA RADVLFI FILIJ COMITIS. *IN LAMBORN HD̄*
.XLVI Radvlfvs fili comitis ten̄ *BOCHENTONE*. Tres liƀi hões
tenuer̄ de rege. E ꝑ. iii. ꟲ in aloð. Tc̄ ꝑ. viii. hið. Modo ꝑ. iii.
hið una v min̄. Tra. ē. iiii. car̄. In dn̄io ſunt. ii. car̄. 7 xi.
borð cū dim car̄. 7 un̄ ſeruus. 7 molin̄ de. v. ſolið. 7 v. ac̄ p̄ti.
Silua de. x. porc̄. De iſto ꟲ ten̄ Odo. i. hið. 7 ibi hr̄. i. car̄.
cū uno borð. Valuit. vii. liƀ. 7 poſt: vi. liƀ. Modo. vii. liƀ.

5 HARTLEY. Ragenhild held it from King Edward. Then it
answered for 2 hides; now for 1 hide. Land for 2 ploughs.
Nothing in lordship but
    2 villagers and 3 smallholders have 2 ploughs.
    Woodland at 15 pigs.
Value 40s.

in ROWBURY Hundred
6 PEASEMORE. Odelard holds from him. Two thanes held it before 1066;
they could go where they would; there were 2 Halls. Then it
answered for 8 hides; now for 3 hides. Land for 6 ploughs.
In lordship 2 ploughs;
    4 villagers and 11 smallholders with 3 ploughs.
    Woodland at 6 pigs.
The value was £6; later 60s; now 100s.

in COMPTON Hundred
7 HODCOTT. Odelard holds from him. Alwin held it from
King Edward. Then and now for 5 hides. Land for ...
In lordship 2 ploughs;
    5 smallholders with ½ plough.
The value was £7; now £4.

47   LAND OF RALPH OF TOSNY

In WANTAGE Hundred
1 Ralph of Tosny holds CHARLTON from the King and Drogo
from him. Three free men held it before 1066. Then and now
for 7 hides. Land for 7 ploughs. In lordship 1 plough;
    4 villagers and 13 cottagers with 1 plough.
    ½ mill at 5s; meadow, 21 acres.
The value was 100s; now £6.
This land is of Earl Roger's Holding.

48   LAND OF RALPH SON OF THE EARL

In LAMBOURN Hundred
1 Ralph, son of the Earl, holds BOCKHAMPTON. Three free men
held it from King Edward as 3 manors in freehold.
Then for 8 hides; now for 3 hides less 1 virgate.
Land for 4 ploughs. In lordship 2 ploughs;
    11 smallholders with ½ plough; 1 slave;
    a mill at 5s; meadow, 5 acres; woodland at 10 pigs.
Odo holds 1 hide of this manor; he has 1 plough with
    1 smallholder.
The value was £7; later £6; now £7.

TERRA RADVLFI FILIJ SEIFRIDE *IN RIPLESMERE HD̄.*

.XLIX R̄ADVLF filī Seifrid ten̄ de rege *CLIVORE*. Herald com̄ tenuit.

T̄c̄ ſe defđ ꝑ. v. hiđ. modo ꝑ. IIII.. hiđ 7 dimiđ. 7 caſtellū de Windeſores. ē in dimiđ hida. T̄ra. ē. In dn̄io. ē una car̄.

7 dimiđ. 7 IX. uiłłi 7 VI. borđ cū. IIII. car̄. 7 molin̄ de. X. ſoliđ.

7 XX. ãc p̃ti. Silua de. X. porc̄. De hac tra ten̄ gener ej Rađ dimiđ hiđ. 7 nichil ē ibi. Valuit. VII. liƀ. Modo. IIII. liƀ 7 X. ſoł.

R̄og filī Seifrid ten̄ de rege *FOLLESCOTE.* *IN BLITBERIE HD̄.*

Lodric q̇dā liƀ hō tenuit T.R.E. T̄c̄ ꝑ. III. hiđ ſe defđ ꝑ. I. hiđ m̄ ſimilit. T̄ra. ē. II. car̄. In dn̄io. ē una. 7 IIII. uiłłi 7 V. cot cū. I. ☞ car̄. 7 XXX. ãc p̃ti. Valuit. XL. ſoł. modo. IIII. liƀ.

TERRA ERNVLFI DE HESDING. *IN TACEHĀ HVND̄.*

.L. H̄ERNVLF de Heſding ten̄ de rege *VLVRITONE*. Vluuard tenuit de rege. E. in alođ. T̄c̄ ſe defđ ꝑ. X. hiđ. m̄ ꝑ. II. hiđ.

7 dim. T̄ra. ē XII. car̄. In dn̄io. ē una car̄. 7 XI. uiłłi 7 XI. borđ cū. VII. car̄. Ibi. II. molini de. L. ſoliđ. 7 XXVII. ãc p̃ti. Silua de. XXV. porc̄. 7 .LI. haga de. XX. ſoliđ 7 VII. denar̄.

T.R.E. ualuit. IX. liƀ. 7 poſt. VIII. liƀ. Modo. XXIIII. liƀ.

TERRA HVGON FILIJ BALDRICI. *IN TACEHĀ HVND̄.*

.LI. H̄VGO filī Baldrici ten̄ de rege *ESSAGES*. Aluric tenuit de rege. E. in alođ. T̄c̄ ꝑ. V. hiđ. modo ꝑ. II. hiđ 7 dimiđ.

T̄ra. ē. V. car̄. In dn̄io. ē dimiđ car̄. 7 IIII. uiłłi 7 XII. borđ cū IIII. car̄. ibi. III. ſerui. 7 molin̄ de. XX. ſoliđ. 7 V. ãc p̃ti. Silua de. L. porc̄. Val 7 ualuit. VI. liƀ.

.LII. TERRA HVGONIS DE PORTH. *IN EGLEI HVND̄.*

H̄VGO de port ten̄ *SIFORD*. de rege. Vlueua tenuit in alođ de rege. E. T̄c̄ ꝑ. XX. hiđ. Modo ꝑ. VII. hiđ 7 II. acris.

49   LAND OF RALPH SON OF SIEGFRIED

In RIPPLESMERE Hundred

1   Ralph son of Siegfried holds CLEWER from the King. Earl Harold
held it. Then it answered for 5 hides; now for 4½ hides;
Windsor Castle is in the ½ hide. Land for ...
In lordship 1½ ploughs;
    9 villagers and 6 smallholders with 4 ploughs.
    A mill at 10s; meadow, 20 acres; woodland at 10 pigs.
    Ralph, his son-in-law, holds ½ hide of this land; nothing there.
The value was £7; now £4 10s.

In BLEWBURY Hundred

2   Roger son of Siegfried holds FULSCOT from the King. Lodric,
a free man, held it before 1066. Then for 3 hides; it answered
for 1 hide, now the same. Land for 2 ploughs. In lordship 1.
    4 villagers and 5 cottagers with 1 plough.
    Meadow, 30 acres.
The value was 40s; now £4.

†   *(3 is placed after 52,1, at the foot of col. 62 d)*

50   LAND OF ARNULF OF HESDIN

In THATCHAM Hundred

1   Arnulf of Hesdin holds NEWBURY from the King. Wulfward (White)
held it from King Edward in freehold. Then it answered for
10 hides, now for 2½ hides. Land for 12 ploughs. In lordship 1 plough;
    11 villagers and 11 smallholders with 7 ploughs.
    2 mills at 50s; meadow, 27 acres; woodland at 25 pigs;
      51 sites at 20s 7d.
Value before 1066 £9; later £8; now £24.

51   LAND OF HUGH SON OF BALDRIC

In THATCHAM Hundred

1   Hugh son of Baldric holds SHAW from the King. Aelfric held it
from King Edward in freehold. Then for 5 hides; now
for 2½ hides. Land for 5 ploughs. In lordship ½ plough;
    4 villagers and 12 smallholders with 4 ploughs.
    3 slaves; a mill at 20s; meadow, 5 acres; woodland at 50 pigs.
The value is and was £6.

52   LAND OF HUGH OF PORT

In EAGLE Hundred

1   Hugh of Port holds (Great) SHEFFORD from the King. Wulfeva
held it in freehold from King Edward. Then for 20 hides;
now for 7 hides and 2 acres.

IN REDINGES HD̅.Ifd Rog̃ ten̅ *PORLEI*.Brifteuuard tenuit de rege.E.

Tc̅ fe defd̅ ꝑ.IIII.hid̅ 7 dimid̅.Modo ꝑ.IIII.hid̅.

Tra.ē.IIII.car̃.In dn̅io funt.II.

7 IX.uiłłi 7 III.bord̅ cũ.III.car̃.7 XVI.ac̅ p̃ti.

Valuit.c.foł.7 p̃.IIII.lib̅.M̃.c.foł.

63 a

Tra.ē.x.car̃ .In dn̅io funt.III.car̃.7 xv.uiłłi 7 VIII.bord̅

cũ.VI.car̃.Ibi.VI.ferui.7 VI.ac̅ p̃ti.Silua de.xxx.porc̃.

Ibi moliñ de.x.folid̅.Valuit.VI.lib̅.Modo.xII.lib̅.

TERRA HVNFRIDI CAMERARIJ. *IN TACEHĀ HVND̃.*

.LIII **H**VNFRID̃ camerarius ten̅ de rege *BAGENORE*.

Vlueua tenuit in alod̅ de rege.E.Tc̅ fe defd̅ ꝑ III.hid̅

Modo ꝑ una hida.Tra.ē.III.car̃.In dn̅io.ē una.7 III.uiłłi

7 III.bord̅ cũ.II.car̃.Ibi un̅ feruus.7 moliñ de xx.folid̅.

7 xx.II.ac̅ p̃ti.Silua de.IIII.porc̃.Vał 7 ualuit.IIII.lib̅.

TERRA HVNFRIDI VIS DE LEW. *IN TACEHĀ HD̅.*

.LIIII **H**VNFRID̃ Vis de Leuu.ten̅ de rege *SPONE*.Carlo

tenuit de rege.E.in alod̅.Tc̅ ꝑ.x.hid̅.modo ꝑ.v.hid̅.

Tra.ē.IX.car̃.In dn̅io funt.III.car̃.7 IX.uiłłi 7 x.bord̅.

cũ.VI.car̃.Ibi æccła 7 VII.ferui.7 moliñ de.xxII.folid̅.

7 LX.ac̅ p̃ti.Silua de.III.porc̃.Valuit.VIII.lib̅.Modo.x.lib̅.

Æcclæ p̃tiñ dim̅ hida de ipfa tra. *IN CHENETEBERIE HD̅.*

Ifd Hunfrid ten̅ *BOCHESORNE*.Tres fr̃s tenuer̃ de rege.E.in

alod̅.Tc̅ ꝑ.IX.hid̅ fe defd̅.modo ꝑ.IIII.hid̅.Tra.ē.II.car̃.

In dn̅io.ē una.7 un̅ uiłłs 7 VI.bord̅ cũ.I.car̃.Ibi un̅ feru.7 moliñ

de.xxVII.foł.7 VI.den̅.7 VI.ac̅ p̃ti.

De ifto c̃ ten̅ Aluric.I.hid̅.7 Almær.II.hid̅.7 ibi.ē.I.car̃ in dn̅io.

Tot T.R.E.ualuit.VIII.lib̅.Modo.VI.lib̅ 7 x.foł.

† *(Directed to its proper place by transposition signs)*

49) In READING Hundred
3   Roger also holds PURLEY. Brictward held it from King Edward.
Then it answered for 4½ hides; now for 4 hides.
Land for 4 ploughs. In lordship 2;
  9 villagers and 3 smallholders with 3 ploughs.
  Meadow, 16 acres.
The value was 100s; later £4; now 100s.

(52,1 *continued*)
Land for 10 ploughs. In lordship 3 ploughs;   63 a
  15 villagers and 8 smallholders with 6 ploughs.
  6 slaves; meadow, 6 acres; woodland at 30 pigs; a mill at 10s.
The value was £6; now £12.

53   LAND OF HUMPHREY THE CHAMBERLAIN

In THATCHAM Hundred
1   Humphrey the Chamberlain holds BAGNOR from the King. Wulfeva
held it in freehold from King Edward. Then it answered for 3
hides; now for 1 hide. Land for 3 ploughs. In lordship 1;
  3 villagers and 3 smallholders with 2 ploughs.
  1 slave; a mill at 20s; meadow, 22 acres; woodland at 4 pigs.
The value is and was £4.

54   LAND OF HUMPHREY VISDELOUP

In THATCHAM Hundred
1   Humphrey Visdeloup holds SPEEN from the King. Karl held it
from King Edward in freehold. Then for 10 hides; now for 5
hides. Land for 9 ploughs. In lordship 3 ploughs;
  9 villagers and 10 smallholders with 6 ploughs.
  A church; 7 slaves; a mill at 22s; meadow, 60 acres;
    woodland at 3 pigs.
The value was £8; now £10.
½ hide of this land belongs to the church.

In KINTBURY Hundred
2   Humphrey also holds BOXFORD. Three brothers held it from
King Edward in freehold. Then it answered for 9 hides;
now for 4 hides. Land for 2 ploughs. In lordship 1;
  1 villager and 6 smallholders with 1 plough.
  1 slave; a mill at 27s 6d; meadow, 6 acres.
Of this manor Aelfric holds 1 hide; Aelmer 2 hides.
In lordship 1 plough.
Value of the whole before 1066 and later £8; now £6 10s.

Iſd Hunfrid ten *BENHA̅*. Tres taini tenuer̄ in aloď de rege . E.

Tc̄ ℈ p . v . hiď . m̊ ℈ p . iiii . hiď . Tra . e̅ . iii . car̄ . In dn̄io . e̅ una . 7 vi . uiłłi

7 viii . borď . cū . v . car̄ . Ibi . ii . ſerui . 7 cxx . ac̅ p̊ti.

De iſto ☧ ten Anſchitil . ii . hiď . 7 Wiłłs . ii . hiď . 7 ibi ſunt . ii . car̄.

Tot̄ T.R.E . 7 poſt 7 m̊ . ual̄ . vi . liḃ.   *IN BLITBERIE HD̄.*

Iſd Hunf ten *MORTVNE* . Oſmund un̄ liḃ hō tenuit T . R . E.

Tc̄ ℈ p . v . hiď . m̊ ℈ p . ii . hiď 7 dim̄ . Tra . e̅ . iii . car̄ . In dn̄io ſunt . ii.

7 iiii . uiłłi 7 iiii . cot cū . i . car̄ . Ibi æcc̄la 7 vi . ſerui . 7 xl . ac̅ p̊ti.

Val̄ 7 ualuit . vi . liḃ.

TERRA TVRTINI FILIJ ROLF.   *IN WIFOL HD̄*

.LV. Tvrstin̄ fili Rolf ten̄ de rege *COLESELLE* . Brictric tenuit in

aloď de rege . E . Tc̄ ſe deſď ℈ p . viii . hiď . modo ℈ p . v . hiď . Tra . e̅ . iii . car̄.

In dn̄io ſunt . ii . car̄ . 7 vii . borď 7 v . ſerui . cū dimiď car̄ . Iḥi

tcia pars molini de . x . ſol̄ . 7 lxix . ac̅ p̊ti.

Valuit . vii . liḃ . 7 poſt . xl . ſol̄ . Modo . c . ſoliď . *IN BLITBERIE HD̄.*

Iſd Turſt ten *OPTONE* . Brictric un̄ liḃ hō tenuit . Tc̄ ℈ p x . hiď.

modo ℈ p . v . hiď . Tra . e̅ . ix . car̄ . In dn̄io ſunt . ii . 7 xvi . uiłłi . 7 vii.

cot cū . vi . car̄ . Ibi . vii . ſerui . 7 xxx . ac̅ p̊ti . Val̄ 7 ualuit . xiii . liḃ.

Iſd Turſtin ten *CELREA* . 7 Roger de eo . *IN ELETESFORD HD̄.*

Brictric un̄ liḃ hō tenuit . T . R . E . Tc̄ ℈ p . x . hiď . modo ℈ p . viii . hiď.

Tra . e̅ . iiii . car̄ . In dn̄io . e̅ una . 7 v . uiłłi 7 vi . cot cū . i . car̄ . Ibi . iii.

ſerui . 7 molin̄ de . ii . ſoliď . 7 æcc̄la . De iſto ☧ ten alt̄ Roger . vi . hiď.

7 una v . 7 ibi . i . car̄ in dn̄io . 7 vi . uiłłi 7 ii . cot cū . i . car̄ . 7 ii . ſerui.

T . R . E . ual̄ḃ . x . liḃ . 7 poſt . viii . liḃ . Modo . ix . liḃ . 7 v . ſoliď.

3 Humphrey also holds BENHAM. Three thanes held it in
freehold from King Edward. Then for 5 hides; now for 4 hides.
Land for 3 ploughs. In lordship 1;
   6 villagers and 8 smallholders with 5 ploughs.
   2 slaves; meadow, 120 acres.
Of this manor Ansketel holds 2 hides; William 2 hides.
   2 ploughs there.
Value of the whole before 1066, later and now £6.

In BLEWBURY Hundred
4 Humphrey also holds (South)MORETON. Osmund, a free man,
held it before 1066. Then for 5 hides; now for 2½ hides.
Land for 3 ploughs. In lordship 2;
   4 villagers and 4 cottagers with 1 plough.
   A church; 6 slaves; meadow, 40 acres.
The value is and was £6.

55   LAND OF THURSTAN SON OF ROLF

In WYFOLD Hundred
1 Thurstan son of Rolf holds COLESHILL from the King. Brictric
held it in freehold from King Edward. Then it answered
for 8 hides; now for 5 hides. Land for 3 ploughs.
In lordship 2 ploughs;
   7 smallholders and 5 slaves with ½ plough.
   The third part of a mill at 10s; meadow, 69 acres.
The value was £7; later 40s; now 100s.

In BLEWBURY Hundred
2 Thurstan also holds UPTON. Brictric, a free man, held it.
Then for 10 hides, now for 5 hides. Land for 9 ploughs.
In lordship 2;
   16 villagers and 7 cottagers with 6 ploughs.
   7 slaves; meadow, 30 acres.
The value is and was £13.

In SLOTISFORD [WANTAGE] Hundred
3 Thurstan also holds CHILDREY, and Roger from him. Brictric,
a free man, held it before 1066. Then for 10 hides; now for
8 hides. Land for 4 ploughs. In lordship 1;
   5 villagers and 6 cottagers with 1 plough.
   3 slaves; a mill at 2s; a church.
Another Roger holds 6 hides and 1 virgate of this manor.
1 plough in lordship;
   6 villagers and 2 cottagers with 1 plough; 2 slaves.
Value before 1066 £10; later £8; now £9 5s.

Iſd Turſt ten SPERSOLT.7 Roger de eo.Brictric un lib ho tenuit
T.R.E.Tc 7 m̃ ℈.11.hid 7 dim|Tra.e.1.car.7 ibi.e in dnio.7 11.ſerui.
7 xvi.ac p̃ti.Valuit.xxx.ſolid.7 poſt:′xx.ſol.Modo:′xxx.ſol.

TERRA ALBERTI.　　　　IN RIPLESMERE HD.

.LVI ALBERTVS ten de rege DIDEORDE.Hugo camerari tenuit
de rege.E.Tc 7 m̃ ſe defd ℈ una hida.　　In dnio.e.1.car.7 1111.
uilli 7 1.bord.cũ.11.car.7 xx.ac p̃ti.Silua de.v.porc.
Valuit.1111.lib.7 poſt 7 modo:′xxx.ſolid.

TERRA AIVLFI VICECOMITIS.　　IN EGLEI HD.

.LVII AIVLFVS ten de rege SIFORD.Brictric tenuit in alod de rege.E.
Tc ſe defd ℈.x.hid.modo ℈.v.hid.Tra.e.v.car.In dnio ſunt
.11.car.7 viii.uilli 7 v.bord.cũ.111.car.Ibi.v.ſerui.7 11.molini
de.xxii.ſolid.7 vi.den.7 viii.ac p̃ti.Silua de.x.porc.
Valuit.x.lib.7 poſt:′ix.lib.Modo:′x.lib.

63 b
TERRA HVGONIS STIRMAN.　IN CHENETEBERIE HD.

LVII HVGOLIN ten de rege HAMESTEDE.Eduuard tenuit ℈ co
de rege.E.in alod.Tc ſe defd ℈.1111.hid.Modo ℈.1.hida.
Tra.e.v.car.In dnio ſunt.11.7 1111.uilli 7 viii.bord cũ.111.car.
Ibi.x.ſerui.7 molin de.xx.ſolid.7 vi.ac p̃ti.Silua.de.x.porc.
Val 7 ualuit.1111.lib.

Iſd Hugolin tenuit hacten EBRIGE.Herleng tenuit T.R.E.℈ co
Tc 7 m̃ ℈ una hid.Tra.e.11.car.In dnio nichil.e.ſed.1111.uilli
7 1111.bord hñt.111.car.Ibi.111.ſerui.7 molin de.xxx.ſolid.7 111.
ac p̃ti.Silua ad clauſurā.Valuit.1111.lib.modo:′111.lib.

4 Thurstan also holds SPARSHOLT, and Roger from him. Brictric,
a free man, held it before 1066. Then and now for 2½ hides
and a virgate. Land for 1 plough. It is there in lordship;
2 slaves.
Meadow, 16 acres.
The value was 30s; later 20s; now 30s.

56   LAND OF ALBERT

In RIPPLESMERE Hundred
1 Albert holds DEDWORTH from the King. Hugh the Chamberlain
held it from King Edward. Then and now it answered for 1 hide.
In lordship 1 plough;
4 villagers and 1 smallholder with 2 ploughs.
Meadow, 20 acres; woodland at 5 pigs.
The value was £4; later and now 30s.

57   LAND OF AIULF THE SHERIFF

In EAGLE Hundred
1 Aiulf holds (East) SHEFFORD from the King. Brictric held it
in freehold from King Edward. Then it answered for 10 hides;
now for 5 hides. Land for 5 ploughs. In lordship 2 ploughs;
8 villagers and 5 smallholders with 3 ploughs.
5 slaves; 2 mills at 22s 6d; meadow, 8 acres;
woodland at 10 pigs.
The value was £10; later £9; now £10.

58   LAND OF HUGOLIN THE STEERSMAN   63 b

In KINTBURY Hundred
1 Hugolin the Steersman holds HAMSTEAD (Marshall) from the King.
Edward held it as a manor from King Edward in freehold. Then it
answered for 4 hides; now for 1 hide. Land for 5 ploughs.
In lordship 2;
4 villagers and 8 smallholders with 3 ploughs.
10 slaves; a mill at 20s; meadow, 6 acres;
woodland at 10 pigs.
The value is and was £4.
2 Hugolin also held IRISH HILL hitherto. Herling held it before
1066 as a manor. Then and now for 1 hide. Land for 2 ploughs.
In lordship nothing, but
4 villagers and 4 smallholders have 3 ploughs.
3 slaves; a mill at 30s; meadow, 3 acres;
woodland for fencing.
The value was £4; now £3.

De hoc ꝏ̄ teſtat̄ ſcira qd n̄ ꝑtinuit ad anteceſſorē Hugonis.

ꝑ quē reclamat. hōēs aut̄ ej⁹ noluer̄ inde reddc̄ rationē.

Ipſe q̇q̇ tranſportauit hallā 7 alias domos 7 pecuniā in alio ꝏ̄.

Iſd Hugoł ten unā v̄ in BORGELDEBERIE .7 nunq̄ geldau.

In Hameſteda jacet 7 jacuit . Vał . x . ſolid.

TERRA MATHIV DE MORETANIA *In Lamborne* HD̄.

.LIX MACI de moretania ten̄ de rege LAMBORNE . Vluuard

tenuit de rege . E . in alod ꝑ ꝏ̄ . Tc̄ 7 m̄ ſe defd ꝑ . IIII . hid.

Tra . ē . II . car̄ . In dn̄io dim̄ car̄.7 II . uiłłi 7 VIII . bord cū . I . car̄.

Valuit . LX . ſoł.7 poſt.̓ xxx . ſoł . Modo.̓ L . ſolid.

TERRA BERNARDI AÇCIPITRARIJ. *In Taceha hvnd*.

.LX BERNARD⁹ Accipitrari⁹ ten̄ de rege WALSINCE . Aluuin⁹ tenuit

de rege . E . in alod . Tc̄ ſe defd ꝑ una hida . m̄ ꝑ dimid . Tra . ē

IIII . car̄ . In dn̄io ſunt . II.7 v . uiłłi 7 I . bord . cū . II . car̄.7 un ſeru⁹.

7 molin̄ de . xvi . ſolid.   Vał 7 ualuit . III . lib.

TERRA RAINBALDI DE CIRECESTRE *In Blitberie* HD̄.

.LXI REIMBALD⁹ de Cireceſtre ten̄ de rege HACHEBORNE . Ipſe

tenuit de rege . E . Ibi . xv . hid . ſed tc̄ 7 m̄ ſe defd ꝑ XII . hid

una v̄ min⁹ . Tra . ē . XII . car̄ . In dn̄io ſunt . II . car̄.7 XVIII . uiłłi.

7˙XVI . cot̄ . cū . x . car̄ . Ibi . VI . ſerui.7 molin̄ de . XII . ſoł.7 VI . den̄.

7 xxx . ac̄ ꝑti . Valuit . xv . lib . Modo.̓ XVIII . lib.

Iſd Reinbald ten̄ ESTONE . Eileua q̄dā libera femina

tenuit T.R.E. Tc̄ . x . hidæ ibi . ſed ꝑ . VI . hid 7 dimid ſe defd

tc̄ 7 m̄ . Tra . ē . VII . car̄ . In dn̄io ſunt . II . car̄.7 x . uiłłi 7 XII.

cot̄ cū . v . car̄ . Ibi . III . ſerui.7 XLI . ac̄ ꝑti . Valuit . x . lib . M̊.̓ XII . lib.

Of this manor the Shire testifies that it did not belong to
Hugolin's predecessor through whom he claims it; but his men
did not wish to give an account thereof. He also transferred the
Hall and the other houses and stock to another manor.

3 Hugolin also holds 1 virgate in BUCKLEBURY. It has never paid
tax. It lies and lay in (the lands of) Hamstead (Marshall).
Value 10s.

59   LAND OF MATTHEW OF MORTAGNE

In LAMBOURN Hundred

1 Matthew of Mortagne holds LAMBOURN from the King. Wulfward
held it from King Edward in freehold as a manor. Then and
now it answered for 4 hides. Land for 2 ploughs.
In lordship ½ plough;
2 villagers and 8 smallholders with 1 plough.
The value was 60s; later 30s; now 50s.

60   LAND OF BERNARD THE FALCONER

In THATCHAM Hundred

1 Bernard the Falconer holds WASING from the King. Alwin
held it from King Edward in freehold. Then it answered
for 1 hide; now for ½. Land for 4 ploughs. In lordship 2;
5 villagers and 1 smallholder with 2 ploughs; 1 slave.
A mill at 16s.
The value is and was £3.

61   LAND OF REINBALD OF CIRENCESTER

In BLEWBURY Hundred

1 Reinbald of Cirencester holds (East) HAGBOURNE from the King.
He held it himself from King Edward. 15 hides; but then and
now it answered for 12 hides less 1 virgate.
Land for 12 ploughs. In lordship 2 ploughs;
18 villagers and 16 cottagers with 10 ploughs.
6 slaves; a mill at 12s 6d; meadow, 30 acres.
The value was £15; now £18.

2 Reinbald also holds ASTON (Upthorpe). Aelfeva, a free woman,
held it before 1066. Then 10 hides; but it answered for 6½ hides
then and now. Land for 7 ploughs. In lordship 2 ploughs;
10 villagers and 12 cottagers with 5 ploughs.
3 slaves; meadow, 41 acres.
The value was £10; now £12.

TERRA GRIMBALDI   IN WANETINZ HD̄.

.LX̄ GRIMBALD ten de rege HENRET . Achi un lib̄ hō tenuit

T.R.E.Tc̄ ꝑ.v.hid . Modo ꝑ una hida.Tra.e̅.II.car̄.In dn̄io

e̅ una.7 II.uilti 7 v.cot cū.I.car̄.7 moliñ de.x.folid.7 xv.ac̄

p̄ti Valuit.IIII.lib̄.7 poſt.′xxx.ſot.Modo.′IIII.lib̄.

TERRA TEODRICI AVRIFABRI. IN NACHEDEDORN HD̄.

.LXĪI THEODRIC Aurifab̄ ten de rege ELLEORDE . Eduuard tenuit

de rege.E.in alod.Tc̄ ꝑ.v.hid.Modo ꝑ.II.hid.Tra.e̅.v.car̄.

In dn̄io ſunt.II.car̄.7 vI.uilti 7 IIII.bord.cū.III.car̄.Ibi.IIII.

ſerui.Silua de x.porc̄.Valuit 7 uat.c.ſolid.

Iſd Theod ten HANSTEDE .Lanc tenuit IN BORGELDEBERIE HD̄.

de rege.E.Tc̄ ꝑ.xvII.hid.Modo ꝑ.vI.hid.Tra.e̅.xII.car̄.

In dn̄io ſunt.II.car̄.7 xIII.uilti 7 IX.bord cū.vIII.car̄.

Ibi.vIII.ſerui.7 IIII.ac̄ p̄ti.Silua de.xL.porc̄.De hac

tra ten p̄br æcctæ in elemoſina dim̄ hid.7 nichil ibi hr̄.

Valuit.xII.lib̄.7 poſt.′Ix.lib̄.Modo.′x.lib̄. IN REDINGES

Iſd Theod ten SOLEHA .Eduuard tenuit de rege.E. ꜰ HVND.

Tc̄ ꝑ una hida.m̄ ꝑ dim̄.Tra.e̅.II.car̄.In dn̄io.e̅ una car̄.

cū.v.bord.7 II.ſerui.7 II.ac̄ p̄ti.Vat 7 ualuit.xxx.ſot.

Iſd Theod ten in PORLAA dimid hid.Eduuard tenuit

7 ꝑ tanto ſe defd tc̄ 7 m̄.Tra.e̅.II.car̄.In dn̄io.e̅ una.

7 un uilts 7 III.bord cū.I.car̄.7 v.ac̄ p̄ti.Valuit.xL.ſot.M̊.L.

62   LAND OF GRIMBALD

In WANTAGE Hundred
1 Grimbald holds (West) HENDRED from the King. Aki, a free
   man, held it before 1066. Then for 5 hides; now for 1 hide.
   Land for 2 ploughs. In lordship 1;
       2 villagers and 5 cottagers with 1 plough.
       A mill at 10s; meadow, 15 acres.
   The value was £4; later 30s; now £4.

63   LAND OF THEODORIC THE GOLDSMITH

In COMPTON Hundred
1 Theodoric the Goldsmith holds ALDWORTH from the King.
   Edward held it from King Edward in freehold. Then
   for 5 hides; now for 2 hides. Land for 5 ploughs.
   In lordship 2 ploughs;
       6 villagers and 4 smallholders with 3 ploughs.
       4 slaves; woodland at 10 pigs.
   The value was and is 100s.

Theodoric also holds
in BUCKLEBURY Hundred
2 HAMPSTEAD (Norris). Lank held it from King Edward. Then
   for 17 hides; now for 6 hides. Land for 12 ploughs.
   In lordship 2 ploughs;
       13 villagers and 9 smallholders with 8 ploughs.
       8 slaves; meadow, 4 acres; woodland at 40 pigs.
       The priest of the church holds ½ hide in alms from
           this land; he has nothing there.
   The value was £12; later £9; now £10.

in READING Hundred
3 SULHAM. Edward held it from King Edward. Then for 1 hide;
   now for ½. Land for 2 ploughs. In lordship 1 plough with
       5 smallholders and 2 slaves.
       Meadow, 2 acres.
   The value is and was 30s.

4 in PURLEY ½ hide. Edward held it and it answered for as
   much then and now. Land for 2 ploughs. In lordship 1;
       1 villager and 3 smallholders with 1 plough.
       Meadow, 5 acres.
   The value was 40s; now 50[s].

Iſd Theod teñ *WITELEI*. Eduuard tenuit de rege. E.

Tc ſe deſd .p. III. hid. M .p una hida. Tra. e̅. III. car̅. In dn̅io

e̅ una car̅. 7 II. uilti 7 II. bord. cu̅. I. car̅. Ibi. IIII. ſerui.

7 XII. ac̅ p̅ti. 7 piſcaria de. XL. denar̅. Val 7 ualuit. XL. ſol.

TERRA STEFANI FILIJ EIRARDI. *IN REDINGES HD.*

.LXIIII. STEFAN fil̅ Eirardi teñ de rege *PETEORDE*. Tres taini

tenuer̅ in paragio. 7 potuer̅ ire cu̅ terris ſuis quo uoluer̅.

Ibi. VII. hidæ 7 dim. ſed tc̅ 7 m̅ geld .p. v. hid 7 dimid.

Tra. e̅. v. car̅. In dn̅io. e̅ una. 7 III. uilti 7 II. bord cu̅. I. car̅.

Ibi. II. molini 7 dimid de. XXXVII. ſol 7 VI. denar̅. 7 XLVIII.

ac̅ p̅ti. Ex his hid teñ Nigell̅. I. hid. 7 qda̅ miles dim hid.

Ibi in dn̅io. I. car̅. 7 IIII. uilti 7 III. bord cu̅. II. car̅ 7 dim.

Tot T.R.E. ualb. c. ſol. 7 poſt. IIII. lib. Modo: IIII. lib 7 x. ſol.

Iſd Stefan teñ. I. hid in *SOLAFEL*. 7 Aluric de eo. Tres

alodiarij tenuer̅. T.R.E. 7 potuer̅ ire quolibet. Tc̅ 7 m̅

ſe deſd .p una hida. Tra. e̅. II. car̅. Ibi ſunt. v. alodiarij

cu̅. II. car̅. 7 bord uno.   Valuit 7 ualet. XX. ſolid.

TERRA ODONIS & ALIO� TAINO�. *IN GAMESFEL HD.*

.LXV. ODO De Winceſtre teñ de rege *HENTONE*. Vluuen

tenuit T.R.E. 7 potuit ire quo uoluit. Tc̅ ſe deſd

.p x. hid. Modo .p. VII. hid 7 dim. Tra. e̅. VIII. car̅.

In dn̅io ſunt. III. car̅. 7 XIII. uilti 7 VIII. bord cu̅. v. car̅.

Ibi æccła 7 VIII. ſerui. 7 II. piſcariæ de. XX. ſol. 7 XL. ac̅ p̅ti.

Valuit T.R.E. XI. lib. 7 poſt. c. ſol. Modo: IX. lib.

In ead uilla h̅t Odo. III. hid. has tenuer̅. II. taini.

7 habuer̅. II. hallas. 7 potuer̅ ire quo uoluer̅. 7 .p. III. hid

ſe deſd tc̅ 7 m̅. Tra. e̅. I. car̅ 7 dimid. Ibi. e̅ cu̅. III. uiltis

7 XII. ac̅ p̅ti. Ad ſupi M̅ jacet. Valuit. L. ſol. m̅. XXX. ſol.

5 WHITLEY. Edward held it from King Edward. Then it answered
for 3 hides; now for 1 hide. Land for 3 ploughs.
In lordship 1 plough;
    2 villagers and 2 smallholders with 1 plough.
    4 slaves; meadow, 12 acres; a fishery at 40d.
The value is and was 40s.

64   LAND OF STEPHEN SON OF ERHARD   63 c

In READING Hundred
1 Stephen son of Erhard holds PADWORTH from the King.
Three thanes held it jointly; they could go where they would
with their lands. 7½ hides, but then and now it pays tax
for 5½ hides. Land for 5 ploughs. In lordship 1.
    3 villagers and 2 smallholders with 1 plough.
    2½ mills at 37s 6d; meadow, 48 acres.
Of these hides Nigel holds 1 hide; a man-at-arms ½ hide.
In lordship 1 plough;
    4 villagers and 3 smallholders with 2½ ploughs.
Value of the whole before 1066, 100s; later £4; now £4 10s.

[In CHARLTON Hundred]
2 Stephen also holds 1 hide in SWALLOWFIELD and Aelfric
from him. Three freeholders held it before 1066; they could
go wherever they would. Then and now it answered for 1 hide.
Land for 2 ploughs.
    5 freeholders with 2 ploughs and 1 smallholder.
The value was and is 20s.

65   LAND OF ODO AND OTHER THANES

In GANFIELD Hundred
1 Odo of Winchester holds HINTON (Waldrist) from the King.
Wulfwen held it before 1066; she could go where she would.
Then it answered for 10 hides; now for 7½ hides.
Land for 8 ploughs. In lordship 3 ploughs;
    13 villagers and 8 smallholders with 5 ploughs.
    A church; 8 slaves; 2 fisheries at 20s; meadow, 40acres.
Value before 1066 £11; later 100s; now £9.

2 In the same village Odo has 3 hides which two thanes held;
they had 2 Halls and could go where they would. It answered
for 3 hides then and now. Land for 1½ ploughs.
It is there, with
    3 villagers.
    Meadow, 12 acres.
It lies in the manor above.
The value was 50s; now 30s.

Iſd Odo ten̅ ibid̄ *DVDOCHESFORDE* . Aluui tenuit.

7 potuit ire quo uoluit . Tc̅ 7 m̊ ꝑ . iii . hid̄ . T̊ra . e̅ . ii . car̅.

In d̅nio . e̅ . i . car̅ . 7 i . uilłs 7 iiii . bord̄ cu̅ dimid̄ car̅ . Ibi

ii . ſerui . 7 molin̅ de . v . ſolid̄ . 7 piſcaria de . xxv . ſoł . 7 ii . den̊.

7 xvi . ac̅ p̊ti . Vał 7 ualuit . iiii . lib̅ . *IN HILLESLAVE*

Iſd Odo ten̊ *NISTETON* . Quiṇq̦ libi hōes   *HVND.*

in alod̄ de rege . E . Tc̅ ſe defd̄ ꝑ . v . hid̄ . Modo ꝑ . ii . uirg̊

7 ii . partiꝺ virgæ . T̊ra . e̅ . iiii . car̅ . In d̅nio dimid̄ car̅.

7 iii . uiłł 7 . vi . bord̄ cu̅ . ii . car̅ 7 dimid̄ . Ibi . iii . ſerui.

Valuit . c . ſoł . T . R . E . 7 poſt . lx . ſoł . Modo꞉ vi . lib̅.

A̅LWARD̄ Aurifab̅ ten̊ de rege *SOTESBROC* . *IN BENES HD̅.*

Pat̊ ej tenuit de regina Eddid̄ . Tc̅ 7 m̊ ꝑ . vii . hid̄ . T̊ra . e̅

v꞉ii . car̅ . In d̅nio ſunt . ii . car̅ . 7 xxiiii . uiłł 7 ii . cot̊

cu̅ . x . car̅ . Ibi . æccła 7 ii . ſerui . vii . ac̅ p̊ti.

Valuit . vii . lib̅ . Modo꞉ vi . lib̅ .   *IN BENES HVND̊*

A̅LWIN̄ fili̊ Cheping ten̊ de rege *BRAS* . Toui tenuit

de rege . E . Tc̅ ꝑ . ii . hid̄ . m̊ ꝑ una hida . T̊ra . e̅ . i . car̅ . 7 ibi . e̅

cu̅ . x . uiłi hn̅tib̅ . i . car̅ . Ibi æccła . Valuit . lx . ſoł . Modo꞉ xxx.

A̅LSI de Ferendone ten̊ *LIERECOTE* *IN GAMESFEL HD̅.*

de dono regis . W . Herald̊ tenuit . Tc̅ ſe defd̄ ꝑ . v . hid̄.

modo ꝑ . ii . hid̄ . T̊ra . e̅ . iiii . car̅ . In d̅nio . e̅ . i . car̅ . 7 v . uiłł

7 v . bord̄ cu̅ . ii . car̅ . Ibi . v . ſerui . Valuit . iiii . lib̅ . Modo . v . lib̅.

Iſd Alſi ten̊ de rege dim̊ hid̄   *IN WANETINZ HD̅.*

qua̅ Aluric q̇da̅ lib̅ hō tenuit . T . R . E . Tc̅ 7 m̊ ꝑ dim̊ hida.

Ibi ſunt . ii . cot̊ . 7 vi . ac̅ p̊ti . Vał 7 ualuit . x . ſolid̄.

3 Odo also holds DUXFORD there. Alfwy held it; he could go where
he would. Then and now for 3 hides. Land for 2 ploughs.
In lordship 1 plough;
    1 villager and 4 smallholders with ½ plough.
    2 slaves; a mill at 5s; a fishery at 25s 2d;
        meadow, 16 acres.
The value is and was £4.

In HILLSLOW Hundred
4 Odo also holds KNIGHTON. Five free men (held it) in freehold
from King Edward. Then it answered for 5 hides; now for 2
virgates and 2 parts of a virgate. Land for 4 ploughs.
In lordship ½ plough;
    3 villagers and 6 smallholders with 2½ ploughs. 3 slaves.
Value before 1066, 100s; later 60s; now £6.

In BEYNHURST Hundred
5 Alfward the Goldsmith holds SHOTTESBROOK from the King.
His father held it from Queen Edith. Then and now for 7 hides.
Land for 8 ploughs. In lordship 2 ploughs;
    24 villagers and 2 cottagers with 10 ploughs.
    A church; 2 slaves; meadow, 7 acres.
The value was £7; now £6.

In BEYNHURST [BRAY] Hundred
6 Alwin son of Chipping holds BRAY from the King. Tovi held
it from King Edward. Then for 2 hides; now for 1 hide.
Land for 1 plough. It is there with
    10 villagers who have 1 plough. A church.
The value was 60s; now 30[s.]

In GANFIELD Hundred
7 Alfsi of Farringdon holds BARCOTE by King William's gift.
Harold held it. Then it answered for 5 hides; now for 2 hides.
Land for 4 ploughs. In lordship 1 plough;
    5 villagers and 5 smallholders with 2 ploughs. 5 slaves.
The value was £4; now £5.

In WANTAGE Hundred
8 Alfsi also holds ½ hide from the King which Aelfric, a free man,
held before 1066. Then and now for ½ hide.
    2 cottagers.
    Meadow, 6 acres.
The value is and was 10s.

E<small>DWARD</small> teñ de rege.ɪ.hid.in C<small>OSERIGE</small>. I<small>N</small> T<small>ACEHÁ</small> H<small>D</small>.

Ipfe tenuit in alod de rege.E.7 ᵱ.ɪ.hida fe defd t̄c 7 m̄.

Tra.ē.ɪ.car̄.7 ibi.ē in dñio.cū.ɪɪɪ.bord.Val 7 ualuit.v.fol.

C<small>OLA</small> teñ de rege A<small>CENGE</small>.Briſtric   I<small>N</small> T<small>ACEHÁ</small> H<small>D</small>.

tenuit in alod de rege.E.Tc̄ ᵱ.ɪɪɪ.hid.modo ᵱ.ɪɪ.hid.

In dñio.ē una car̄.7 v.uiłłi 7 ɪɪɪ.bord.cū.v.car̄.Ibi

ɪɪɪɪ.ferui.7 moliñ de xv.folid.7 xxv.ac̄ ꝑti.Silua

de.ɪɪɪ.porc̄.Val 7 ualuit.ɪɪɪ.lib.   I<small>N</small> C<small>HENETEBERIE</small>

W<small>IGAR</small> teñ de rege.ɪɪ.hid in B<small>ENNEHA</small>.   H<small>I'ND</small>.

Ormar tenuit in alod   ᵱ m̄ de rege.E.

63 d

Tc̄ fe defd ᵱ.ɪɪ.hid.modo ᵱ dim̄ hida.Tra.ē.ɪ.car̄.7 ibi.ē

in dñio.cū.ɪɪ.bord.7 ʟx.ac̄ ꝑti.Val 7 ualuit.xʟ.fol.

E<small>DWARD</small> teñ de rege B<small>OCHENTONE</small>. L<small>ÁBORNE</small> H<small>D</small>.

Anfchil tenuit in alod de rege.E.Tc̄ ᵱ.ɪɪɪ.hid.m̄ ᵱ dim̄

hida.Tra.ē.ɪɪ.car̄.In dñio.ē una car̄.cū.v.bord.

Valuit.ʟx.folid.Modo.ʹxʟ.folid. I<small>N</small> W<small>ANETINZ</small> H<small>D</small>.

C<small>OLA</small> teñ de rege.H<small>ENRET</small>.Sauuiñ q̃dã lib hō tenuit

.T.R.E.Tc̄ ᵱ.vɪɪ.hid.Modo ᵱ una hida 7 ɪɪɪ.uirg̃.Tra.ē

ɪɪɪ.car̄.Ibi funt.vɪɪɪ.cot 7 moliñ de xx.folid.7 vɪɪɪ.ac̄

ꝑti.Valuit.c.folid.Modo.ɪɪɪɪ.ʹlib.

In THATCHAM Hundred

9 Edward holds 1 hide from the King in CURRIDGE. He held it
himself in freehold from King Edward; it answered for 1
hide, then and now. Land for 1 plough. It is there,
in lordship, with
   3 smallholders.
The value is and was 5s.

In THATCHAM [WANTAGE] Hundred

10 Cola holds (East)GINGE from the King. Brictric held it in
freehold from King Edward. Then for 3 hides; now for 2 hides.
In lordship 1 plough;
   5 villagers and 3 smallholders with 5 ploughs.
   4 slaves; a mill at 15s; meadow, 25 acres;
      woodland at 3 pigs.
The value is and was £3.

In KINTBURY Hundred

11 Wigar holds 2 hides from the King in BENHAM. Ordmer held it
in freehold as a manor from King Edward. Then it answered
for 2 hides; now for ½ hide. Land for 1 plough. It is there,   6 3 d
in lordship, with
   2 smallholders.
   Meadow, 60 acres.
The value is and was 40s.

In LAMBOURN Hundred

12 Edward holds BOCKHAMPTON from the King. Askell held it in
freehold from King Edward. Then for 3 hides; now for ½ hide.
Land for 2 ploughs. In lordship 1 plough, with
   5 smallholders.
The value was 60s; now 40s.

In WANTAGE Hundred

13 Cola holds (East)HENDRED from the King. Saewin, a free
man, held it before 1066. Then for 7 hides; now for 1 hide
and 3 virgates. Land for 3 ploughs.
   8 cottagers.
   A mill at 20s; meadow, 8 acres.
The value was 100s; now £4..

Ibi hr quedā Ældeua liba femina. i. hid de rege in elemos.

quā ead tenuit T.R.E.7 quo uellet ire potuiffet. Tc 7 m

p una hida. Ibi funt. ii. cot. 7 una ac pti. Valuit. xx. fot. M.v. fot.

IN GAMESFEL HD. hr Eddid quedā femina. i. uirg de

rege in elemofina. quā ipfa tenuit T.R.E.7 quo uellet

ire potuiffet. Tc p una v. modo p nichilo. Vat. xii. den.

ALWOLD camerari ten de rege   IN SVDTONE HD.

CHERSVELLE. Eddida regina tenuit. Tc fe defd p.v. hid.

Modo p una hida. Tra. e. ii. car. Ibi funt in dnio.7 iiii.

uitti 7 vi. bord cu. i. car. Ibi. ix. ferui.7 pifcaria

de xl. denar.7 lix. ac pti. Vat 7 ualuit. iiii. lib.

ALBERIC camerari regine ten. i. hid IN REDINGES HD.

de regina in BVRLEI. Aluuard tenuit de rege. E.7 po

tuit ire quo uoluit. Tc fe defd p una hida. m p nichilo.

Tra. e. i. car 7 dimid.   Valuit. xxx. fot M xx. fot.

HERDING ten. i. hid in BVRLEI.

Hanc ipfe tenuit de regina Eddid. Alueua tenuit T.R.E.

7 potuit ire quo uoluit. Tc p una hida. m p nichilo.

Tra. e. i. car 7 dim. Nichil in dnio. fed ibi. iii. uitti hnt

unā car. Silua de. v. porc. Valuit. xx. folid. Modo. xii. fot.

IN CHENETEBERIE HD. e Ingleflot qd ten Polcehard

de Witto. i. hid cu. i. bord. Vat. iii. fot.

Aldeva, a free woman, has 1 hide there from the King, in alms,
which she also held before 1066; she could have gone where she would.
Then and now for 1 hide.
2 cottagers.
Meadow, 1 acre.
The value was 20s; now 5s.

In GANFIELD Hundred
14 Edith, a woman, has 1 virgate from the King, in alms, which
she held herself before 1066; she could have gone where she would.
Then for 1 virgate; now for nothing.
Value 12d.

In SUTTON Hundred
15 Alfwold the Chamberlain holds CARSWELL from the King.
Queen Edith held it. Then it answered for 5 hides; now
for 1 hide. Land for 2 ploughs. They are there, in lordship;
4 villagers and 6 smallholders with 1 plough.
9 slaves; a fishery at 40d; meadow, 59 acres.
The value is and was £4.

In READING Hundred
16 Aubrey the Queen's Chamberlain holds 1 hide from the Queen
in 'BURLEY'. Alfward held it from King Edward; he could go where
he would. Then it answered for 1 hide; now for nothing.
Land for 1½ ploughs.
The value was 30s; now 20s.

17 Harding holds 1 hide in 'BURLEY'. He held it himself
from Queen Edith. Aelfeva held it before 1066; she could
go where she would. Then for 1 hide; now for nothing.
Land for 1½ ploughs. Nothing in lordship; but
3 villagers have 1 plough.
Woodland at 5 pigs.
The value was 20s; now 12s.

In KINTBURY Hundred
18 is INGLEWOOD which Fulchard holds from William. 1 hide with
1 smallholder.
Value 3s.

7 Alured hɫ.ɪ.hid in eod ꝳ.7 ɪ.caɼ in dñio.Vaɫ.xv.foɫ.

7 Godebold.ɪ.hid 7 dim cū.ɪɪɪ.bord. Vaɫ.x.foɫid.

7 Radulf de Felgeres.ɪɪ.hid 7 dim.que jacueɼ in Ingepene
fic dicit fcira.

IN MERCEHĀ HD.

Berneri nepos.R.de perone ten *Apletone*.de feudo eꝑi baioc.
Aluuin tenuit de rege.E.Tc fe defd ꝑ.v.hid.modo ꝑ.ɪɪ.hid
7 dimid.Ʇra.ē.ɪɪɪɪ.caɼ.In dñio.ē una.7 ɪɪɪ.uiɫɫi 7 v.bord
cū.ɪ.caɼ.Ibi.ɪɪɪ.fcrui.Valuit.ɪɪɪɪ.liƀ.7 poft.ɪx.foɫ.M.ʟ.foɫ.

Rodbert ten.de rege *Ingheflot*.
Duo taini tenueɼ de.R.E.ꝑ.ɪɪ.ꝳ.Tc 7 ɱ.ꝑ.ɪɪɪ.hid.Terra.
Ibi.ɪ.caɼ in dñio.Ibi.ɪ.uiɫɫ.7 vɪɪ.bord.cū.ɪ.caɼ.7.ɪ.feruus.
7.ɪɪɪɪ.ac ꝑti.7 paɫua filua.Valuit.xxx.foɫ.7 ꝑ.xx.7 ɱ fimiɫ

Eldit ꝗdā femina ten de rege in elemofina.unā v træ. *In Games*
Ipfa tenuit T.R.E.Tc geldƀ ꝑ una v træ.ɱ ꝑ nichilo. *ꝼ FELLE HD.*
Valuit.xxx.denaɼ.Modo.xɪɪ.denaɼ. *In Ʇacehā HD.*
Aluui tenuit T.R.E.crochehā.7 defd fe ꝑ.ɪ.hida.Idē ten
Ʇra.ɪ.caɼ.Ibi.ɪɪɪ.uiɫɫi.Vaɫ.xx.foɫid.

63 d

Alfred has 1 hide in the same manor. 1 plough in lordship.
Value 15s.
Godbald, 1½ hides with
3 smallholders.
Value 10s.
Ralph of Feugères, 2½ hides, which lay in Inkpen (lands),
as the Shire states.

In MARCHAM Hundred
19 Berner nephew of R(obert) of Peronne holds APPLETON from
the Bishop of Bayeux's Holding. Alwin held it from
King Edward. Then it answered for 5 hides; now for 2½ hides.
Land for 4 ploughs. In lordship 1;
   3 villagers and 5 smallholders with 1 plough. 3 slaves.
The value was £4; later 60s; now 50s.

[In KINTBURY Hundred]
20 Robert son of Rolf holds INGLEWOOD from the King.
Two thanes held it from King Edward as two manors.
Then and now for 3 hides. Land for ... 1 plough in lordship.
   1 villager and 7 smallholders with 1 plough; 1 slave.
   Meadow, 4 acres; a little woodland.
The value was 30s; later 20; now the same.

In GANFIELD Hundred
21 Aldith, a woman, holds 1 virgate of land from the King
in alms. She held it herself before 1066. Then it paid tax
for 1 virgate; now for nothing.
The value was 30d; now 12d.

In THATCHAM Hundred
22 Alfwy Chafersbeard held CROOKHAM before 1066. It answered
for 1 hide. He still holds it. Land for 1 plough.
   3 villagers.
Value 20s.

BERKSHIRE HOLDINGS
ENTERED ELSEWHERE IN THE SURVEY

The Latin text of these entries is given in the County volumes concerned

In WILTSHIRE
49
EW 1

1 a   Roger of Lacy, Thurstan son of Rolf and William Leofric   72 d
hold 1 hide in COLESHILL. Three thanes held it before 1066.
Value of the part of all of them, £4.

Misplaced entry. See Wilts., notes 49,1a.

In BUCKINGHAMSHIRE
11   LAND OF REINBALD THE PRIEST   146 a
EB 1

In BURNHAM Hundred

1   Reinbald the Priest holds 1 hide from the King in BOVENEY,
which lies in (the lands of) the Church of Cookham. Land
for 1 plough; it is there, with
1 villager.
Meadow for 1 plough.
The value is and always was 10s.
He held it himself in alms from King Edward.

In HAMPSHIRE
29   LAND OF RALPH OF MORTIMER   47 a
EH 1

In BOUNTISBOROUGH Hundred

16   Ralph also holds one manor, STRATFIELD (Mortimer), which
Chipping held before 1066. Then it answered for 5 hides;
now for 1 hide. Land for 5 ploughs. In lordship 2;
4 villagers and 9 smallholders with 1 plough.
6 slaves; meadow, 2 acres.
Before 1066 the value was £12; later £10; now £6.

NOTES ON THE TEXT AND TRANSLATION

INDEX OF PERSONS

SYSTEMS OF REFERENCE

INDEX OF PLACES

NOTES

ABBREVIATIONS used in the notes. Ab ... *Chronicon Monasterii de Abingdon,* ed. J. Stevenson (Rolls Series, 1858). DB ... Domesday Book. DG ... H. C. Darby and G. R. Versey, *Domesday Gazetteer,* Cambridge 1975. EPNS ... English Place-Name Society Survey (xlix-li, Berkshire). MS ... Manuscript. OE ... Old English. OEB ... G. Tengvik, *Old English Bynames,* (Uppsala 1938*). PNDB ... O. von Feilitzen, *The Pre-Conquest Personal Names of Domesday Book,* Uppsala 1937*. VCH ... Victoria County History (Berkshire volume 1).
Nomina Germanica, volumes 3 and 4.

The manuscript is written on leaves, or folios, of parchment (sheepskin), measuring about 15 ins. by 11 ins. (38 by 28 cm.), on both sides. On each side, or page, are two columns, making four to each folio. The folios were numbered in the 17th century, and the four columns of each are here lettered a, b, c, d. The manuscript emphasises words and usually distinguishes chapters and sections by the use of red ink. Underlining here indicates deletion.

BERKSHIRE. In red, across the top of the page, spread above both columns.
BERROCHESCIRE 56 ab, *BERCHESCIRE* 56 cd, abbreviated to *BERCHSCIRE* after 58 ab.

L   LANDHOLDERS. The order of the Holdings of Battle Abbey, 16, and the Abbess of Winchester, 15, is reversed in the text.

B   WALLINGFORD. The Borough is described in exceptional detail. The wording distinguishes between *hagae* and *mansurae* (sites and dwellings), and gives individual values for each, with a separate category of houses (*domus*). It lists both sites and dwellings within the Borough, held by landholders in Berkshire and Oxfordshire, and sites in many villages which belong to Wallingford, but were held by landholders. The meaning of much of the material is not clear and awaits further study.

B 1   8 VIRGATES. 2 hides, or 240 acres on DB reckoning, with 286 sites (276 less 13, plus 23 held by William of Warenne and the Frenchmen), an average of a little under an acre for each site. The area enclosed by the walls of the Old English Borough is only about 100 acres. The details do not add up to the total and are probably not meant to; listed are 132 *mansurae*, 72 *hagae* and 10 *domus*, in all 214. The 286 sites are probably those within the walls; those not listed as held by various persons were probably the King's.
THE CASTLE. Built by 1071 when the Abbot of Abingdon, Ealdred, was imprisoned there, Ab i, 486.

B 3   HUGH GRANT. *Hugo Magnus = Hugo Grandus,* possibly the same man as Hugh Grant of Scoca, see note B 9.
BOLBEC. MS error for *Molebec,* repeated at B 5, and common elsewhere in DB, OEB 73, 127.

B 4   BISHOP PETER. Of Chester 1072 - 1085. The see was transferred from Lichfield in 1075, and to Coventry in 1102.
BISHOP REMIGIUS of Lincoln. Remigius of Fécamp, promised the Bishopric of Dorchester in 1066 in return for ships furnished to William, succeeded Wulfwin of Dorchester who died in 1067, and translated the see to Lincoln between 1072 and 1086.

B 6   RALPH PIERCEHEDGE. Son-in-law of Gilbert Latimer who held Garsington (Oxon. 9,7) from the Abbey of Abingdon, Ab ii, 34-35, 89.
SINGA. Unintelligible, probably a copyist's error. VCH proposes *singula* but that would be redundant. In the light of the following clause Dr. Morris supposed some unidentified original word meaning 'contested'.
Palaeographically (given long *s*; flat topped 3 for *g* in error for short *t* involved with some loop or ascender from a following line; the bow and tongue of *e* involved in the cross of *t;* the copyist's omission of a first syllable; and perhaps a transliteration from Insular to Caroline miniscule) *singa* could be a mistake for a garbled form of, say, (con)sueta or (di)ruta. Both 'disused, discontinued' and 'ruined, broken down' would be sensible in the context.
BRISTIST. OE Brictric (final -*c* assibilated 'rich'); PNDB 198 reports the spellings *Bristrix, Brictricius* in which *x, ci* probably represent phonetic [ts], here metathesised and represented *st.*

B 8   ADBREI. Dr. Morris thought this a place-name A(l)d(e)beri (? Albury, Oxfordshire, see EPNS xxii, 191, cf. B 3), rather than a personal name, but it is in a list of persons, and it is a feasible mistake for *adƀt,* ad(el)bert(us), (OE Aeðelbeorht, or *Eadbeorht.*)

MILES MOLAY. Presumably Miles Crispin; *Moli*, presumably his place of origin is probably Molay in Calvados, OEB 128.

B 9 THANES HAD LAND. 'Thane' is an unusual description of ecclesiastical and secular magn̄ so is the statement that a dozen magnates, who held land in many Counties, had held Wallingford in the past, but evidently no longer held it. No emendation or transpositioṅ the heading offers any practicable alternative. The circumstances of the change in landholding are not explained.

The named places are all in Oxfordshire. All but Wace are named there as holders in th places named.

ABBOT R....... Possibly Abbot Rhiwallon of the New Minster at Winchester (later Hyde Aḃ 1072-1088.

CREM. VCH Crowmarsh. This supposes a miscopied abbreviation form such as *Crau'* (for *Craumares*).

SCOCA. An unidentified place, perhaps in France. However, the first *c-* may be a misreadiṅ *t-*, whence *Stoca*, 'Stoke' (usually spelt *Stoch(e)*, *Stocha* in DB, but *Stoc(a)* appears in, Stoke Fleming, Devon; Stoke Prior, Herefordshire; Stoke sub Hamdon, Somerset).

B 10 ONE MAN-AT-ARMS ... 5 HIDES. At some point during the OE period the assessment for military service was reduced from one man from each hide (an obligation based on the family) to one man from a number of hides. The reduction is assumed to have been to ȯ man from 5 hides, or in the Scandinavian counties to one man from 6 carucates. Much ȯ the evidence is given by J.H. Round, *Feudal England* (1968 reprint), p.47 ff., and the b of the reduction is here clearly stated in the Berkshire entry. It is recalled in the commȯ DB p.n. *FIVEHIDE*, (see Fyfield 21,15-16) where the assessment was often higher; the allusion of the place-name being to a common unit of assessment rather than a statemeṅ extent, see EPNS 408 and refs.

(THE REASON TO) STAY BEHIND. The meaning of the passage is clear; but the grammaṙ *remanendi habens ... mittere permitterent* is unusual.

The second paragraph, Stenton argued (*The First Century of English Feudalism*, 2nd ȩ 1961, p.119), recalled a more universal obligation of service upon the thanes, but in the context a back reference to the 'one man-at-arms from 5 hides' seems more likely.

DEATH-DUTY. The *relevatio*, *relevium*, the 'relief' or 'heriot', was paid by the heir on tak̇ his inheritance. The scale of rates was laid down in the law codes, especially 2Canute71 'Laws of King William' 20. The *villanus* paid an ox, cow or horse, the *censarius* a year's tribute.

HAD DOGS. The French construction *essent ei* for 'had' is unusual in DB.

1,1 ALBERT THE CLERK. His land in Windsor was granted to Abingdon Abbey c.1110, *terra̅* *illam et domum de Windresores quae fuit Alberti*, Ab ii, 112.

1,3 [£?] 50s. MS 50s, probably in error.

1,4 WALTHAM. Probably Waltham St. Lawrence.

1,5 WILLIAM BEAUFOUR. Bishop of Thetford 1085-1091, succeeded by Herbert Losinga wḣ transferred the see to Norwich.

1,8 EARL ROGER of Hereford, son of William fitzOsbern, forfeited his lands after the rebelliȯ of 1075. His lands had not yet been granted to others.

AELFEVA. *Eileva* 61,2; probably the same woman as *Ailueua* 65,17; both are OE *Aelfgif* PNDB 173.

1,9 DOES NOT PAY TAX. Or 'did not pay tax'.

1,10 SPARSHOLT. (see also note 7,38 Fawler). Entered under Wantage Hundred here and at 21 35,5 but under Slotisford Hundred at 55,4. Like Childrey (see note 28,2), mostly under Wantage, partly under Slotisford.

FROGER THE SHERIFF. Of Berkshire. According to the Abingdon chronicler he had beeṅ responsible for the despoliation of the Abbey and its estate after the Conquest. 'In thesȩ acts Froger, then sheriff of Berkshire, was prominent. But God the Judge later punished this mighty man who persecuted the humble, for the royal justice deprived him of the office which he had turned into a tyranny, and he spent the remainder of his life in brutish want despised by all.', Ab i, 486, 494. Translation given in *English Historical Documents 1042-1189*, ed. D.C. Douglas, p.901.

1,12 WULFLED. A woman, OE *Wulflaed*, PNDB 418. Cf. *Leflet*, Leofled 1,13, OE *Leofflaed*, PNDB 309.

ROBERT Perhaps D'Oilly, cf. 1,13 and note 41.

1,13 'SUTTON'. Probably part of the manor of Sutton (Courtenay), see below 1,37, which belonged to Wantage Hundred. Compare East Hendred, EPNS 38, a manor territorially i̇ Wantage Hundred, but assessed under Sutton Hundred.

1,14   LEOFLED. See note 1,12 under Wulfled.
HIS LORD'S MANOR. Probably adjacent to Wargrave (1,15), perhaps in Hurley (Beynhurst Hundred), 38,5.

1,17   SWALLOWFIELD. Entered here under Charlton Hundred; under Reading Hundred at 1,46 for 1 hide which 'lies in Swallowfield which is in Charlton Hundred' (see note 7,14); and under Reading Hundred at 64,2 where a Hundred rubric is probably missing.
MS GAP. Hants. 43,4 records that 'Gilbert (of Bretteville) also holds Bramshill with the King's manor Swallowfield that is in Berkshire'. Bramshill is just across the border. The MS gap is long enough to have been left for an allusion to Gilbert's holding here.
FREEHOLD. A continental term, *alodium*, defined as *haereditas quam vendere et donare possum .. mea propria;* as *praedium, id est alodium,* from the 9th century. Used in DB in the south-east, often with *sicut,* 'like a', for holdings that resembled continental *alodium.* The Sussex returns identify the DB meaning; the same holding, held by the same person, is described first as *sicut alodium* and later as 'he could go where he would.' Elsewhere *libere tenuit, se recedere* and similar phrases have the same meaning. The word is not, of course, at all points identical with modern 'freehold'. In DB it is virtually confined to the south and south-east. See Sussex note 10,51.

1,20   VALUE. Possibly, but less likely, 'Value before 1066 and later £4; now £3.'
1,21   VALUE. See note 1,20.
1,22   BRAY. Entered here under Bray Hundred and under Beynhurst Hundred at 65,6. The west part of the territory of Bray adjoins White Waltham which is Beynhurst territory; but in 65,6 the church is in the Beynhurst manor, so the geography is not that simple: compare Childrey 55,3 (see note 28,2), whose church-village was in the 'other' Hundred.
1,24   *NACHEDEDORNE* . 'Bare thorn'. The earlier name (and meeting place?) of Compton Hundred, possibly part of the later manor of Compton (see EPNS 495). Possibly 'Unica spinosa arbor', the single tree where Alfred beat the Danes at Ashdown in 870, Asser ed. W.H. Stephenson, 238.
1,26   KNOW HOW. Or 'by what authority'.
1,27   SHALBOURNE. Now in Wiltshire. At DB there were 4 manors here, the largest in Berkshire. The County boundary divided the parish until the late 19th century.
REEVE'S LAND. *Una hida fuit de Reue Land .. in which Reue Land* is obviously a technical term or a name in OE not translated into Latin. It would be OE *gerefan land,* 'land of the steward of the manor, the Reeve's land'.
1,31   BOOR. MS *burs* (usually Latinized *buri*), OE *(ge)bur.* For the status and function of the *(ge)bur* and other ranks of rural society as described in 11th century documents see the *Survey of Tidenham (Gloucs)* in Robertson *Anglo-Saxon Charters* 204-7, 452-4 which distinguishes the *thegn, (ge)neat, cotsetla* and *(ge)bur.*
Most authorities avoid either an adequate translation or explanation. DB does equate the *buri* with the *coliberti* (see note 7,6) on two occasions, both in Hampshire, where *vel coliberti* is interlined (see Maitland DBB p.62, Fontana edition). They appear in 14 shires. The drift of Maitland's argument is that they are less free than the smallholder and cottager, but often possessors of two plough beasts.
1,32   KINGSTON LISLE. See note 7,38.
GODRIC LOST THE SHERIFFDOM. Ab 1, 484, 491 reports that Godric was killed at Hastings, 'Godric likewise was killed in the same battle (of Hastings)'. Perhaps here, but certainly below at 21,13 ('Godric appropriated it .. after the Battle of Hastings') DB assumes that he had survived the battle.
1,34   BISHOP OSMUND. Of Salisbury, 1087-1099.
1,37   SUTTON (COURTENAY). The exactions of its reeve, Alfsi, on the Abingdon estates are reported in Ab 11, 10-11.
1,38   EAST HENDRED. Entered under Wantage Hundred at 3,2; 17,9; 65,13 and under Sutton Hundred here and at 21,17. It may be that the irregular shape of East Hendred parish (when compared with that of West Hendred) may be due to the inclusion of part of the territory of Sutton Hundred.
DOGS. Modern breeds of hunting dogs are termed 'hounds'; it is doubtful if the specialised strains had been bred by 1086.
1,39   VALUE ... NOW £32. Farler error £22 for £32.
AS THEY SUPPOSE ... HOLDS IT. MS *Robertus ... istud ten(et) ut suspicant* not, as Farley, *tenut.*
1,41   55s. MS *xxxv* with *l* written above; that is 35s corrected to 55s.
17s 6d. MS altered from xiiii by joining together the first two minims.

1,42   LODGING. *Hospitium,* probably as his town house rather than as a guest house.
       THEREFORE. *Ido* probably *ideo*, 'therefore', rather than *idonee* 'properly'.
2,1   Marginal *fac* note reproduced by Farley. Its meaning obscure.
2,2   OF HIS BISHOPRIC. That is not for the monks and not held personally.
       STIGAND. Bishop of Winchester 1047-1070 and Archbishop of Canterbury 1052-1070.
3,1   MS *tenuit Albericus de Coci*, Farley *tenuit de*..
3,2   1½ HIDES. Probably at East Hendred.
       BISHOP HERMAN. Of Sherborne 1058-1078; a German from Lotharingia, PNDB 290n.
4,1   WALTHAM ABBEY. The Abbey of Waltham Holy Cross in Essex founded by Earl Harold
       in 1060. The coincidence of the name of the manor and its owner is confusing, see
       EPNS 70.
5,1   BUCKLAND. See note 7,47.
       WEYS. *Pensis caseorum,* a weight or 'wey' of cheese was several hundredweight (OE *waeg*
       'a weight').
       VALUE 32s 4d. The figure does not divide by 10. Possibly an error for 33s 4d, or 10 weys at
       40d.
6,1   ODDA   or Odo, perhaps Odo of Winchester, see 10,1
7   ABINGDON CHURCH. The Abingdon Chronicle, composed by a monk of the house during
       the early twelfth century, survives in two MSS of the thirteenth century; it transcribes
       early charters and preserves the Abingdon tradition of events on the monastic estate in the
       aftermath of the Conquest. Perhaps its best known passages deal with the imposition of
       military service upon the ecclesiastical estate shortly after the Conquest. 'The affairs of
       the kingdom being in such a state of uproar, the lord Abbot Aethelhelm safely guarded
       with a strong force of men-at-arms the place committed to him (that is Windsor Castle);
       and at first indeed he used stipendaries for this purpose. But after the disturbances had
       died down, since it was noted in the annals by command of the King how many men-at-
       arms were to be exacted from Bishops and Abbots for the defence of the realm should
       need arise, the Abbot, having previously refrained from such grants, thenceforth assigned
       to kinsmen manors from the Church's possessions, in each case in return for the
       stipulated service from the manor thus given. These lands had been held by those called
       thanes who had fallen in the Battle of Hastings'. Ab ii, 3.
         The relationship of Abbot Aethelhelm's list of knights, composed before 1084, to
       the DB (Berks.) entries is given below:-

Abingdon ii, 4-5			DB		
Warriss of Palences*	4 men-at-arms				
Dry Sandford	7 hides		7,9	Hugh Cook	2 hides
Leverton			7,35	Hezelin	4½ hides
Chilton	5 hides		7,34	Wynric	5 hides
Denton (Oxon.)	2 hides				
Wadley	1 hide				
Bayworth	4 hides		7,10	Askell & Gilbert	10 hides
Sunningwell			7,11	Berner	5 hides
Reginald of St. Helens	3 men-at-arms				
Garsington (Oxon.)	5 hides				
Frilford	4 hides		7,18	Reginald	4 hides
Lyford	3 hides		7,25	Reginald	3 hides
West Hendred	2 hides				
Askell	2 men-at-arms				
Seacourt			7,2	Askell	5 hides
Bayworth	5 hides		7,10	Askell & Gilbert	10 hides
Marcham	1 hide		7,17	Askell	1 hide
Warin	½ man-at-arms				
Sugworth	4 hides		7,11	Warin	4 hides
Hubert	1 man-at-arms				
Wytham	5 hides		7,3	Hubert	5 hides

Reinbald	*1½ men-at-arms*			
Sunningwell	2 hides	7,11	Berner	5 hides
Kennington	3 hides			
Garford	2 hides	7,21	Berner	2 hides
Boxford	2 hides	7,14	Berner	2 hides
Cumnor	2 hides	7,1	Abingdon	30 hides
Frilford	1 hide	7,18	Reinbald	1 hide
Longworth	1 hide	7,39	Abingdon	8 hides
Reinbald	*1 man-at-arms*			
Tubney		7,19	Reinbald	1 hide
Herbert son of Herbert	*1 man-at-arms*			
Leckhampstead	10 hides	7,14	Reinbald	10 hides
Walter of Rivers	*2½ men-at-arms*			
Beedon		7,15	Walter of Rivers	8 hides
	½ man-at-arms			
Bradley (in Chieveley)		7,12	William (of Jumièges)	5 hides
Walter Giffard	*1 man-at-arms*			
Lyford	7 hides	7,24	Walter Giffard	7 hides
Hugh of Buckland	*1 man-at-arms*			
Buckland	10 hides	7,47	Abingdon	5 hides
Gilbert of Colombières	*2 men-at-arms*			
Horduuelle(?)				
Uffington	6 hides	7,37	Gilbert	6 hides
Gilbert	*1 man-at-arms*			
Pusey	2 hides	7,43	Gilbert	2 hides
Draycott Moor	2 hides	7,26	Gilbert	1 hide
East Lockinge	1 hide	7,44	Gilbert	1 hide
Baldwin of Colombières	*1 man-at-arms*			
Fawler		7,38	Askell	10 hides

*Warriss of Palences. MS *Gueres de Palences,* see 'A Dictionary of British Surnames', ed. P.H. Reaney (2nd edition), s.n. Werry.

7,3   HUBERT. Granted the land after his capture in the Channel by pirates, see note 7,23.

7,6   COLIBERTUS. A continental term not otherwise found in England; used in DB to render a native term, stated on two occasions to be *(ge)bur* (see above note 1,31). The *coliberti* are found mainly in the counties of Wessex and western Mercia, particularly in Wiltshire and Somerset. As the name suggests they had originally (that is in France) been slaves freed in groups, although by the 11th century the name preserved only the memory of superior status.

7,7   EARL HUGH GAVE IT. Reported in Ab ii, 19-20 to have been in return for £30 and a promise of confraternity at the house, although entered there under the date 1090.

7,11   5 HIDES. Three at Sunningwell and two at Kennington, see D.C. Douglas *Some Early Surveys from the Abbey of Abingdon* English Historical Review (1929), 623.
OTHER. MS *aliis,* not as Farley *Aliis.*

7,12   WILLIAM of Jumièges. He appears later under the protection of Henry I when he quitclaimed this land, 'which Abbot Reginald (1084-1097) gave him unjustly,' to Abbot Faritus, Ab ii, 93, 129. The 5 hides lay in Bradley, EPNS 242. See above note 7. Both Aethelhelm and Reginald had been monks of Jumièges.

7,14   BOXFORD. Entered under Kintbury Hundred at 54,2. This entry describes land in Boxford territory which belongs to the manor of Welford in Rowbury Hundred. The Wickham Heath quarter of Boxford parish is called after Wickham Green in Welford. Boxford has since been a parish in Faircross Hundred which includes the DB Rowbury Hundred. Either a wrong or omitted Hundred rubric, or Boxford an outlier of Kintbury Hundred which has since been absorbed into different, surrounding, Hundreds to which some of its territory belonged. Compare the instance of Swallowfield (note 1,17) where the *caput manerii* is in Charlton Hundred but some of the ground in Swallowfield territory is assessed or owes suit in Reading Hundred. The *Hundred* is not necessarily a geographical entity.

7,15 RIVERS. Surname from one of the French places named *La Riviere* (Calvados, Pas de Calais) OEB 109-110. For the modern form, cf. Wooton Rivers (EPNS xvi, 357).

7,16 BENHAM. Entered here under Rowbury Hundred and under Kintbury Hundred at 54,3; 65,11. Marsh Benham (SU 4267) and Benham Park (SU4367) in Speen in Faircross Hundred (includes DB Rowbury Hundred); Benham Burslot (SU 4070) and Hoe Benham (SU 4169) now in Welford in Faircross Hundred; all the parts of Benham except Hoe and Burslot form a district on the north bank of the Kennet (the Hundred boundary) opposite Enborne in Kintbury Eagle Hundred. Perhaps part of Benham owed suit in Kintbury, part in Rowbury (the entry here could refer to Benham Burslot and Hoe Benham: these adjoin Wickham Heath, SU 4169 see note 7,14, in Rowbury territory); perhaps the Kintbury Hundred boundary here crossed the River Kennet to take in the Benham district.

7,18 REGINALD of St. Helens, a man-at-arms of the Abbey (see above note 7). So named because he presumably lived at St. Helens near the Church, EPNS 438-9.

REINBALD, 1 HIDE. Described in Abbot Aethelhelm's list (see above note 7), 'et in Frileford, i hida, quam dedit Bernerus Turstino de Sancta Helena'. Several of the lands held by Reinbald were later held by Berner in DB.

7,21 *DE EO*. 'Of it', of 'from him'.

7,22 EAST HANNEY. Entered under Marcham Hundred, but under Wantage Hundred at 17,8 (as also West Hanney at 20,1-2), and under Bucklebury Hundred at 36,2 (in the latter case a Hundred rubric has probably been omitted). It is possible that East Hanney was held under more than one Hundred. The territory adjoins Marcham parish and Hundred on the River Ock at SU 4595; the place-name Landmead (SU 440947) thought by EPNS 478 (on rather tentative grounds) to mean 'boundary meadow' might suggest an old manorial division of the township, not coincident with the present parish boundary; and note also in EPNS loc. cit. that there were three manors in Hanney in late medieval times.

7,23 HERMER. Returning from Normandy several of the Abbot's men-at-arms were involved in an attack by pirates. Hermer, who had not yet been provided with land (see above note 7, 'at first he used stipendaries'), was mutilated by the loss of his hands. Out of pity the King ordered the Abbot to provide for him at Denchworth *de victualio monachorum*, probably included here at Goosey, an adjacent place. Ab ii,6, see above note 7,3.

RACHENESTE. For *Radchenest*, OE *rad-cniht*. Literally a man who rides (a horse); free men who performed riding services as messengers or escorts.

7,29 ALWIN THE PRIEST. 'Erat enim legibus patriae optime institutus', Ab ii,27. He later obtained this land and the Church at Sutton for his son, Siward, on payment of a fine of £5, Ab loc.cit.

7,30 MS *teñuit*, corrected by Farley to *tenuit*.

7,31 KING'S FOREST. ' ... regis arbitrio, ad forestam illic amplificandum, iiii hidae tunc exterminatae sunt.' Walter son of Othere, the Keeper of the Forest (see note 31), also took possession of woodland belonging to the Abbey near Bagshot (in Surrey) and *Jerdelea* (EPNS 42), Ab ii, 7. The creation of the Forest did not pass without opposition; 'Praedictae autem villae Uuinkfeld regis forestarii plurimum infesti fiebant'. The Abbot was later able to produce a writ of William Rufus calling on Walter to allow the Abbot to enjoy the wood of Winkfield without harassment, Ab ii, 29.

7,34 BLACKMAN. A wealthy priest who went into exile with Gytha, Harold's mother, and Abbot Ealdred of Abingdon. 'When he left England, everything which he possessed was taken into the hands of the King since he was held to be a renegade, and it was with the greatest difficulty that the Abbot secured the restoration of his lands to the Church.' Ab i, 484.

7,35 *IN FEUDO T.R.E.* The circumstances of Blackman's exile (see above) may account for the claim here that Blackman had held his land as a Holding before 1066. DB does not recognise the previous possession of the Abbey, and *in alodio* and *in feudo T.R.E.* may perhaps be unwarranted glosses advanced by a Norman clerk.

HEZELIN. The same name as Azelin (7,27), cf. T. Forssner, *Continental-Germanic Personal-Names in England*, Uppsala (1916), p.39.

7,38 ASKELL. '..held (Fawler) for the service of 1 man-at-arms in the time of Abbot Reginald (1084-1097)'. Ab ii, 125-6, see above note 7. William Rufus seized the land after Askell's disgrace, although it was restored to the Abbey by Henry I, Ab ii, 36-37.

FAWLER. In Kingston Lisle; one of the three manors in the pre-Conquest estate named Sparsholt, now Fawler, Kingston Lisle and Sparsholt. EPNS 372.

PROVIDE. The son should maintain his father and inherit the manor after the father's death. The estate is now in the hands of the church, but the text does not make it clear how it was transferred. 'He put', *misit*, subject either Edric's son or the Abbot of Abingdon; 'where it was' or 'where he was', *erat*, subject either 'it' the manor (hence Fawler church), or 'he' Edric's son (hence Abingdon).

7,40 2 VIRGATES. Perhaps in error for 2 hides.

7,41 ½ HIDE. In Charney Bassett, Douglas, op.cit., p.623.

7,43 PUSEY. Entered under Ganfield Hundred here and at 13,1; 44,5 and under Sutton Hundred at 21,19, although geographically the place is in Ganfield Hundred (see note 21,18; 36,4). A Hundred rubric may have been omitted at 21,18.

7,46 2 HIDES. In West Ginge, Douglas, op.cit., p.623.

7,47 BUCKLAND. Entered here under Wantage Hundred, but under Ganfield Hundred at 5,1 and 17,12-13. Unless there is a lost and unidentified 'Buckland' in Wantage Hundred, either there is a Hundred rubric error, or different parts of Buckland territory owed suit in different Hundreds. The latter is perhaps more probable in view of the appearance of the Abingdon land at Buckland under Wantage Hundred in a pre-DB record of hidage on the Abbey estate, Douglas, loc.cit.

8,1 Farley error, £20 for £12.

10,1 COUNTESS GYTHA. Wife of Earl Godwin of Wessex.

EARL GYRTH. Son of Godwin and Earl of East Anglia from 1057. Killed at Hastings.

14,1 GAVE THE CHURCH AND HIS DAUGHTER. That is so that she might become a nun.

15,2 A CHURCH IN READING. Assumed to be one of the pre-Conquest nunneries originally founded by St Edward the Martyr's mother, Queeen Elfrida, although according to the Anglo-Saxon Chronicle much of Reading, including the religious houses, was destroyed by the Danes in 1006.

ABBESS LEOFEVA. Perhaps identical to Abbess Leofeva of Shaftesbury.

17,1 MS. The chapter number is written within the *C* of *Comes*.

SHEFFIELD. MS *Sewelle* recte *Seuuelle* a farm in Burghfield, EPNS 206.

17,2 PEASEMORE. Entered under Rowbury Hundred at 46,6; here under Reading Hundred and under Marcham Hundred at 36,6. Geographically the place is in Rowbury territory (later included in Faircross Hundred).

JOINTLY. *In paragio; paragium* 'joint tenure'. It appears widely in the south-western counties, especially Somerset (see Somerset notes). Either Alwin was the only heir, the land itself remaining subject to partible inheritance, or else the only heir mentioned.

17,3 Farler error, 7 slaves for 8 slaves.

17,4 *CROCHESTROPE*. Dr Morris suggested that the location might be about Cold Ash (SU 5169). Perhaps the place-name Westrop (SU 5170) in Bucklebury parish commemorates the location, EPNS 158; the common element is OEÞrop, 'an outlying farm, hamlet'.

17,5 CALCOT. About SU 3370, near Leverton in Hungerford (formerly in Chilton Foliat, Wilts), see EPNS 302.

17,8 EAST HANNEY. See note 7,22.

17,9 EAST HENDRED. See note 1,38.

17,10 HIDES. Probably also at East Hendred.

17,12 HIDES. Probably at Buckland, later held by the Priory of Noyon which acquired much of the Count's Berkshire land, VCH p.346. See note 7,47

17,13 HIDES. See above note 17,12.

18,1 DRAYTON. Entered here under Sutton Hundred and under Lambourn Hundred at 35,4. The Drayton territory is situated in Sutton Hundred (there is no other mention of a *Drayton* in Lambourn Hundred), but the jurisdiction may have lain in two different Hundreds.

18,2 ROBERT. Probably D'Oilly, VCH p.346.

DROGO. Probably of Les Andilys, VCH p.346.

19,1 THE ABBEY OF PREAUX HOLDS. In exchange for the village of St. Clair in Normandy, VCH p.288.

20,1-2 WEST HANNEY. See note 7,22.

21,2   EAST ILSLEY. Entered here under Compton Hundred and under Kintbury Hundred at 38,1 (as also West Ilsley 38,2). Geographically the two places lie in Compton Hundred. Perhaps a Hundred rubric error.

21,3   'ASHDEN'. About SU 5281, in Compton, see EPNS 498; spellings in other sources indicate the final el. OE *denu* 'a valley' (i.e., the valley in which Compton village lies), not *dun* 'an upland, a hill' as the DB spelling had suggested to the sources of DG which propose Ashridge (SU 4978) in Beedon.
       RALPH OF BAGPUIZE. Bachepuz in Eure (Evreux), VCH p.347; J.H. Round, *Ancestor* 1 p.152, L.C. Loyd, *Origins of Some Anglo-Norman Families*, Harleian Society (Leeds 1953), p.10.

21,5   SIWARD (BAIRN). Henry's predecessor elsewhere too, see Warwickshire 19,1-3. He joined Hereward, Edwin and Morcar in the Ely revolt of 1070. 'Bairn' (OE *bearn*) probably had the same significance as OE *cild* 'Childe'; born to an inheritance, well born.

21,6   BAGSHOT. Now in Wiltshire.

21,7   ARPENT. A French measure of uncertain and probably variable size, usually applied in DB to vineyards, but occasionally to meadow and woodland.

21,8   WILLINGTON'S. Willington's Farm, Willington's Farm, Wigbald Farm, in the west part of Long Wittenham, cf. EPNS 429. The p.n. was OE *Wigbaldincgtune* 'a farm calle after one Wigbald'.

21,9   (SOUTH) DENCHWORTH. Testa de Nevill, p.109, cited VCH p.348.

21,11 CURZON. Notre Dame de Courson, south of Lisieux, L.C. Loyd, op.cit., p.37. Robert of Courson, a landholder in Suffolk and Norfolk, probably came from Curson by St. Sever north-east of Avranches, OEB 85.

21,12 SPARSHOLT. See notes 1,10; 7,38.
       FULCHARD. MS *Polcehard*, obviously an error (no known personal-name prototheme in *polce-*); Insular miniscule *p* and *f* are similar; *Folcehard* would represent OGerman *Fulchard*, Forssner, op.cit., p.98, PNDB 256.

21,14 STANKELL. Ab i, 484, 491 reports that a certain rich man called Thorkell had commende himself and this land to Abingdon with the consent of Earl Harold. Thorkell appears as the T.R.E. landholder in Kingston at 22,12. Stankell is perhaps a scribal error.
       KINGSTON. 'When this man (Stankell) fell in the famous battle (of Hastings) Henry of Ferrers seized this land for himself despite the protests of the Abbot'. Ab i, 484, 491.

21,15 FYFIELD. 'There a certain Godric, who was Sheriff, had held from the Church on a lease for three lives, on the understanding that whatever mischance might befall the tenants, the Church should suffer no loss therefrom. But when Godric was likewise killed in the same battle, Henry of Ferrers added this village also to his possessions.' Ab i, 484, 491.

21,17 AELFRIC BORE WITNESS. See above 1,38.

21,18 STANFORD. Entered under Sutton Hundred, although geographically in Ganfield Hundre as also part of Pusey 21,19 (and cf. Hatford, note 36,4). A Hundred rubric may have be omitted here. But observe that the adjacent Goosey was a detached parish of Ock Hund in medieval times, so there may well have been outlying estates under Sutton Hundred which lay in the territory of Ganfield Hundred.

21,19 PUSEY. See note 7,43.

21,20 BONDI. MS has *Bondinus*, see PNDB 206.
       A MILL. Probably in error for *dimidia molin* as at Burghfield 46,4, where *dimidia* is interlined and the value (5s 10d) the same.

21,21 'BURLEY'. Cf. 65,16-17. EPNS 149 does not identify; but Burleigh (SU 9070) in Winkfiel parish, EPNS 39, and Burley (SU 9171) in Sunninghill parish, EPNS 89, may preserve the name, although not observed before the early 17th century.

22,5   UFTON (ROBERT) and Ufton (Nervet) 34,3. There are two manors in the one village, which takes its name from one of them, EPNS 224.
       HORLING. 'Adulterer', PNDB 292, from OE *horling*, ME *horling* 'adulterer (whoreling)'.

22,7   EAST ILSLEY. See note 21,2.

23,1   ALSTAN of Boscombe, a Wiltshire thane and predecessor of William of Eu in that county, VCH 289, 351.

23,3   (NORTH) DENCHWORTH. At SU 3893, a farm in West Hanney parish, EPNS 473, 478.

25,1   SOUTHCOTE. A house in Reading, EPNS 177.

28,2   CHILDREY. Entered under Wantage Hundred here and at 45,2-3, but under Slotisford Hundred at 55,3. As with Bray (see note 1,22) the church-village is in the 'other' Hund Sparsholt (see notes 1,10; 7,38) like Childrey was mostly under Wantage Hundred, but partly under Slotisford.

30,1 THEY HAVE NOT PAID TAX. The words should refer to the hides, not the slaves; probably miscopied.
31 WALTER SON OF OTHERE. Castellan of Windsor, where Abbot Aethelhelm's men-at-arms owed service, and keeper of the Forest of Berkshire, Ab ii, 7. The latter point is implied in 31,4 ' .. because of the Keeping the Forest'.
31,1 ORTONE. In Ripplesmere Hundred. This might be somewhere near Windsor. The name would be OE *Ortune* '(at) the farm at the bluff', from OE *ora* ' a steep bank, hillside, bluff' (as in Windsor EPNS 26). It is tempting to compare *Underore* (lost in New Windsor, about SU 9777), EPNS 29, '(place) under the bluff'.
30s. *xl* deleted, *xxx* substituted.
31,2 1½ PLOUGHS. No figure given, probably 1.
31,3 AELFHILD DESE. PNDB 175. The by-name is probably an aphetic form of the OE poetic word *idese, -an,* a weak form (BT Suppl) of *ides,* 'a lady'.
32,1 'LOSFIELD'. The old name of the district about St. Leonard's in Clewer, EPNS 20.
33,1 NOTHING IN LORDSHIP. Presumably meaning that there are no ploughs in lordship.
33,3 CLAPCOT. Outside the north-east corner of the Borough and the Castle at Wallingford. EPNS 563.
33,9 LONCHELEI, GRATENTUN. The former is described as lying in, and assessed in, the latter, which is in Oxfordshire. *Gratentun* is not identified in either EPNS Oxon. or Berks.; but *Longhelei* tentatively with Langley (SU 6775) in Ticehurst EPNS 194, so *Gratentun* ought to be south of the Thames in Ticehurst.
WIGOT. Probably of Wallingford, cf. 41,2.
34,2 MAIDENHEAD. Formerly *Ellington,* EPNS 53, 54-55.
34,3 UFTON (NERVET). See note 22,5
35 HASCOIT. Hascoit Musard, a Breton and landholder in many counties.
35,4 DRAYTON. See note 18,1.
35,5 SPARSHOLT. See note 1,10.
36,2 EAST HANNEY. So in VCH 357, see note 7,22.
36,4 MS *haula,* not as Farley *Haula.*
HATFORD. Entered under Marcham Hundred, although geographically in Ganfield Hundred, cf. Pusey note 7,43, Stanford note 21,18. Quite a number of places situated in Ganfield Hundred are entered under other Hundreds.
36,6 HUNDRED. Marcham repeated, evidently in error for Rowbury.
PEASEMORE. See note 17,2.
HERLWIN. MS *Urleuuine,* OGerman *Erlewin, Herlewin* PNDB 248.
37,1 MANOR. Possibly Langley (SU 5076) in Hampstead Norris, EPNS 251, VCH 357 cites Testa de Nevill 124.
VILLAGERS. MS error *vill(an)i* for *vill(ano)s.*
38,1 EAST ILSLEY. So VCH 358, see note 21,2.
38,2 WEST ILSLEY So VCH 358.
38,3 EAST GARSTON. Here included in Lambourn. The name is a corruption of *Esgarston,* from the name of its holder, Asgar the Constable. EPNS 330.
41 ROBERT D'OILLY. Sheriff of Warwickshire, Oxfordshire and perhaps Berkshire. A formidable neighbour of the Abbot of Abingdon who had acquired several of the Abbey lands in Oxfordshire. He later repented and was buried in the Abbey after his death, Ab ii, 7, 12-15, 24, 284.
41,2 WIGOT or Wigod of Wallingford, butler and kinsman of King Edward, father-in-law of Robert D'Oilly who inherited his estates, cf. 33,9. He is 'of Wallingford' in Bucks, 23,7; 12; 33. Most of the instances of plain *Wigot, Wigod* etc., in Sussex, Surrey, Hants., Berks., Herts., and Bucks., probably refer to him (see PNDB 404n). His personal name is ODanish (*Vigot*) as was his son's (*Toki*).
41,3 SHEFFORD . Robert D'Oilly, a sworn brother or Roger of Ivry in a report in the 13th century Oseney Cartulary, 'Fratres jurati et per fidem et sacramentum confederati', cited in R. Lennard, *Rural England* p.65. Their DB holdings were often divided equally, as here at Shefford, see 44,2.
42,1 MS *v cotarii,* corrected from *ii cotarii.*
SOUTH DENCHWORTH. The present village of Denchworth, EPNS 473. See above note 23,3.
44,1 ELING. In Hampstead Norris, EPNS 250. For Saewin's holding in East Hendred see note 65,13 and note 1,38; for Harwell see below 44,3-4.
44,5 PUSEY. See note 7,43.

45,2	CHILDREY. See note 28,2.
46,4	ABBOT ALFSI. Of St. Augustine's Canterbury (1061-?1070), and later of Ramsey (1080-1087).
	UNTIL HE WAS AN OUTLAW. In exile in Denmark from about 1070 (see Hunts., D8 'when the Abbot was in Denmark'.), D. Knowles, *The Heads of Religious Houses in England and Wales 940-1216*, (1972), pp.35-36 and refs.
	THE OLD MONASTERY. The Cathedral Church. See note B 9.
46,6	PEASEMORE. See note 17,2.
47,1	EARL ROGER. See note 1,8.
49,2	LODRIC. OGerman *Lud(e)ric*, PNDB 321.
	THEN FOR 3 HIDES. Perhaps in error for *iii.hid.ibi.*
49,3	MS *i.ii.hid.*, corrected by Farley to *iiii.hid.*
50,1	WULFWARD (WHITE). See Oxon., 40,3. PNDB s.n. *Wulfweard*.
54	VISDELOUP. 'Wolf's face', OEB 340. Also in Hampshire (69,40) and perhaps related to Ralph Visdeloup in Norfolk.
54,2	BOXFORD. See note 7,14.
54,3	BENHAM. See note 7,16.
55,3	CHILDREY. See note 28,2.
55,4	SPARSHOLT. See note 1,10.
57	AIULF THE SHERIFF. Of Dorset. The personal-name is the Anglo-Norman form for OE *Athulf/AEthelwulf*, PNDB 191. He was a brother of Humphrey the Chamberlain, see above 53; VCH 291.
58,2	IRISH HILL. At SU 4066 in Hamstead Marshall. The identification is the more likely as DB *Ebrige* (for *Ev-*, *Eu-*) and the other spellings cited in EPNS 299 are consistent with an OE *iw-hrycge* 'at the yew-covered ridge'; this solves the anomaly in form and topography discussed by EPNS loc.cit.
62,1	WEST HENDRED. See note 1,38.
63,2	LANK. MS *Lanc*, PNDB 308 s.n. OE *Lang*.
64,2	SWALLOWFIELD. See note 1,17.
65,6	BRAY. See note 1,22.
65,7	BARCOTE. In Buckland, EPNS 386; DB *Li-* represents miscopied *b* at some stage before the final MS.
65,10	*ACENGE*. East Ginge in Ardington, EPNS 469, citing B.R. Kemp, *The Mother Church of Thatcham*, Archaeological Journal 67 (1967-8), p.21. Geographically in Wantage Hundred, it is entered here under Thatcham.
65,11	WIGAR. Probably OE *Wihtgar*, PNDB 413.
	BENHAM. See note 7,16.
65,13	EAST HENDRED. See notes 1,38 and 44,1.
65,15	CARSWELL. In Buckland, EPNS 286; entered under Sutton Hundred although geographically in Ganfield Hundred, see Note 7,43.
65,16	'BURLEY'. See note 21,21.
65,18	FULCHARD. See note 21,12.
65,22	CHAFERSBEARD. *Ceuresbert* OEB 301, PNDB 158 line 4.

INDEX OF PERSONS

Familiar modern spellings are given where they exist. Unfamiliar names are usually given in an approximate late 11th century form, avoiding variants that were already obsolescent or pedantic. Spellings that mislead the modern eye are avoided where possible. Two, however, cannot be avoided: they are combined in the name of 'Leofgeat', pronounced 'Leffyet', or 'Levyet'. The definite article is omitted before bynames, except where there is reason to suppose that they described the individual. The chapter numbers of listed landholders are printed in italics.

Aelfeva	1,8. 61,2. 65,17	Aubrey of Coucy	*3,1*
Aelfhild Dese	31,3	Azelin	7,27
Aelfric	1,1; 5. 7,14; 19. 21,17.	Azor	1,28. 41,6
	32,1. 36,3. 41,5. 44,5.	Bagpuize, see Ralph	
	51,1. 54,2. 64,2. 65,8	Baldric, see Hugh	
another Aelfric	1,1	Baldwin	22,6-8. 33,1-2. 46,2
Aelfric of Thatcham	1,38	Beaufour, see William	
Aelmer	1,11; 20-21. 7,47.	Bellett, see William	
	22,11. 34,1. 43,1.	Bernard the Falconer	*60*
	54,2	Berner	7,11; 14; 21
Aelmer the priest	B 7	Berner nephew of Robert	
another Aelmer the priest	B 7	of Peronne	65,19
Aethelhelm	22,12	Blackman	7,34-35
Aiulf the Sheriff	*57*	Bolbec, see Hugh	
Aki	44,4. 62,1	Bondi	21,3; 7; 20
Albert	*56*	Bosi	33,8
Albert Clerk	1,1	Braose, see William	
Aldeva	65,13	Bretteville, see Gilbert	
Aldith	65,21	Brictheah	35,1-3. 41,3. 44,2
Alfgeat	1,40	Brictric	B 6. 35,5. 40,1. 55,1-4.
another Alfgeat	1,40		57,1. 65,10
Alfred	7,43. 22,3. 33,8.	Brictward	1,45. 17,1; 5; 7. 25,1.
	65,18		49,3
Alfsi	1,40	Brictwin	7,14
Abbot Alfsi	46,4	Bruman	B 7
Alfsi of Faringdon	65,7-8	Cailly, see William	
Alfsi (of Faringdon)	1,34	Chafersbeard, see Alfwy	
Alfsi of Faringdon's son	B 1	Chipping	46,3 EH 1
Alfward	23,2-3. 65,16	Chipping, see Alwin	
Alfward the Goldsmith	65,5	Cola	41,5. 65,10; 13
Alfward the priest	7,8	Colman	17,1
Alfwold	B 7	Corbucion, see William	
Alfwold the Chamberlain	1,43. 65,15	Coucy, see Aubrey	
Alfwy	65,3	Coutances, see Geoffrey	
Alfwy Chafersbeard	65,22	Crispin, see Miles	
Alfyard's sons	7,24	Dese, see Aelfhild	
Algar	B 4. 21,2	Doda	B 4
Algot	37,1	Domnic	21,19
Alric	21,9. 36,5	Drogo	B 9. 18,2. 47,1
Alstan	23,1	Dunn	39,1
Alwin	B 6. 7,11; 17. 8,1. 17,	Edith	7,16. 65,14
	2; 9. 22,1. 31,5. 36,1.	Queen Edith	1,4; 14-16; 47. 20,3.
	41,5. 46,7. 60,1.		21,20. 65,5; 15-17
	65,19	Edmund	B 7. 14,1. 45,1-2
Alwin the priest	7,29	Ednoth	18,1
Alwin son of Chipping	65,6	Ednoth the Constable	7,7
Ansketel	54,3	Edred the priest	1,10
Ansculf, see Giles, William		Edric	1,24. 7,38. 22,9
Armentières, see Robert		Edsi	21,1
Arnulf of Hesdin	*50*	Edward	8,1. 65,9; 12
Asgar	38,3; 5-6	Edward	13,2. 41,1. 58,1. 63,1; 3-5
Askell	7,2; 10; 17; 38. 19,1.	Edwin (free man)	20,1. 41,4
	65,12	Edwin (thane)	46,3
Aubigny, see Nigel		Edwin the priest	7,22
Aubrey the Queen's		Edwy	B 7
Chamberlain	65,16	Erhard, see Stephen	

Ernucion 12,1
Eu, see William
Eudo the Steward 32. 1,1
Count of Evreux 17. B 5
Faringdon, see Alfsi
Ferrers, see Henry
Feugères, see Ralph
Flambard, see Ranulf
Froger the Sheriff 1,10; 43
Fulchard 21,12. 65,18
Geoffrey 27,3
Bishop Geoffrey of
  Coutances 6
Geoffrey de Mandeville 38. 1,14
Gerald, see Robert
Ghent, see Gilbert
Giffard, see Osbern, Walter
Gilbert 1,7. 7,10; 26; 36-37;
  42-44. 22,1. 34,1
Gilbert of Bretteville 36
Gilbert of Ghent 37. B 3
Gilbert Maminot 1,1
Giles brother of Ansculf 34
Godbald 22,8. 65,18
Godfrey 7,12. 28,2
Godric B 4; 7. 21,6; 12; 16.
  29,1. 31,1. 36,2
Godric the Sheriff 1,26-27; 32; 37-38;
  42. 21,13; 15; 17; 22
Godric's wife 1,38
Godwin B 6. 35,4. 36,6. 41,5.
  46,1
Grimbald 62
Gunnar 43,2
(Earl) Gyrth 10,1
Gyrth 30,1
Countess Gytha 10,1
Haldane 33,6-7
Harding 65,17
Harold 1,34-36; 39-40; 44.
  18,1. 33,4. 65,7
Earl Harold 1,19. 4,1. 7,34.
  15,1. 18,2. 49,1
Hascoit (Musard) 35
Henry of Ferrers 21. B1; 4.1,25 -27; 32;
  37-38; 42
a second Henry 21,15; 17; 19
Henry the Steward 21,18
Herling 58,2
Herlwin 36,6
Bishop Herman (of
  Salisbury) 3,2-3
Hermer 7,23
Hervey 1,7
Hezelin 7,35
Horling 22,2; 5
Hubert 7,3
Hubert (of Curzon) 21,11
Hugh 1,7. 34,2
Hugh Grant of Scoca B 3; 9

Hugh son of Baldric 51
Hugh of Bolbec B 3; 5; 9
Hugh the Chamberlain 53
Hugh Cook 7,9
Earl Hugh 18. B 4; 9. 7,7
Hugh of Port 52. 10,1-2
Hugolin the Steersman 58
Humphrey the
  Chamberlain 53
Humphrey Visdeloup 54. B 1
Ilbert of Lacy B 9
Ivry, see Roger
Jocelyn 23,1; 3. 36,2
Karl 54,1
Kemp, see Wulfric
Kenmarchuc 35,1
Lacy, see Ilbert, Roger, Walter
Lambert the priest B 7
Landri 34,2
Archbishop Lanfranc B 3; 9
Lank 1,47. 63,2
Lank's wife 1,6
Lawrence 42,1
Leofeva B 6. 42,1
Abbess Leofeva 15,2
Leofled B 7. 1,13
Leofric the monk 33,5
Leofward 33,9
Leofwin 7,9. 17,3. 21,21. 45,3
Leofwin the Goldsmith 7,8
Lindbald the monk 7,25
Lodric 49,2
Lovett, see William
Maminot, see Gilbert
Mandeville, see Geoffrey
Matthew of Mortagne 59
Miles Crispin 33. B 1-2
Miles Molay B 8
Count of Mortain 19
Mortimer, see Ralph
Musard, see Hascoit
Nicolas 7,22
Nigel B 1. 21,8. 64,1
Nigel of Aubigny 12,1
Norman 7,2; 9; 15; 19-20; 46.
Odda 6,1
Odelard 46,6-7
Odo 48,1
Odo of Winchester 65. 10,1
Oilly, see Robert
Ordgar B 9
Ordmer 65,11
Ordwulf 38,1-2
Osbern 7,4. 20,1
Bishop Osbern (of Exeter) 5
Osbern Giffard 39
Osgot 28,1-3
Osmund, see William
Osmund 54,4
Bishop Osmund (of
  Salisbury) 3. B 6. 1,34

Othere, see Walter
Oxford, see Saewulf
Payne   36,4-5
Peronne, see Berner, Robert
Bishop Peter (of Lichfield) B 4. 1,9; 11; 42
Peverel, see William
Piercehedge, see Ralph
Port, see Hugh
Poynant, see Richard
Poyntz, see Walter
Abbot R......   B 9
Ragenhild   46,5
Ralph   27,2
Ralph son of the Earl   48
Earl Ralph   24,1
Ralph of Bagpuize   21,3; 14
Ralph of Feugères   65,18
Ralph of Mortimer   46. EH 1
Ralph Piercehedge   B 6
Ralph the priest   1,24
Ralph son of Siegfried   49. B 3
Ralph of Tosny   47
Ranulf   18,2
Ranulf Flambard   3,3
Ranulf Peverel   B 3
Rayner   21,9. 34,1
Reginald   B 3; 8. 1,24. 7,5; 7; 18; 25; 27; 46
Reinbald   1,22. 7,14; 18-19
Reinbald son of
  Bishop Peter   1,42
Reinbald the priest   B 6. 1,3 EB 1
Reinbald of Cirencester   61
Bishop Remigius
  (of Lincoln)   B 4; 9
Rhiwallon, see Abbot R...
Richard   33,6-7. 36,6
Richard, see William
Richard Poynant   43. 1,7
Rivers, see Walter
Robert   1,12-13. 7,28. 18,2. 21,10. 31,5. 37,1
Robert of Armentières   B 9
Robert son of Gerald   40
Robert Hugh of Port's
  Steward   10,2
Robert d'Oilly   41. B 3; 5-6; 9. 1,39. 8,1
R(obert) of Peronne, see Berner
Robert son of Rolf   65,20
Robert of Stafford   42
Roger   21,2; 4. 55,3-4
another Roger   55,3
Earl Roger   1,8. 47,1
Roger of Ivry   44. 2;1
Roger of Lacy   45. B 5-6; 8. EW 1
Roger the priest   3,1
Roger son of
  Siegfried   B 9. 49,2-3

Rolf, see Robert, Thurstan
Saewin   41,5. 44,1. 65,13
Saewulf   34,3-4
Saewulf of Oxford   B 1
Salvi   7,18
Saswalo   38,1-2
Saxfrid   33,4
Saxi   1,17-18; 46
Scoca, see Hugh Grant
Siegfried, see Ralph, Roger
Siward   34,2. 38,4
Siward (Bairn)   21,5; 11; 18
Stankell   21,14
Stephen   22,4; 6-7
Stephen son of Erhard   64
Bishop Stigand
  (of Winchester)   2,2-3
Swarting   B 1
Thatcham, see Aelfric
Theodoric   1,47. 20,1
Theodoric the Goldsmith   63
Thori   3,2
Thorkell   21,8. 22,12
Thorold   11,1
Thorold the priest   20,2
Thurstan son of Rolf   55. EW 1
Tonni   37,1
Tosny, see Ralph
Earl Tosti   20,2
Toti   26,1-3
Tovi   21,10. 27,1; 3. 65,6
Visdeloup, see Humphrey
Wace   B 9
Bishop Walkelin
  of Winchester   2. B 2
Walter Giffard   20. B 1; 3; 9. 1,11. 7,24
Walter of Lacy   14,1
Walter son of Othere   31. B 3. 1,1
Walter son of Poyntz   30
Walter of Rivers   7,15-16
Warin   7,11; 41
Wibert the priest   38,6
Wictric   31,6
Wigar   65,11
Wigot   33,9. 41,2
William   1,7. 7,12; 14; 20. 18,1. 33,1-2; 5. 36,1. 54,3. 65,18
Earl William   44,4
William son of Ansculf   22
William Beaufour   1,5
William Bellett   1,1
William of Braose   25
William of Cailly   29
William son of
  Corbucion   27
William the Deacon   1,9
William of Eu   23
William Leofric   EW 1
William Lovett   26. B 3

William Peverel 24
William son of
  Osmund B 7
William son of Richard 28
William of Warenne B 1
Winchester, see Odo
Wimund 7,36; 42
Wulfeva 52,1. 53,1
Wulfgar 17,11
Wulfled 1,12
Wulfmer 22,4

Wulfnoth 33,3
Wulfric 1,12. 7,10. 44,3
Wulfric Kemp 5,1
Wulfward 59,1
Wulfward (White) 50,1
Wulfwen 65,1
Wulfwin 7,22; 41. 17,12
Canon Wulfwin 4,1
Wulfwy 7,22
Wynric 7,34
Wynsi 31,2

Churches and Clergy. **Archbishop** ... (of Canterbury) B 3, see also Lanfranc. **Bishop** ... of Bayeu 41,3. 44,2; 5. 65,19. Chester, see Peter. Coutances 6. Durham 4. Exeter 5. Lincoln, see Remigius. Salisbury 3, see also Herman, Osmund. Winchester 2, see also Stigand, Walkelin. **Abbeys** ... Abingdon 7. B 2; 8. Amesbury 16. Battle 15. Chertsey 11. Glastonbury 8. Mont St. Michel 1,7. Preaux 19,1. Reading 15,2, see also Leofeva. St Albans 12.B 6; 9. St. Pierre-sur-Dives 13. Waltham 4,1. Westminster 9. Winchester 10. 14, see also Alfsi, Rhiwallon. **Canon** ... see Wulfwin. **Clerk** ... see Albert. **Deacon** ...see William. **Monks** ... see Leofric, Lindbald. **Priests** ... see Aelmer, Alfward, Alwin, Edred, Edwin, Lambert, Ralph, Reinbald, Roger, Thorold, Wibert.
Secular Titles and Occupational Names. **Bursar** (dispensator) .. Azor. **Chamberlain** (camerariu .. Alfwold, Aubrey, Hugh, Humphrey. **Constable** (stalre) .. Ednoth. **Cook** (cocus) .. Hugh. **Count** (comes) .. of Evreux, of Mortain. **Countess** (comitissa) .. Gytha. **Earl** (comes) .. Gyrth, Harold, Hug Ralph, Roger, Tosti, William. **Falconer** (accipitrarius) .. Bernard. **Goldsmith** (aurifaber) .. Alfward, Leofwin, Theodoric. **Queen** (regina) .. Edith. **Sheriff** (vicecomes) .. Aiulf, Froger, Godric. **Steermai** (stirman) .. Hugolin. **Steward** (dapifer) .. Eudo, Henry, Robert. **Thane** (teignus) .. Chipping, Edwin

SYSTEMS OF REFERENCE TO DOMESDAY BOOK

The manuscript is divided into numbered chapters, and the chapters into sections, usually marked by large initials and red ink. Ferley, however, did not number the sections. References have therefor been inexact, by folio numbers, which cannot be closer than an entire page or column. Moreover, half a dozen different ways of referring to the same column have been devised. In 1816 Ellis used th separate systems in his indices; (i) on pages i-cvii; 435-518; 537-570; (ii) on pages 1-144; (iii) on page 145-433 and 519-535. Other systems have since come into use, notably that used by Vinogradoff, here followed. This edition numbers the sections, the normal practicable form of close reference; but since all discussion of Domesday for three hundred years has been obliged to refer to page or columr a comparative table will help to locate the references given. The five columns below give Vinogradof notation, Ellis' three systems, and that employed by Welldon Finn and others. Maitland, Stenton, Darby and others have usually followed Ellis (i).

Vinogradoff	Ellis (i)	Ellis (ii)	Ellis (iii)	Finn
152 a	152	152 a	152	152ai
152 b	152	152 a	152.2	152a2
152 c	152 b	152 b	152 b	152bi
152 d	152 b	152 b	152 b	152b2

In Berkshire, the relation between the Vinogradoff column notation, here followed, and the chapters and sections is

56 a	Landholders			59 a	7,21	-	7,30		62 a	36,2	-	39,1
b	B 1	-	B 4	b	7,31	-	7,39		b	39,1	-	43,1
c	B 4	-	B 11	c	7,39	-	8,1		c	43,1	-	46,3
d	1,1	-	1,7	d	9,1	-	15,1		d	46,4	-	49,3
57 a	1,7	-	1,13	60 a	15,2	-	17,10		63 a	52,1	-	57,1
b	1,14	-	1,23	b	17,11	-	20,3		b	58,1	-	63,5
c	1,24	-	1,32	c	21,4	-	21,15		c	64,1	-	65,11
d	1,32	-	1,39	d	21,16	-	22,4		d	65,11	-	65,22
58 a	1,40	-	1,47	61 a	22,4	-	24,1					
b	2,1	-	4,1	b	25,1	-	28,3					
c	5,1	-	7,9	c	31,1	-	33,5					
d	7,9	-	7,20	d	33,6	-	34,4					

INDEX OF PLACES

As in most counties some Hundred rubrics are missing. Others seem to be wrongly entered, as occasionally elsewhere, notably in Staffordshire. In most counties these omissions and errors are easily corrected, since the Hundreds were often geographical units, and their boundaries remained unchanged, apart from amalgamation, subdivision and the transfer of some monastic holdings to the Hundred of the Church concerned. In others, eg. Buckinghamshire (see Bucks. note 1,1) the Hundred order is often the same within each chapter and throughout the County.

In Berkshire, however, the Hundreds were rearranged and renamed in and after the 12th century (see below), with a considerable number of places annexed to Hundreds with which they had not a geographical connection. The process had already begun before 1086, since in DB some manors are divided by Hundred boundaries, and others are detached geographically from their Hundreds. Therefore, although it is probable that many of the anomalies are, as elsewhere, the result of errors and omissions in the MS., there is not always sufficient evidence to prove such errors. Manors which may have been divided by Hundred boundaries are here indexed under their geographical Hundreds, although the possibility that part of their territory may have lain or owed service elsewhere is indicated by the use of a dagger (†) and in the map keys by their appearance in square brackets at the foot of each Hundred key. All anomalies are fully discussed in the notes.

HUNDREDS

Several of the Berkshire Hundreds were reorganized, chiefly in the 13th century. Of the 22 DB Hundreds, 13 retained their identity; Beynhurst, Bray, Charlton, Kintbury, Eagle (the last two joined together as one double Hundred), Ganfield, Hormer, Lambourn, *Nachededorn* (renamed Compton), Reading, Ripplesmere, Shrivenham and Wantage. The other 9 were amalgamated: Hillslow and Wyfold with Shrivenham; Bucklebury, Rowbury and Thatcham into a single Hundred named Faircross; Blewbury and Slotisford into Moreton; Marcham and Sutton into Ock. 3 of the DB Hundreds were also subdivided in the late 12th/early 13th century, Cookham, Sonning and Theale were separated from Beynhurst, Charlton and Reading respectively to become separate Hundreds. These changes entailed the detachment of some 15 parishes from their geographical Hundreds (8 of them, including Thatcham, Blewbury and Cholsey, were assigned to the new Reading Hundred, formed from a collection of manors belonging to the Abbey); and were accompanied by a few minor adjustments of Hundred boundaries. The boundaries of the reorganized Hundreds are fully described in EPNS.

The editor is grateful to Dr. Margaret Gelling for her advice on the place-names and Hundreds of Berkshire.

The name of each place is follwed by (i) the initial of its Hundred and its location on the Map in this volume; (ii) its National Grid reference; (iii) chapter and section reference in DB. Bracketed figures denote mention in sections dealing with a different place. Unless otherwise stated, the identifications of EPNS and the spellings of the Ordnance Survey are followed for places in England , of OEB for places abroad. Inverted commas mark lost places with known modern spelling; unidentifiable places are given in DB spelling, in italics. The National Grid reference system is explained on all Ordnance Survey maps, and in the Automobile Association Handbooks; the figures reading from left to right are given before those reading from bottom to top of the map. Places marked with (*) are in the 100 kilometre grid square lettered SP; all others are in square SU. The Berkshire Hundreds are Beynhurst (Be), Bucklebury (Bu), Blewbury (Bw), Bray (Br), Charlton (Ch), Compton (Co), Ganfield (G), Eagle (E), Hillslow (Hi), Hormer (Ho), Kintbury (K), Lambourn (L), Marcham (M), Reading (Re), Ripplesmere (Ri), Rowbury (Ro), Shrivenham (Sh), Slotisford (Sf), Sutton (Su), Thatcham (T), Wantage (Wa), Wyfold (Wy).

	Map	Grid	Text		Map	Grid	Text
Abingdon	Ho 10	49 97	7,38	Bagnor	T 2	45 69	53,1
Albury* (Oxon)		65 05	B3;8. See	Bagshot	K 9	31 65	21,6
			note B8	Barcote	G 4	31 97	65,7
Aldermaston	Re 18	59 65	B5. 1,44-45	'Barethorn'	- -	- -	1,24
Aldworth	Co 9	55 79	63,1	Barkham	Ch 7	78 66	1,20
Appleford	Su 3	52 93	7,28	Barton	Ho 11	50 97	7,6;9
Appleton*	M 2	44 01	33,6. 65,19	Basildon	Sf 7	60 78	1,8
Ardington	Wa 5	43 88	41,4;5	Bayworth*	Ho 5	50 01	7,10
Ashbury	Hi 8	26 85	8,1	Beckett	Sh 3	23 88	17,6
'Ashden'	- -	- -	21,3	Beedon	Ro 2	48 78	7,15
Aston Tirrold	Bw11	55 85	1,6. 19,1	Benham†	K 5	43 67	7,16. 54,3.
Aston Upthorpe	Bw10	55 86	61,2				65,11
Avington	K 4	37 68	43,2	Benson (Oxon)		61 91	B1

Name	Map	Grid	Text
Bessels Leigh*	M 3	45 01	7,20
Betterton	Wa 13	43 86	1,12. 33,5
Bisham	Be 1	84 85	21,7
Blewbury	Bw 9	53 85	B1. 1,5. 17,7
Bockhampton	L 2	33 78	48,1. 65,12
Boxford†	Ro 8	42 71	7,14. 54,2
Bradfield	Re 7	60 72	22,2
Bray†	Br 1	90 79	B2. 1,22. 65,6
Brightwalton	Co 6	42 79	15,1
Brightwell	Sf 1	57 90	B2. 2,3
Brimpton	T 11	55 64	40,1. 46,1
Buckland†	G 5	34 98	5,1. 7,47. 17,12-13
Bucklebury	Bu 5	55 70	1,23. 17,3. 31,3. 58,3
Burghfield	Re 13	66 68	21,20. 46,4
'Burley'	- -	- -	21,21. 65,16;17
Buscot	Wy 1	22 97	18,2
'Calcot'	- -	- -	17,5
'Carswell'	- -	- -	65,15
Catmore	Co 7	45 80	21,1
Caversham (Oxon)		72 74	B9
Chaddleworth	E 8	41 77	10,1. 41,1
Chalgrove (Oxon)		63 96	B2
West Challow	E 1	36 88	16,2
Charlton	Wa 4	40 88	1,11. 20,2. 21,10. 27,3. 47,1
Charney Bassett	G 10	37 94	7,40-41
Chieveley	Ro 7	47 73	7,12
Childrey†	Wa 9	36 87	28,2. 45, 2-3. 55,3
Chilton	Co 1	48 85	7,34. 31.2
Cholsey	Sf 4	58 86	1,7. 43,1
Cirencester (Gloucs.)		- -	61,1-2
Clapcot	Sf 3	60 89	33,3;4
Clewer	Ri 2	95 76	49,1
Coleshill	Wy 4	23 93	14,1. 28,1. 55,1. EW 1
Compton	Co 8	51 79	1,25. 6,1
Compton Beauchamp	Hi 6	28 87	22,11
Cookham	Be 2	89 85	1,3. EB1
Great Coxwell	Wy 5	26 93	1,35
Little Coxwell	Wy 6	28 93	1,36
Crochestrope	- -	- -	17,4
Crookham	T 10	53 64	65,22
Cumnor*	Ho 3	04 46	7,1;4;5
Curridge	T 1	48 71	13,2. 46,2. 65,9
Crowmarsh (Gifford)* (Oxon)		61 89	B9
Dedworth	Ri 1	94 76	56,1
Denford	K 3	36 69	23,2
North Denchworth	Wa 1	38 92	23,3
South Denchworth	Wa 1	38 92	21,9. 42,1
Donnington	T 3	46 69	26,1
Dorchester (Oxon)		57 94	B9
Draycott (Moor)	M 4	40 99	7,26
Drayton†	Su 1	47 94	18,1. 35,4
Duxford	G 1	36 99	65,3
Earley	Ch 4	75 72	1,21;42 39,1
East Garston	L 3	36 76	38,3
Easthampstead	Ri 7	86 67	9,1
Eaton*	M 1	44 03	33,7;8
Eaton Hastings	Wy 2	26 98	30,1
Eddington	K 2	34 69	1,28
Eling	Bu 3	52 75	44,1
Enborne	K 12	43 65	26,2. 27,1. 34,4. 45,1
Englefield	Re 8	62 72	22,1;4
Ewelme (Oxon)		64 91	B9
Great Faringdon	Wy 3	28 95	1,34
Farnborough	Co 2	43 81	7,33
Fawler	Hi 4	31 88	7,38
Great Fawley	E 4	39 81	16,3
Little Fawley	E 5	39 80	1,30
Finchampstead	Ch 9	79 63	1,19
Frilford	M 9	44 97	7,18
Frilsham	Bu 4	53 73	21,4
Fulscot	Bw 4	54 88	49,2
Fyfield	M 6	42 98	21,15;16
Garford	M 8	42 96	7,21
East Ginge†	Wa 15	44 86	65,10
West Ginge	Wa 14	44 86	7,45-46
Goosey	M 12	35 91	7,23 33,9
Gratentun (Oxon)			
Greenham	T 9	47 65	21,5
East Hagbourne	Bw 3	53 88	61,1
West Hagbourne	Bw 6	51 87	31,5
Hamstead Marshall	K 11	41 65	58,1;3
Hampstead Norris	Bu 1	52 76	63,2
East Hanney†	Wa 3	41 92	7,22. 17,8. 36,2
West Hanney	Wa 2	40 92	20,1;2
Hartley	Re 14	70 68	46,5
Hartridge	Re 1	57 77	22,3
Harwell	Bw 2	49 89	2,2. 44,1; 3;4
Haseley* (Oxon)		64 01	B2
Hastings (Sussex)	- -	- -	21,13
Hatford†	G 9	33 94	36,4
East Hendred†	Wa 7	45 88	1,38. 3,2. 17,9-10. 21 44,1. 65,15
West Hendred	Wa 6	44 88	12,1. 62,1
Hinton Waldrist	G 2	38 99	65,1;2
Hodcott	Co 4	47 81	22,6. 46,7
Hurley	Be 3	82 83	38,5

Name	Map	Grid	Text
East Ilsley†	Co 5	49 81	B4. 3,1. 21,2. 22,7. 38,1
West Ilsley	Co 3	47 82	38,2
Inglewood	K 6	36 66	40,2. 65,18; 20
Inkpen	K 10	35 64	22,10. 65,18
Irish Hill	K 8	66 40	58,2
Kennington*	Ho 4	02 52	7,11
Kingston Bagpuize	M 5	40 98	21,14. 22,12
Kingston Lisle	Hi 7	32 87	1,32
Kintbury	K 7	38 66	1,26. 16,1. 31,4
Knighton	Hi 2	28 87	65,4
Lambourn	L 1	32 78	1,29. 35,3. 59,1
Langley	Re 4	67 75	33,9
Leckhampstead	Ro 3	43 75	7,14
Letcombe Bassett	E 2	37 85	41,2
Letcombe Regis	E 3	38 86	1,31
Leverton	K 1	33 70	7,35
Littleworth	G 7	31 97	1,40
East Lockinge	Wa 12	42 87	7,44
West Lockinge	Wa 11	42 87	21,11
Lollingdon	Sf 5	57 85	43,1
Longworth	G 3	38 99	7,39
'Losfield'	Ri 4	93 94	32,1
Lyford	M 11	39 94	7,24;25
Maidenhead	Be 4	88 81	34,2
Marcham	M 10	45 96	7,17
Midgham	T 8	55 67	34,1
Milton	Su 7	48 92	7,27
South Moreton	Bw 7	56 88	26,3. 54,4
North Moreton	Bw 5	56 89	27,2
Newbury	T 6	47 66	50,1
Newington (Oxon.)		61 96	B9
Newnham Murren (Oxon.)		61 88	B2
Newton	G 6	36 98	36,5
Odstone	Hi 5	27 86	28,3
Ortone	- -	- -	31,1
Oxford (Oxon.)	- -	51 06	B2. 1,39. 38,6
Padworth	Re 16	61 66	23,1. 64,1
Pangbourne	Re 2	63 76	1,43. 33,1
Peasemore†	Ro 1	45 77	17,2. 36,6. 46,6
Purley	Re 3	65 76	49,3. 63,4
Pusey†	G 8	35 96	7,43. 13,1. 21,19. 44,5
Pyrton (Oxon.)		68 95	B9
Reading	Re 6	71 73	B1. 1,41; 42. 15,2
Remenham	Ch 1	77 84	1,16
St. Albans (Herts.)	- -	- -	B6
Dry Sandford*	Ho 6	46 00	7,9
Seacourt*	Ho 2	48 07	7,2
Scoca	- -	- -	B9.
Shalbourn	K 13	31 63	1,27
Shaw	T 4	47 68	51,1

Name	Map	Grid	Text
Sheffield	Re 12	65 69	17,1
East Shefford	E 10	38 74	57,1
Great Shefford	E 9	38 75	41,3. 44,2. 52,1
Shellingford	G 11	31 93	7,42
Shinfield	Ch 6	72 68	1,18
Shippon	Ho 9	47 98	7,7-8
*Shirburn (Oxon.)	- -		B9
Shottesbrook	Be 6	84 77	65,5
Shrivenham	Sh 2	23 88	1,33
Sonning	Ch 3	75 75	3,1
Sotwell	Sf 2	58 90	10,2
Southcote	Re 9	68 71	25,1
Sparsholt†	Wa 8	34 87	1,10. 21,12. 35,5. 55,4
Speen	T 5	46 67	54,1
Stafford (Staffs)	- -	- -	42,1
Stanford Dingley	Co 11	57 71	22,9
Stanford in the Vale†	G 12	34 93	21,18
Steventon	Su 6	47 91	1,39
Stoke Talmage (Oxon.)			B9
(North) Stoke (Oxon.)		61 86	B2
Stratfield Mortimer	Re 19	66 64	46,3. EH1
Streatley	Sf 6	59 80	38,6
Sugworth*	Ho 8	51 00	7,11
Sulham	Re 5	64 74	29,1. 33,2. 63,3
Sunningwell*	Ho 7	49 00	7,11
'Sutton'			1,13
Sutton Courtenay	Su 2	50 94	B1;2. 1,37. 7,29
Swallowfield†	Ch 8	71 64	1,17;46. 64,2
Thatcham	T 7	51 67	1,2
Tubney	M 7	43 98	7,19
Uffington	Hi 1	30 89	7,37
Ufton Nervet	Re 17	63 67	34,3
Ufton Robert	Re 11	62 68	22,5
Upton	Bw 8	51 86	55,2
Wallingford	W	60 89	B. 1,37. 2,3. 3,1. 15,1. 20,3. 27,2
Waltham	Be 5	82 77	1,4
White Waltham	Be 7	85 77	4,1. 11,1
Wantage	Wa 10	39 87	1,9
Warfield	Ri 5	88 72	1,14
Wargrave	Ch 2	78 78	1,15
Wasing	T 12	57 64	60,1
Watchfield	Sh 1	24 90	7,36
Waterperry* (Oxon.)		62 06	B9
Watlington* (Oxon.)		68 94	B9
Welford	Ro 5	40 73	7,13
Weston	Ro 4	39 73	7,14
South Weston (Oxon.)		70 98	B9
Whatcombe	E 7	39 78	38,4

	Map	Grid	Text		Map	Grid	Text
Whistley	Ch 5	79 73	7,32	Long Wittenham	Su 4	54 93	B1. 20,3
Whitley	Re 10	71 70	63,5	Wokefield	Re 20	67 65	1,44;45.
Willington	Bw 1	54 91	21,8				31,6
Windsor	Ri 3	96 76	1,1;3.	Woolhampton	Re 15	57 66	21,22
			41,6. 49,1	Woolley	E 6	41 80	24,1
Winkfield	Ri 6	90 72	7,31	Woolstone	Hi 3	29 87	2,1
Winterbourne	Ro 6	45 72	1,47. 3,3.	Wyld	Bu 2	54 76	36,1
			35,1;2	Wytham	Ho 1	47 09	7,3
Little Wittenham	Su 5	56 93	7,30	Yattendon	Co 10	55 74	22,8

Places not named

In Ganfield Hundred 17,12-13. 65,14;21. In Rowbury Hundred 37,1. [In Wantage Hundred] 36,3. In Wantage Hundred 3,2. 17,10-11. 21,13. 41,6. 45,3. 65,8.

Places not in Berkshire

References are to entries in the Indices of Persons and Places.

Elsewhere in Britain

GLOUCESTERSHIRE...Cirencester, see Reinbald. HERTFORDSHIRE...St. Albans. OXFORDSHIR ...Albury, Benson, Caversham, Chalgrove, Crowmarsh Gifford, Dorchester, Ewelme, *Gratentun,* Haseley, Newington, Newnham Murren, Oxford, Pyrton, Shirburn, Stoke Talmage, North Stoke, Waterperry, Watlington, South Weston. WILTSHIRE...Shalbourn. STAFFORDSHIRE...Stafford, see Robert. SUSSEX...Hastings. *See also Index of Churches and Clergy.*

Outside Britain

Armentières...Robert. Aubigny...Nigel. Bagpuize...Ralph. Bayeux...Bishop. Bolbec...Hugh. Braose... William. Bretteville...Gilbert. Cailly...William. Coutances...Bishop. Curzon...Hubert. Eu...William. Evreux...Count. Ferrers...Henry. Feugères...Ralph. Ghent...Gilbert. Hesdin...Arnulf. Ivry...Roger. Lacy...Ilbert, Roger, Walter. Mandeville...Geoffrey. Mortagne...Matthew. Mortain...Count. Mortimer...Ralph. Oilly...Robert. Peronne...Robert. Port...Hugh. Preaux...Abbey. Rivers...Walter. St. Pierre-sur-Dives...Abbey. *Scoca*...Hugh.

MAP AND MAP KEYS

TECHNICAL TERMS

On the map the County Boundary is marked by thick lines; Hundred boundaries by thin lines, dotted where uncertain.

National Grid 10-kilometre squares are shown on the map border.

Each four-figure grid square covers one square kilometre, or 247 acres, approximately 2 hides, at 120 acres to the hide.

BERKSHIRE HUNDREDS

Wyfold (Wy)
1 Buscot
2 Eaton Hastings
3 Great Faringdon
4 Coleshill
5 Great Coxwell
6 Little Coxwell

Shrivenham (Sh)
1 Watchfield
2 Shrivenham
3 Beckett

Hillslow (Hi)
1 Uffington
2 Knighton
3 Woolstone
4 Fawler
5 Odstone
6 Compton
7 Kingston Lisle
8 Ashbury

Lambourn (L)
1 Lambourn
2 Bockhampton
3 East Garston

[Drayton]

Kintbury (K)
1 Leverton
2 Eddington
3 Denford
4 Avington
5 Benham
6 Inglewood
7 Kintbury
8 Irish Hill
9 Bagshot
10 Inkpen
11 Hamstead Marshall
12 Enborne
13 Shalbourne
'Calcot'

[Boxford]

Ganfield (G)
1 Duxford
2 Hinton Waldrist
3 Longworth
4 Barcote
5 Buckland
6 Newton
7 Littleworth
8 Pusey
9 Hatford
10 Charney Bassett
11 Shellingford
12 Stanford in the Vale [Benham]

Wantage (Wa)
1 North and South
  Denchworth
2 West Hanney
3 East Hanney
4 Charlton
5 Ardington
6 West Hendred
7 East Hendred
8 Sparsholt
9 Childrey
10 Wantage
11 West Lockinge
12 East Lockinge
13 Betterton
14 West Ginge
15 East Ginge
'Sutton'

[Buckland]

Eagle (E)
1 West Challow
2 Letcombe Bassett
3 Letcombe Regis
4 Great Fawley
5 Little Fawley
6 Woolley
7 Whatcombe

8 Chaddleworth
9 Great Shefford
10 East Shefford

Rowbury (Ro)
1 Peasemore
2 Beedon
3 Leckhampstead
4 Weston
5 Welford
6 Winterbourne
7 Chieveley
8 Boxford

Thatcham (T)
1 Curridge
2 Bagnor
3 Donnington
4 Shaw
5 Speen
6 Newbury
7 Thatcham
8 Midgham
9 Greenham
10 Crookham
11 Brimpton
12 Wasing

[East Ginge]

Marcham (M)
1 Eaton
2 Appleton
3 Bessels Leigh
4 Draycott Moor
5 Kingston Bagpuize
6 Fyfield
7 Tubney
8 Garford
9 Frilford
10 Marcham
11 Lyford
12 Goosey

[Hatford]
[Peasemore]

Hormer (Ho)
1 Wytham
2 Seacourt
3 Cumnor
4 Kennington
5 Bayworth
6 Dry Sandford
7 Sunningwell
8 Sugworth
9 Shippon
10 Abingdon
11 Barton

Sutton (Su)
1 Drayton
2 Sutton Courtenay
3 Appleford
4 Long Wittenham
5 Little Wittenham
6 Steventon
7 Milton
'Carswell'

[East Hendred]
[Pusey]
[Stanford in the Vale]

Blewbury (Bw)
1 Willington's
2 Harwell
3 East Hagbourne
4 Fulscot
5 North Moreton
6 West Hagbourne
7 South Moreton
8 Upton
9 Blewbury
10 Aston Upthorpe
11 Aston Tirrold

Compton (Co)
1 Chilton
2 Farnborough

3 West Ilsley
4 Hodcott
5 East Ilsley
6 Brightwalton
7 Catmore
8 Compton
9 Aldworth
10 Yattendon
11 Stanford Dingley
'Ashden'
'Barethorn'

Bucklebury (Bu)
1 Hampstead Norris
2 Wyld
3 Eling
4 Frilsham
5 Bucklebury
Crochestrope

Slotisford (Sf)
1 Brightwell
2 Sotwell
3 Clapcot
4 Cholsey
5 Lollington
6 Streatley
7 Basildon

[Childrey]
[Sparsholt]

Reading (Re)
1 Hartridge
2 Pangbourne
3 Purley
4 Langley
5 Sulham
6 Reading
7 Bradfield
8 Englefield
9 Southcote
10 Whitley
11 Ufton Robert
12 Sheffield
13 Burghfield
14 Hartley
15 Woolhampton
16 Padworth
17 Ufton Nervet
18 Aldermaston
19 Stratfield Mortimer
20 Wokefield
'Burley'

[Peasemore]

Charlton (Ch)
1 Remenham
2 Wargrave
3 Sonning
4 Earley
5 Whistley
6 Shinfield
7 Barkham
8 Swallowfield
9 Finchampstead

Beynhurst (Be)
1 Bisham
2 Cookham
3 Hurley
4 Maidenhead
5 Waltham
6 Shottesbrook
7 White Waltham

[Bray]

Ripplesmere (Ri)
1 Dedworth
2 Clewer
3 Windsor
4 'Losfield'
5 Warfield
6 Winkfield
7 Easthampstead
Ortone

Bray (Br)
1 Bray

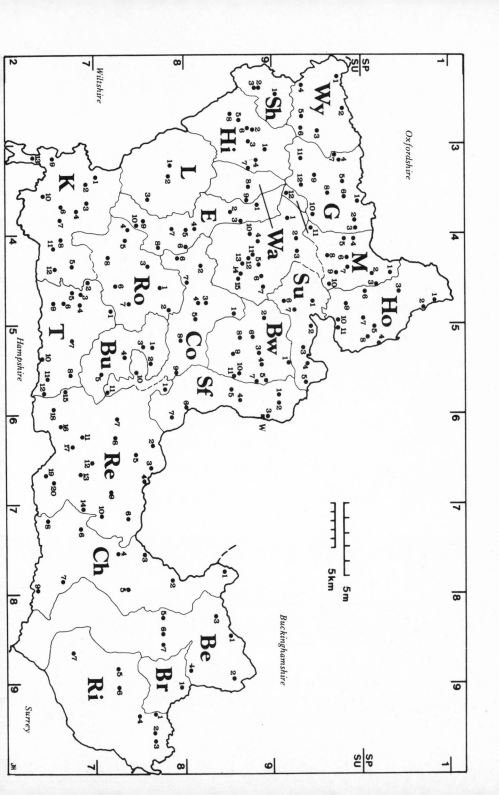

TECHNICAL TERMS

Many words meaning measurements have to be transliterated. But translation may not dodge other problems by the use of obsolete or made-up words which do not exist in modern English. The translations here used are given in italics. They cannot be exact; they aim at the nearest modern equivalent.

BORDARIUS. Cultivator of inferior status, usually with a little land. *s m a l l h o l d e r*

CARUCA. A plough with the oxen who pulled it, usually reckoned at 8. *p l o u g h*

DOMINIUM. The mastery or dominion of a lord *(dominus)*; including ploughs, land, men, villages, etc., reserved for the lord's use; often concentrated in a *home farm* or *demesne*, a 'Manor Farm' or 'Lordship Farm'. *l o r d s h i p*

FEUDUM. Continental variant of *feuum*, not used in England before 1066; either a landholder's total holding, or land held by special grant. *H o l d i n g*

FIRMA. Old English *feorm*, provisions due to the King or lord; a fixed sum paid in place of these and other miscellaneous dues. *r e v e n u e*

GELDUM. The principal royal tax, originally levied during the Danish wars, normally at an equal number of pence on each *hide* of land. *t a x*

HIDA. The English unit of land measurement or assessment, often reckoned at 120 acres; see Sussex, Appendix. *h i d e*

HUNDRED. A district within a shire, whose assembly of notables and village representatives usually met about once a month. *H u n d r e d*

SOCA. *'Soke'*, from *socn*, to seek, comparable with Latin *quaestio*. Jurisdiction with the right to receive fines and a multiplicity of other dues. District in which such *soca* is exercised; a place in a *soca*. *j u r i s d i c t i o n*

TAINUS, TEGNUS. Person holding land from the King by special grant; formerly used of the King's ministers and military companions. *t h a n e*

T.R.E. *tempore regis Edwardi*, in King Edward's time. *b e f o r e   1 0 6 6*

VILLA. Translating Old English *tun*, town. The later distinction between a small *village* and a large *town* was not yet in use in 1086. *v i l l a g e* or *t o w n*

VILLANUS. Member of a *villa*, usually with more land than a *bordarius*. *v i l l a g e r*

VIRGATA. A quarter of a hide, reckoned at 30 acres. *v i r g a t e*